ALSO BY THOMAS MALLON

FICTION

Arts and Sciences
Aurora 7
Henry and Clara
Dewey Defeats Truman
Two Moons
Bandbox
Fellow Travelers

NONFICTION

Edmund Blunden
A Book of One's Own
Stolen Words
Rockets and Rodeos
In Fact
Mrs. Paine's Garage

Yours Ever

Yours Ever

PEOPLE AND THEIR LETTERS

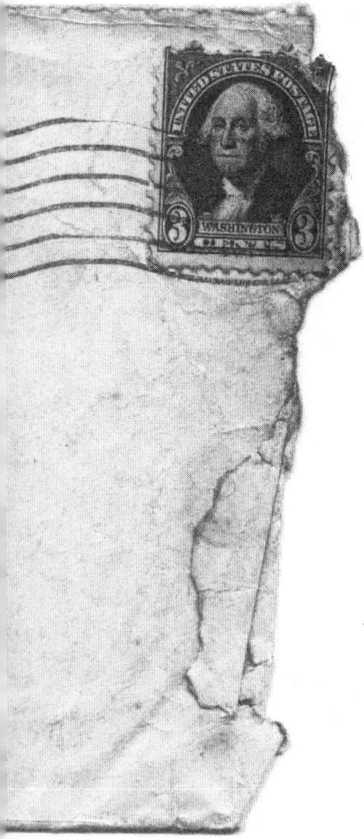

Thomas Mallon

PANTHEON BOOKS, NEW YORK

 Published in the United States by Pantheon Books, a division of Random House, Inc., New York, and in Canada by Random House of Canada Limited, Toronto.

Pantheon Books and colophon are registered trademarks of Random House, Inc.

Portions of this book appeared, often in very different form, in *The New Yorker*, *The Atlantic Monthly*, *The American Scholar*, *GQ*, *The New York Times Book Review*, and other publications.

Library of Congress Cataloging-in-Publication Data

Mallon, Thomas [date]
Yours ever : people and their letters / Thomas Mallon.
p. cm.
Includes bibliographical references and index.
ISBN 978-0-679-44426-8
1. Letters. I. Title.
PN6131.M35 2009 808.86—dc22 2009006315

www.pantheonbooks.com

Printed in the United States of America

First Edition

9 8 7 6 5 4 3 2 1

In memory of

FRAN WALKER
(1927–2003)

faithful correspondent, fast friend

Contents

Yours Ever

Introduction

IT EMBARRASSES ME to admit that I began writing this book when a first-class stamp cost twenty-nine cents. Well, here we are, the price half again as much and I a third again as old, and my excuses no better than what one usually offers when finally answering a letter that's been under the paperweight for ages longer than one ever meant it to be.

But a person can't adequately procrastinate without at least one semi-valid rationalization, and so here's mine: if this book had come out, as it was supposed to, around 1997, it would have appeared just as e-mail was reaching Everyman and beginning to kill, or revive (there are both schools of thought), the practice and art of letter writing. Whichever the case, the book would have come ashore just as a sea change was making the waters even more interesting.

Letters had always defeated distance, but with the coming of e-mail, time seemed to be vanquished as well. It's worth spending a minute or two pondering the physics of the thing, which interested Charles Lamb even early in the nineteenth century. Domestic mail was already a marvel—"One drops a packet at Lombard Street, and in twenty-four hours a friend in Cumberland gets it as fresh as if it came in ice"*—but in his essay "Distant Correspondents" (1822), Lamb seemed to regard remoteness and delay as inherent, vexing elements of the whole epistolary enterprise. Con-

*More or less foreseeing the telephone, Lamb writes that posting a letter is like "whispering through a long trumpet."

sidering the gap between the dispatch and receipt of a far-traveling letter, hewrote: "Not only does truth, in these long intervals, unessence herself, but (what is harder) one cannot venture a crude fiction, for the fear that it may ripen into a truth upon the voyage." In Lamb's view, sentiment, unlike revenge, "requires to be served up hot . . . If it have time to cool, it is the most tasteless of all cold meats." He even imagines poor sentiment being "hoisted into a ship . . . pawed about and handled between the rude jests of tarpaulin ruffians."

And yet, once the sentiment-carrying letter arrives, Lamb will be "chatting" to his distant correspondent "as familiarly as when we used to exchange good-morrows out of our old contiguous windows." The letter will have reconnected them, however imperfectly, by the slenderest and most improbable of threads. With e-mail and its even realer-time progeny, the IM and the text message and the Tweet, we get to ask simply "how have you been?"—in, that is, the twelve minutes since we were last in touch.

In a history of the mails that he published in the frantic year 1928, Alvin F. Harlow proudly insisted that "the history of postal service has been the history of civilization," and he debunked the idea that Queen Atossa, daughter of Cyrus the Great, wrote the first letter, from Persia, sometime in the sixth century B.C. Mr. Harlow felt certain that these civilizing instruments had been on the road, if not the wing, "hundreds of years" before that. Setting aside the question of precedence, we do know that Greeks had their fleet-footed *hemerodromes* and the Romans their *Cursus publicus* for the delivery of communications between one part of the government and another. Couriers and messengers made the Dark Ages a little less so, before Louis XI established what Mr. Harlow calls "the first royal, regular message service" in the fifteenth century, which allowed Henry VIII to imitate and expand the institution forty years later, across the Channel. Not long after that, private carriers began servicing non-royal folk, bequeathing us the phrase "post haste"—a shortening of the injunction ("Haste, Post, haste!") that customers sometimes inscribed on their dispatches.

During the seventeenth century, government delivery service appeared in England, along with postmarks and complaints from messenger boys against the unfair competition. (One thinks of how the lethal bicycle messengers of 1980s Manhattan cursed the faxes that suddenly ran them off the road.) The mail coach transported England into its golden epistolary age, a time of such confidence in the quality of letters that, as Daniel Pool points out in his book about nineteenth-century British life, the recipient paid the postage. That changed with the advent of the penny post, around 1840, by which time envelopes had replaced sealing wax.

In America, as the Pony Express began racing alongside train tracks, speed of delivery came to trump all else, though the cozy convenience of home delivery did not arrive in most places until after the Civil War. Here, where I live in Washington D.C., a walk down F Street will take you past the building that served as the city's post office in Lincoln's time; the sidewalk that's now filled with tourists—the building has become a hotel—once teemed with wives and sweethearts and women who didn't yet know they were widows, all of them come to collect the mail they hoped was arriving from the battlefield.

Anthony Trollope arrived in the capital just a few years later—"in June the musquito of Washington is as a roaring lion"—to negotiate a postal treaty between the United States and England. (The Victorian appetite for work being what it was, writing several dozen books didn't mean Trollope couldn't hold a full-time government job, too.) According to R. H. Super, the treaty "settled almost nothing." Trollope's real postal success would remain more domestic than international: his introduction of the red pillar box that allowed for easy mailing of the letters upon which events in his novels so often turn.

WHAT HATH GOD WROUGHT. Trollope may not have lived into the age of air mail, but his postal career was spent under the whizzings and clicks of the telegraph wires, through which some could hear the first of many premature dirges for the old-fashioned letter. Writing to Flaubert in 1869, the ever-forward-looking George Sand considered "What an effect telegrams have had on things" and imagined "how full of fact and free of uncertainty life will be when such procedures have been still more simplified." One can almost hear the electronic in-box beginning to chime.

A few intermediate marvels, like the radio and telephone, were enough to make Alvin Harlow put the word "so-called" before one late reference to the "civilization" he hymned in the pages of his history. "The art of beautiful letter writing has declined" with our supposed advances, he lamented—a cry we have been hearing ever more often in the eighty years since his book appeared. Those of us with a strong inclination toward the past must remember that, to its early writers, the handwritten or even chiseled letter must itself have seemed a marvel of modernity, and surely, even in Queen Atossa's time, there were those who complained that letter writing—by its nature a "virtual" activity—was cutting down on all the face time that civilized Persians had previously enjoyed.

Is e-mail even mail? It's a question that's provoked more debate than margarine and the aluminum bat. In terms of its transmittal—in its first years over phone lines and these days via satellite—it would indeed seem closer to a telephone call. But its mode of composition argues for classifying it as a form of the letter, and to anyone who's ever used it, e-mail's quaint, snail-mail iconography—a blank pad and pencil for the "Compose" function, an "envelope" that lights up with a message's arrival—makes perfect sense. (E-mail "arrives," of course, at the big central computer of one's Internet service provider, and when we log on, we're more or less taking the sort of trip to the post office that those Civil War sweethearts had to make.)

More than one fine literary stylist has found e-mail actually to be more in keeping with letter writing's early vitality than were the stuffy epistolary conventions that grew up over later centuries. Reflecting on her correspondence with a friend in France, Phyllis Rose writes, in *The Year of Reading Proust:* "Like a collagen cream or estrogen which restores to the skin its lost elasticity, e-mail has given me back the spontaneity I had lost to the laziness of age. I can receive Jack's newsletter at noon, read it after dinner, write him a note, and it will pop up on his computer screen when he arrives at work the next morning in Paris."

It's peculiar how much less effort e-mail seems to require compared to its predecessors. But really: how difficult was it to roll paper into the typewriter, extract an envelope from the drawer, lick a stamp and then set the finished production upon that table in the hall? Not very, and yet the relative ease of e-mail feels undeniable, as does—to give the downside its due—the glaze of impersonality over what pops up on that computer screen. Even if nowadays, thanks to the computer, everybody can type, we once got to know and recognize the quirks of a person's typing, and typewriter, almost as readily as his penmanship. In retrospect, one realizes that typewriting had more in common with the ink of a pen than the uniform pixels on a monitor. Of course, handwriting, that even more irreducible mode, has an intimacy and force that can never be matched by either medium. The reader of this book will meet several presidents in its pages, and it's worth noting here the biographer Edmund Morris's point about how, because it was handwritten, Ronald Reagan's letter announcing his Alzheimer's disease had a distinctly greater public impact than it would have had otherwise.

For all the wild calamities of indiscretion that cyber communication has excited, in and of itself it is far less sexy than a gartered clutch of letters that were once sealed with a kiss and had the words "I Love You" secretly written under the stamps. Does anyone really want to buy Casanova's hard drive, or Milady's printouts, at auction? And yet, to flip sides once again, electronic mail has a few of its own oddball, endearing traits: the subject line that hangs around long past the point at which it has anything to do with what the correspondence is now discussing; the whimsical screen names that it shuttles between. Shipboard cable addresses, temporary handles for the transoceanic traveler, used to have something of the same charm. Jessica Mitford's was ELKSHATRACK, chosen after a friend told her "You need news from home like an elk needs a hat rack."

But the lack of emotional affect to much e-mail is a trait conceded even by the form's enthusiasts. E-mail is so bluntly efficient that it often seems downright angry. When it *means* to be angry, it is sent in haste and repented not at leisure—no one has any of that anymore—but in a horrified burst, about three minutes after the offending words have been dispatched. In their book *Send: The Essential Guide to Email for Office and Home*, David Shipley and Will

Schwalbe take a sensible, mixed view of what's out there in the ether, and they exonerate e-mail from the most serious charge against it: "Email has been blamed for the death of the letter. We think that's unfair. Email is responsible for the death of the useless phone call. (And, by the way, it was the telephone that killed the letter.)"

People complain about e-mail's supposed evanescence, but Shipley and Schwalbe argue that its actual cockroachlike endurance is greater cause for concern: "Not only everything you've sent but also everything you've received can come back to bite you." The authors warn against the form's indiscriminate movements with the sternness of an old army training film: "Never forward anything without permission, and assume everything you write will be forwarded."

If you've bought or borrowed this book, I'm guessing you're the sort of person who deplores the absence of salutations and polite closings in electronic correspondence. And yet, I'll bet that, like me, at some point in the last couple of years, on your own digital road to Damascus, you've been thunderstruck by the realization that you'd just sent a text message that read, in its entirety: "r u there?" We are all living in Mr. Jobs's world now. Its addictive instant gratifications have replaced the old, slow anticipation of the daily visit from the mailman, who now brings mostly junk and whose bosses at the United States Postal Service have, for the past dozen or so years, been pleading with customers to come back. One advertisement from 1996 already implored:

> In this electronic age, a letter is personal and permanent. It says you took the time and trouble to communicate. The impact of a letter is unique, whether you're complaining about a disappointing purchase or declaring your love.
>
> The point is, write. A letter or card is truly a unique gift—a piece of yourself.

Lest we over-romanticize letter writing, we should remember that it could sometimes be terrible drudgery. On January 14, 1958, C. S. Lewis reminded one of his correspondents, a bit churlishly, that his letter to her was the eighth one he'd already written that day, and at the end of the following year, he asked the same woman to join him in a pact that "if we are both alive next year, whenever we write to one another it shall *not* be at Christmas time. That period is becoming a sort of nightmare to me—it means endless quill-driving!" (One wonders if he'd have been happy living into the age of the word-processed Christmas letter—"Dear Everybody"—that goes into the mail, or out through the ISP.)

The Christmas card is only one epistolary subgenre of dozens, from the chain letter to the mash note, the Collins (see Jane Austen), the bread-and-butter letter, the ransom note, the begging letter, dunning letters, letters of recommendation and introduction, the unsent letter, letters to the dead (sent by the Egyptians more than four thousand years ago), letters *from* the dead ("to be opened in the event of . . ."). Some of these, along with reports of travel, Valentines, war-zone dispatches, pleas from prison, advice to the lovelorn and j'accusing jeremiads, will surface in the chapters that follow.

AS THEIR CLOSELY variant subtitles indicate, *Yours Ever* has always been intended as a kind of companion volume to *A Book of One's Own*, the study of diaries I published back in 1984. Readers of that earlier volume may find less overlap of its dramatis personae with this book's than they might expect. Only a few of the old cast are back (George Sand and Byron are two of them), mostly because being a "natural" at one of the forms doesn't often extend to a talent for the other. Among plenty of exceptions (I can already hear them coming to your mind), Virginia Woolf may be first and foremost. Her absence here—except as the recipient of Vita Sackville-West's love letters—stems mainly from a sense that I didn't have much to add to all that others have written about her letters. But the sheer uninclusive arbitrariness of this new book (something it has in common with its predecessor) also kept me from laboring to overcome my disinclination—in this instance and some others.

Over the years, diarists who've read *A Book of One's Own* have sent me a wonderful heap of letters ("I guess I just couldn't resist one more opportunity to put my thoughts on paper"), and the only querulous note I believe they've struck has always come as an interrogative: *How could you have left out . . . ?* I'm afraid it will be the same here, with only space limitations, and a belief that it's better to convey enthusiasm than obligation, as my mitigating pleas.

Some things are quite different about this new book. Diarists are a less numerous and *odder* lot than letter writers: the assassin and the masochist and the crackpot Elizabethan astrologer, all denizens of *A Book of One's Own*, are more drawn to unanswerable monologue than to exchange. There are, for sure, plenty of flamboyant characters in the pages that follow—I wouldn't trade Flannery O'Connor, FDR and Madame de Sévigné for any of the aforementioned three—but they are writing in a form, letters, that has been used by almost every literate person. If the material feels less rarefied than the diaries in *A Book of One's Own*, it may also feel more welcoming and accessible. One common feature is indisputable: the pleasure to be had in violating someone's privacy. Whether we're reading his diaries or her letters, we're reading material that wasn't intended for us—at least originally.

If this book seems less antic than the earlier one, so is the author finally publishing it. I was a young man when I wrote *A Book of One's Own*, and while I'm fond of certain stretches, some overeager portions of it make me cringe a little, in the same healthy way one recoils a bit when rereading one's own diaries—or letters. The chance to get your hands on the latter comes infrequently—perhaps when a lover throws them back in your face, or the parent who saved them dies—but if you don't find the experience at least slightly mortifying, then something's gone wrong with your growth.

There's a difference in the *reading* of diaries and letters, not just in the writing of them. From the first genre, one is getting the whole story; however selective, the diary is the total narrative that the author chose to provide. A letter is rarely more than half the story; if its forerunner or reply aren't available, one has to infer the other half of the conversation, which can be as frustrating as listening to a cell-phone caller on the train. There are signs, however, that the genres are blending. The blog would seem to hover between the two, as half diary, half letter-to-the-world, a sign that we are entering the post-private age at least partly of our own free will.

For six months of the year 2000, when blogging barely had a name, a magazine editor named Paul Tough ran a website called Open Letters. As Dinitia Smith reported in *The New York Times:* "There was one from a man confronting his estranged wife, who was spending the night with another man; another from a 29-year-old woman having chemotherapy; and one from a well-known author who uses his bird feeders as a distraction from writing." (How unexotic this already sounds in the age of YouTube and Wonkette!) The real sign that the era of the blog was being hatched came with Smith's taking note of how "Some of the letters became mini-series that readers followed."

Yours Ever is organized roughly around the circumstances motivating each chapter's worth of letters. Life being the chaotic thing it is and letters being the associative catchall they are, there is nothing very categorical about the categories. The chapter divisions are, in fact, even more porous than they were in *A Book of One's Own*, and aside from asking "How could you have left out . . . ," readers are entitled to object that some collection discussed in "Advice" really belongs in "Confession," just as bits of "Friendship," "Complaint," "Love" and "War" may have strayed from their proper habitats. I can only reply that sorting the various bundles and collections has sometimes felt like herding cats.

This judgmental survey is offered not as an exercise in nostalgia but a series of glimpses into a still-living literature. This is a book whose text bows down to its bibliography, one that presents itself as a kind of long cover letter to the cornucopia of titles listed back there. If, from what follows, a reader feels inspired to seek out any of those volumes, to consume them at length or in toto, I will have no cause to regret the anything-but-swift completion of my appointed rounds.

Washington, D.C.
June 4, 2009

CHAPTER ONE *Absence*

We are by September and yet my flowers are bold as June. Amherst has gone to Eden.

Emily Dickinson to Elizabeth Holland, October 1870

"REAL TIME"—which isn't time at all, but rather simultaneity—seems these days always to be our goal in communicating between one place and another. So much so that one must ask: was the old passage of days and weeks, as letters traveled, "false time"?

A telephone call or instant message actually conveys one *place* to another, whereas letters always conveyed not only a place but a time as well, one that had already passed. If written vividly enough, they made the recipient forget that what he was reading about had actually taken place weeks before—the way an astronomer looking at the explosion of a star has to remember that he is in fact looking into the past, at something that happened ages ago and whose light is only now being delivered.

Distance—the fact that you are there and I am not—is the hardest fact against which letters were for centuries written, even if the distance was short and temporary, as it was between Elizabeth Holland in New York and Emily Dickinson in Massachusetts. Letters talked across it with information and sentiment, putting themselves at the service of both practical necessity and emotional luxury. Here in this first chapter we have news from elsewhere, letters containing anything at all and nothing in particular, catchall correspondence that never would have come into existence had its writer, or reader, just stayed home.

THE WARRING red and white roses of Lancaster and York still bloom against all the black ink spilled throughout the fifteenth century by one embattled Norfolk family. The Paston Letters are a medieval document-drama, crammed with besieged castles, arranged marriages, tournaments, knightings, plague, lawsuits, highwaymen, pilgrimages and falconry. The members of the prosperous but always-imperilled Paston clan—along with their retainers, allies, patrons and foes—create, year by year, a sort of prose *Canterbury Tales*, a chronicle ripe with cunning and calamity. Each packet of "tidings" between home and London (where a father or brother is usually pursuing family interests) nearly bursts its seal with urgency. So much *depends* on these letters. When the Pastons ask for news of one another, they're not being polite. They require tidings on the spot. In the decades just before Richard III offered his kingdom for a horse, the Pastons would have given at least one manor house for a telephone.

At the heart of this multigenerational mini-series stand Margaret Paston and her husband John, a lawyer often away at the capital's Inner Temple. Affection and gossip aren't absent from their correspondence, but when Margaret wishes that John "be not chary of writing letters," and tells him she "would have one every day," she's asking that they be stuffed with information, not sealed with a kiss. The two-way traffic is, if anything, more crucial to him than her. Margaret offers, for example, her sense of what the local poor are wishing from the parliament in which her husband now sits: "they live in hope that you should set a way that they might live in better peace in this country than they have done before, and that wool should be provided for so that it should not go out of this land as it has been allowed to do before." She gives John warnings of his enemies ("I pray you heartily beware how you walk there and have a good fellowship with you when you walk out. The Lord Moleyns has a company of scoundrels with him that care not what they do"), and she supplies news of their predations close to home. Most spectacular is her report, on October 27, 1465, of how the duke of Suffolk's men have come to one Paston property and "ransacked the church and bore away all the goods that were left there, both of ours and of the tenants, and even stood upon the high altar and ransacked the images and took away those that they could find, and put the parson out of the church till they had done, and ransacked every man's house in the town five or six times."

At less turbulent moments, Margaret uses her letters to remind John that their sons need hats, or that she had no decent necklace to wear when the queen visited Norwich. She has, to say the least, a strong practical streak. Shortly after John is released from a brief stay in Fleet Prison, she reminds him to bring some "pewter vessels, 2 basins, 2 ewers and 12 candlesticks" home for Christmas. John Paston sometimes complains about how things are being managed in his absence ("I pray you put all your wits together and see to the reform of it"), but more often he has reason to compliment his wife's fearlessness: "I recommend me to you and thank you for your labour and diligence against the unruly fellowship that came before you on Monday last, of which I have heard report by John Hobbs. In good faith you acquit yourself right well and discreetly, and much to your worship and mine, and to the shame of your adversaries."

The Pastons' wealth was vastly increased by an inheritance from Sir John Fastolf, a rich Knight of the Garter to whom John Paston rendered long friendship and legal counsel. Fastolf's last will and testament—itself a sort of letter, through which the author speaks of many matters from beyond the grave—assured a constant volley of arrows and writs between the Pastons and those who sought to overturn their benefactor's wishes.

These struggles lasted many years beyond John Paston's death in 1466, after which two of Margaret's sons, both named John, continued to receive her strong-willed, advice-filled letters. The eldest, Sir John (or John II), was a courtier of King Edward IV, better at holding on to a jouster's lance than money. Having irritated his father ("I see in him," John Sr. wrote Margaret, "no disposition towards discretion nor self-control"), John II is now the constant object of his mother's scoldings. Usually in London instead of at the contested Paston properties, he exasperates her with his absence and pleas of poverty. She can't believe how infrequently he writes or, after five years, that he has still not had his father's gravestone made. She tells him that one lord "reports better of you than I think you deserve," and that she will not be responsible for his debts, not when her own encircled estates are bringing in so little: "We beat the bushes and have the loss and disworship, and other men have the birds."

Sir John will protest that his presence at court is important to the family's interests, but his younger brother (John III) is the one literally left holding the fort. John III warns him that "your folk think that you have forgotten them," and suggests he spend more time with his tenants and less on his tournaments. John II does send some men to help defend the estate at Caister against the duke of Norfolk, but he doesn't show up himself to help, a dereliction that prompts his mother's most bitter letter of all:

> I greet you well, letting you know that your brother and his fellowship stand in great jeopardy at Caister, and are lacking in victuals. Daubeney and Berney are dead and others badly hurt, and gunpowder and arrows are lacking. The place is badly broken down by the guns of the other party, so that, unless they have hasty help, they are likely to lose both their lives and the place, which will be the greatest rebuke to you that ever came to any gentleman . . .

Before one begins thinking of Johns II and III as those latter-day scions of Brideshead—the wastrel Sebastian and the rule-bound Bridey, with Margaret, in between, as Lady Marchmain—one should turn to the non-emergency letters that passed between the brothers, often on the subject of John III's search for a wife. The elder John does his best to help with a number of candidates, including one properous, immovable widow: "she prayed me that I should not labour further therein, for she would hold by such answer as she had given you before." When John III all on his own finally secures a bride, John II appears displeased not to have been needed: "This matter is gone so far without my counsel, so I pray you make an end of it without my counsel."

Even more than a suitable wife, John III craves a serviceable bird, so that he might get some exercise and society through falconry: "If I have not a hawk I shall grow fat for lack of labour and dead for lack of company, by my troth. No more, but I pray God send you all your desires and me my mewed goshawk in haste . . . There is a grocer dwelling right over against the well with two buckets a little way from St. Helen's, who always has hawks to sell . . ." What the older sibling finally produces is "as good as lame in both her legs, as every man's eye may see," but John III thanks him for trying.

The two seem most like brothers when John II writes about the Turk at court with a penis "as long as his leg" (and asks John III to be careful about showing this letter to Mother), or when the two of them ally against the family's chaplain, James Gloys, who has developed too much of a hold over Margaret. "Sir James and I are at odds," reports John III to his older brother. "We fell out before my mother, with 'Thou proud priest' and 'Thou proud squire', my mother taking his side, so I have almost burned my boats as far as my mother's house is concerned; yet summer will be over before I get me any master." A year after this incident, John II congratulates John III on the chaplain's death. "I am right glad that [our mother] will now do somewhat by your advice. Wherefore beware henceforth that no such fellow creeps in between her and you . . ."

Gloys had sometimes composed Margaret's letters for her, an activity that left the younger Pastons open to his manipulations. Margaret should have understood their sensitivity on this point. Shortly after her husband's death, it was she who had counseled John II: "beware that you keep securely your writings that are of value, so that they do not come into the hands of those that may harm you hereafter. Your father . . . in his troublous time set more store on his writings and evidence than he did by any of his movable goods."

Like deeds and wills, letters were instruments that helped a man to hold his place in the turbulent medieval world. The Pastons' constantly challenged claims to land and wealth required, as much as anything, paper proof. More than five hundred years later, the written tidings they sent among themselves are all that remain to vouchsafe even their existence. The family died out in 1732.

IF WE DISPATCH ourselves two centuries ahead and across the Channel to the world of Louis XIV, we will find Marie de Rabutin Chantal—Madame de Sévigné—in a perpetually clever orbit around the Sun King's court. "Receiving and answering letters takes up a large part of our lives," she writes in 1689, toward the end of a twenty-year exchange with Françoise de Grignan, her married daughter in Provence. Indeed, Madame de Sévigné owes her literary survival to the production of mere letters just as surely as her English contemporary Pepys secured his with nothing but a diary. Each made what is supposedly literature's supporting material into a finished product.

If one compares Margaret Paston's letters and Madame de Sévigné's, the most striking difference arises from the lack of necessity attaching to the latter. So *little* depends on them but pleasure. Vital information has become gossip, and letter writing transformed itself from a task into an art.

Though news of Louis XIV's court may not "last from one post to the next," Madame de Sévigné has managed to keep it fresh for three centuries. Even the stock market of the king's female favorites continues, in her reports of it, to absorb the reader. "Here is the present position: Mme de Montespan is furious. She wept a lot yesterday. You can imagine the tortures her pride is going through. It is even more outraged by the high favour of Mme de Maintenon." Part of the punch here derives from Madame de Sévigné's absolute regard for her absolute monarch. Unsparing of anyone else, she remains rapt by the king's generosity, friendliness and general near-divinity.

She declares to Françoise that she "cannot invent anything," pronouncing herself "quite satisfied to be a substance that thinks and reads." But more important, she is a substance on whom "nothing is lost." She more than once expresses contempt for exaggeration and "false details," though there was scarce need for anyone to resort to those in surveying the Sun King's domain. On April 24, 1671, she recounts the catastrophe befalling a Chantilly chef who let down the monarch's hunting party. Milking the suspense, she withholds the crucial verb until both the periodic sentence and no doubt Françoise are ready to burst:

> Vatel, the great Vatel, maître d'hôtel to M. Foucquet and now to Monsieur le Prince, this man whose ability surpassed all others, whose mental capacity was capable of carrying all the cares of a state—this man, then, whom I knew, seeing at eight o'clock this morning that the fish had not come, was unable to face the humiliation he saw about to overwhelm him and, in a word, stabbed himself.

If only poor Vatel had possessed the sangfroid that the Marquise de Brinvilliers would exhibit five years later, after poisoning her husband: "She listened to her sentence in the morning with no fear or weakness, and at the end had it read over again, saying that the tumbril had seized her attention at the beginning and she had not followed the rest . . . She was given a glimpse of a pardon, and such a clear glimpse that she did not think she would die, and said as she climbed the scaffold, 'So it's serious?' "

The letters reveal a markedly modern mother-daughter relationship. Madame de Sévigné has time with Françoise—as Margaret Paston did not with her sons—to indulge feeling for its own sake. More than a soupçon of neurosis and passive aggression go into the envelopes. "When you want to be you are adorable," she writes at the start of their separation; she tells Françoise that her love for her is genuine, "whatever you may think about it." She asks why the daughter doesn't return her demonstrations ("Are you afraid I might die of joy?"), and her response to a report that Françoise has been crying sounds like an ancien-régime version of the classic I'll-just-sit-in-the-dark Jewish-mother joke: "I do urge you, dear heart, to look after your eyes—as to mine, you know they must be used up in your service." She cannot stop crowing once she's found the right wet nurse for her granddaughter ("This is how we manage your affairs").

She appends compliments with nudges ("I am delighted to know you are beautiful, and would like to kiss you. But how silly always to wear that blue dress!"), and she deploys feelings like troops: "Do you think I don't receive your caresses with open arms? Do you think I don't also kiss with all my heart your lovely cheeks and bosom? Do you think I can embrace you without infinite affection? Do you think that affection can ever go further than mine for you?" No, *maman*, no.

But enough about Françoise. Like all great letter-writers, Madame de Sévigné writes mostly for herself, inverting the paradox that governs the best diarists, who whether they admit it or not are really writing for others. She will "make so bold as to quote [herself]," and she knows that she writes too much ("I am producing prose with a facility that will be the death of you"), but what else is she to do when she does it so well?

She makes frequent pronouncements upon the proper way to compose correspondence, an activity so serious that even birdsong is an interruption: "I set aside part of this after-dinner period to write to you in the garden, where I am being deafened by three or four nightingales over my head." She urges Françoise to adopt a natural style, not to skimp on narrative and to put down what's on her mind right at the moment, even if the fifteen-day postman's journey may render it stale. She will give her daughter material to use in provincial conversations but expects a service in return: "Refer to certain people in our letters, so that I can say so to them." Explaining that "I have gone in for a lot of details but I am sending them because on a similar occasion I should like them myself," she promulgates a timeless epistolary standard: send the letter you'd like to receive. In the fall of 1676, she pays Françoise the ultimate compliment: "I have never seen such a brilliant letter as your last. I nearly sent it back to you to give you the pleasure of reading it." Nothing could better illustrate letter writing's movement out of utility and into aesthetics.

As befitting a friend of La Rochefoucauld's, Madame de Sévigné's style rises, at its best, to aphorism: "One can't prove that one is discreet, for by proving it one ceases to be so." Part of an age that knew how to put intellect over feeling, she can appear icily detached in her amusement. Her own granddaughter "is no beauty but she is very nice." If her outpourings of sentiment toward Françoise seem like rhetorical manipulation, the disdain with which she perceives her son's romantic entanglements comes straight from her head-ruled heart: "His emotions are quite genuine and quite false, freezing cold and burning hot, quite villainous and quite sincere; in fact his heart is crazy. [La Rochefoucauld and I] laughed a lot about it, even with my son, for he is good company and can cap anything. We get on very well together." Together they laugh at the spelling and style of his mistress's letters. When the young man distinguishes himself in the king's wars, his mother grows better disposed toward him, even if at the start of one military campaign she wearily notes how "the vogue for being wounded is setting in."

In assessing herself, Madame de Sévigné claims to resist both decorum and licentiousness; declares herself afraid of both other people's sympathy and her own self-reproach. (On the latter score she hasn't much to worry about.) She claims to be "very sorry" about an insufficiency of religious feeling, but the piety that comes most naturally to her is the mock variety, not offered at an altar but cackled behind a fan: "Everything you write about the Marans woman is delightful, and the punishments she will have in hell. But do you realize you will accompany her if you continue to hate her—just think that you will be together for all eternity. Nothing more is needed to persuade you to seek your salvation." She will promise to answer a packet of Françoise's letters when she's feeling "much less devout," and three days later, in reporting an embarrassment suffered by Madame de Gêvres, she announces her own recovery from the lapse into spirituality: "My dear, I'm spiteful—I was delighted."

Three hundred years later, we would no more have her on her knees than we would ask Pepys to stop groping the servant girls.

THE PALACE of the Sun King would probably have rendered Mark Twain less comfortable than King Arthur's court left a certain Connecticut Yankee. Though he had met the czar of Russia in 1867 and found himself well enough treated ("we staid 4 hours and were made a good deal more at home than we could have been in a New York drawing-room"), the passing of the years left Samuel Clemens a strident antimonarchist. "Another throne has gone down," he writes to the *Boston Herald*'s Sylvester Baxter in 1889, when the Brazilian monarchy falls; "I swim in oceans of satisfaction." He came to regard royalism as "the grotesquest of all the swindles ever invented by man"; the czar as "the head slave-driver of Europe"; and the "stench" of titled Englishmen as being so bad it called for shipping to foreign parts. The basic ingredient of Clemens's epistolary humor is usually a deadpan hyperbole, but the very idea of a king makes him lose his head.

On democratic home ground, this first completely American prose writer displays a range of letter-writing moods and methods that can surprise even those who know full well that *Huckleberry Finn* is not a Young Adult novel. The propulsion and vividness of Clemens's letters—his narratives are always descriptive and his descriptions are always narratives—can be seen in especially stunning combination in what he writes from Elmira, New York, to Mr. and Mrs. William Dean Howells on August 25, 1877. He tells them the story of a debt-ridden black farmer who, by some spectacular quick thinking and courage, has just saved the occupants of a runaway horse-and-buggy:

> He saw the frantic horse plunging down the hill toward him on a full gallop, throwing his heels as high as a man's head at every jump. So Lewis turned his team diagonally across the road just at the "turn," thus making a V with the fence. The running horse could not escape that, but must enter it. Then Lewis sprang to the ground and stood in this V. He gathered his vast strength, and with a perfect Creedmoor aim he seized the gray horse's bit as he plunged by and fetched him up standing!

Clemens always appreciates strong, plain style in the letters he receives—praising, for instance, the prose of his daughter Susy for having "no barnacles on it." And when he relaxes into his own epistolary labors, he seems to enjoy them, taking the time to send his wife, Livy, a "rebus," that form of letter in which certain words, mostly nouns, are eliminated in favor of little sketches depicting them.

But he did not like having to put anything conventional or obligatory into his correspondence ("I cannot overcome my repugnance to telling what I am doing or what I expect to do or propose to do") or to keep up with the letter-writing demands of literary success and celebrity. People visiting him with letters of introduction could get a chilly reception, as could those who approached only through the mails. He professed not to understand why strangers should feel the impulse to annoy him with "kindly letters" that left him with the choice of being "rudely silent" or annoyed by the labor and distraction of responding.

Clemens composed unsent letters—those black-inked jeremiads providing so much relief to the writer while doing no damage to the unaware "recipient"—with unusual frequency. He once even wrote an introduction for a collection of them that he contemplated publishing, and he advised all those inclined toward this subgenre to pigeonhole any letters they produced in it for much-later reading: "An old cold letter like that makes you wonder how you could ever have got into such a rage about nothing."

Clemens's letters have retained a full-bloodedness that gives biographies of him a peculiar animation; the reader feels treated by the subject himself to a moving picture instead of the typical collection of stills. Once he leaves Hannibal, Missouri, for New York City in the 1850s, the future Mark Twain sends home repeated, bumptious assurances that success will soon come and be entirely his doing: "I fancy they'll have to wait some time till they see me down-hearted or afraid of starving while I have strength to work and am in a city of 400,000 inhabitants." When he learns to pilot boats along the Mississippi, his self-confidence shows no sign of cooling off: "what vast respect Prosperity commands! Why, six months ago I could enter the 'Rooms' and receive only a customary fraternal greeting, but now they say, 'Why, how *are* you, old fellow—when did you get in?'" After life on the river come his years in the West, with all their adventures in mining and prospecting and journalism, and all their sights and smells, to be mailed to people still in Missouri: "When crushed, sage brush emits an odor which isn't exactly magnolia and equally isn't exactly polecat, but is a sort of compromise between the two."

This description, from 1861, appears in a letter to his mother, whose long life and heart's secrets would excite Clemens's imaginative respect for decades to come. But the family member who would forever provoke his greatest wonder, and exasperation, was his feckless brother Orion, who spent life in a prolonged, cheerful fit of self-delusion, bouncing from one ill-conceived business and belief to the next. In February 1879, while traveling in Munich, Clemens writes to Howells, his own greatest literary supporter, about Orion's scheme to make money by lecturing on his famous brother: "Did you ever see the grotesquely absurd and the heart-breakingly pathetic more closely joined together? . . . Now only think of it! He still has 100 pages to write on his lecture, yet in one inking of his pen he has already swooped around the United States and invested the result!"

Clemens suggests that Orion's ever-shifting allegiances and enthusiasms would make him a great literary character for Howells: "*you* must put him into romance." Or perhaps the two of them can write a play about him: "Orion is a field which grows richer and richer the more he mulches it with each new topdressing of religion or other guano. Drop me an immediate line about this, won't you?" When the brother proves incapable even of hiring a home nurse for their ailing mother, Clemens blows his top: "Jesus *Christ*!" he roars at Orion. "It is perilous to write such a man. You can go crazy on less material than anybody that ever lived." And yet it is Orion, flitting between the Republicans and the Democrats, the Methodists and the Swedenborgians, chicken-farming and the law, who provides the comic material that any reader of Clemens's correspondence winds up craving most.

The Mark Twain letters are replete with Clemens's own failed business ventures, to which he always applied the sort of sustained zeal Orion could never summon. When it came to managing work he created personally, Clemens could be shrewd: he understood immediately that the banning of *Huckleberry Finn* by the public library of Concord, Massachusetts, would prove good for sales; knew enough to squelch hopeless dramatic adaptations of *Tom Sawyer;* fended off requests for product endorsements; and refused newspaper editors' requests for free comment on one thing or another when he could just as easily compose his remarks for money. But his long detours into two different businesses supposedly allied to authorship—publishing and printing—proved slow-motion, draining debacles.

Working with Charles L. Webster, he had a solid success publishing Ulysses Grant's memoirs, whose gallant completion by the dying Grant occasioned Clemens's moving portrait of the persistent old general. Still, Charles L. Webster & Co. went bankrupt in 1894, at roughly the same time Clemens's "ten-year dream" of developing a perfect typesetting machine, the Paige Compositor, came clanging to a dismal close. "All the other wonderful inventions of the human brain sink pretty nearly into commonplace contrasted with this awful mechanical miracle," he had written—to Orion!—in 1889. The old boastfulness of those youthful letters from New York and the Mississippi River balloons once more over the mighty Compositor ("We own the whole field—every inch of it—and nothing can dislodge us"), but in the end, no amount of time and money can make the enterprise go. After it and the publishing business are gone, Clemens will discharge his debts by once more strenuously driving his pen.

How little detachment this greatest of ironists has in the peak moments of his far-flung life. Clemens hated "sham sentimentality" whenever he got wind of its sour sweetness, especially from incoming mail. But his own often exclamatory letters never stint on genuine feeling. He can rhapsodize a "perfect" summer day or unleash a *cri de coeur* of grief and guilt, such as the one he lets loose during his river days over the death of his brother Henry in a shipboard boiler explosion: "Men take me by the hand and *congratulate* me and call me 'lucky' because I was not on the *Pennsylvania* when she blew up!" (This long, despairing letter stands in inverse proportion to the joyous later one about Lewis, the heroic farmhand.)

After the death of his wife, Clemens directs his cry of sorrow toward Howells: "Shall we ever laugh again? If I could only see a dog that I knew in the old times! and could put my arms around his neck and tell him all, everything, and ease my heart." This lord of fictional mischief had been a worshipful husband from the start, introducing Livy to his family in a letter written on February 27, 1869: "She is only a little body but she hasn't her peer in Christendom . . . I warn you that whoever comes within the fatal influence of her beautiful nature is her willing slave for evermore."

On those occasions when Clemens and Livy were apart, letters between them substituted for companionable conversation from pillow to pillow. Having witnessed a spat between the Howellses, Clemens couldn't wait to tell his own wife about it: "It didn't seem to me that I had any right to be having this feast and you not there." It must have been particular torment, during her long last illness, for Clemens—as Charles Neider, the editor of his letters, tells us—to be permitted only forty minutes of daily visiting with Livy, and the dispatch of only two letters per day, preferably newsless and unexciting, into the sickroom.

As he aged and death increased its takings—not just Livy, but two daughters and many friends—Clemens grew more preoccupied with a dark religious determinism that held man to be "a helpless and irresponsible coffee mill ground by the hand of God." The design was anything but intelligent, and the machine ran backward. "The whole scheme of things is turned wrong end to. Life should begin with age and its privileges and accumulations, and end with youth and its capacity to splendidly enjoy such advantages."

As the twentieth century arrived, the big picture began commanding more of his focus than anything small—world disarmament trumping "that sewer—party politics"—but little sublunary concerns could never fully disappear from the letters of a writer so instinctively prescriptive. Near the end of his life, Clemens adds Sir Walter Scott to a list of literary dismissals that already includes Hawthorne, Henry James and *Middlemarch*. Posing a series of innocent-seeming questions to the critic Brander Matthews, he asks, regarding the Scotch novelist: "Has he funny characters that are funny, and humorous passages that are humorous? . . . Did he know how to write English and didn't do it because he didn't want to?"

In the year he turned forty-five, Clemens had found himself reading the "diffuse, conceited, 'eloquent,' bathotic" letters of the youthful Daniel Webster—and musing upon epistolary survival. At that point quite content in the prime of his own life beside a loving wife and healthy new baby, Clemens sat down to write a letter to his best friend, the Reverend Joseph Twichell and to wonder about whoever might be reading this same letter "80 years hence," in the year 1960. Curiously enough, Clemens imagined this reader as a "pitying snob" who would only sneer at the "pathetically trivial" doings of the author's family. Bringing the composition to an abrupt close, Clemens stopped addressing Twichell and issued a warning to the nasty specimen of posterity he was envisioning: "Suffice it you to know, scoffer and ribald, that the little child is old and blind now, and once more toothless, and the rest of us are shadows, these many, many years. Yes, and *your* time cometh!"

Come it does, of course. But a half century beyond 1960, finding ourselves still avid for Clemens's letters—in which the children are still cutting their teeth and the bloom remains on Livy's cheek—we have the pleasure of seeing that the joke, for once, was on him.

THE MOST IMPORTANT letter Jessica Mitford ever wrote was a forgery, addressed to herself ("Darling Decca") at the age of nineteen, on February 3, 1937. Pretending to be a girlfriend traveling on the Continent, the future muckraker issued an effervescent pseudo-invitation to come across the Channel: "We have taken a house in Dieppe—that is, Auntie has taken it! We mean to make it the centre of a sort of motor tour to all the amusing places round. We are going there from Austria on Wednesday, and we should so *love* you to join us next weekend sometime . . ."

The letter made it appear as if Mitford might soon be headed toward a world as stable and socially regulated as Madame de Sévigné's. In fact, her destination was war-torn Spain, which she intended to reach after eloping with her second cousin Esmond

Romilly, a nephew of Winston Churchill's who'd achieved a precocious stardom through his flamboyant rebellion against British public-school culture and his later service with the International Brigade defending Madrid. The Dieppe ruse worked. Shown the letter of invitation, Mitford's mother, Lady Redesdale, let her daughter slip out of England, and before long Decca and Romilly were in Loyalist Bilbao, transmitting news of the Spanish war for a press bureau that had taken them on.

Looked at in class and period terms, all this might be regarded as normal youthful revolt. Lord Redesdale, known to his children as "Farve," was a glowering martinet who used a stopwatch to time the sermons of whatever vicar he hired for the Cotswolds village that the Mitfords dominated. His wife ("Muv") insisted that their six daughters, widely spaced in age but sharing a complicated matrix of games, nicknames and nonsense languages, receive much of their education at home—a confinement especially resented by Decca, who from the start possessed terrific gumption.

She was the fifth of the sisters to make a London debut. All of them had looks, wit and aggression to burn; each was "a terrific hater," Decca would remember. The escapades of the older ones had been harmless enough during the 1920s heyday of the Bright Young Things (Evelyn Waugh even worked twelve-year-old Decca's pet lamb into *Vile Bodies*), but they proved a good deal less amusing when conducted under the darker clouds of the decade that followed. It would be the grotesque doings of her sisters, more than the eccentricities and strictness of her parents, that prompted Decca's flight in 1937.

"Whenever I see the words 'Peer's Daughter' in a headline," sighed Muv, "I know it's going to be something about one of you children." In 1936, after the collapse of her marriage to Bryan Guinness, heir to the brewing fortune, Diana, the greatest beauty among the girls, wed Sir Oswald Mosley, head of the British Union of Fascists. This new connection fired up Nazi enthusiasm in the most physically imposing of the sisters, Unity (middle name Valkyrie), who soon became friendly with Goebbels, Goering and Hitler himself. Nancy Mitford, the eldest and most caustic of the girls, satirized the family's political adventurings in a novel called *Wigs on the Green*, but even she had the Mitford gift for group-loathing; in her case, a weirdly virulent anti-Americanism. When Decca, the clan's only leftist, made her escape, Nancy joined forces with the family in trying to retrieve her.

After a period in Spain, the young Romillys did return, briefly, to England, where the lights in their London flat "blazed away night and day," since nobody had ever informed Decca "that you had to pay for electricity." Following the Munich pact of 1938, the couple were off to America, determined to stay there while Britain's international alignments sorted themselves out. Esmond and Decca sponged and schemed and odd-jobbed their way up and down the East Coast until during the spring of 1940, in response to Hitler's westward invasions, Romilly decided to enlist in the Canadian Air Force. He was killed the next year.

Decca remained in Washington with their baby daughter, Constancia ("Dinky"), finding work with the Office of Price Administration and a social life among the young New Dealers. She lived with Clifford and Virginia Durr, Southern liberals whose guests sometimes included Congressman Lyndon B. Johnson and his wife. ("Who is Lady Bird?" Muv wrote to Decca. "I looked her up in the Peerage, but could find no trace.") By the middle of the war, Mitford had moved to San Francisco and gotten remarried to an OPA lawyer named Robert Treuhaft. She became an American citizen in order to join the Communist Party, in whose activities she and her husband avidly participated for the next fifteen years.

Her natural leftward leanings were no doubt overstimulated by the "very lonely opposition" she recalled maintaining within her family's feathered nest. That she was able to remain a Party member, well past Khrushchev's "secret speech" denouncing Stalin in 1956 and beyond the Soviet invasion of Hungary later that year, suggests a garish, surrogate penitence for the Mitfords' Nazi sinnings. Her eventual resignation from the Party, in 1958, came about "not on any principled issue" but only because the CP had "got rather drab and useless."

A reader of her collected letters can only marvel at how such a lively spirit and instinctive debunker stayed so devoted to the commissars who kept plugging and torturing their way along in the USSR. Unity Mitford lasted several years in Nazi Germany before shooting herself when war broke out with England. It's hard to imagine her mischievous sister surviving a month in Soviet Russia without being sent off somewhere cold for re-education. Mitford loved making fun of the Party's American jargon and forever exhibited her difficulty with any form of piety or political correctness: "I should never have let you inveigle him to that Unitarian Sunday School," she writes a friend in 1959, after her son has criticized her for generalizing about people. California's Communist Party was known for being looser than other state affiliates, but Mitford's joking still got her into trouble. And yet, at no point in her letters does she question the Party's right to shun and chastise its members for the smallest deviations. Her ideological worst and self-mocking best are both on display, in annoyingly peaceful coexistence, in a letter written in 1958:

> Sat. night to Dobby's, a long battle to the end over Dr. Zhivago (Pasternak) with Dobby taking the position the S. U. is completely justified [in ordering the book's suppression], the rest of us agreeing with Laurent who pointed out that the Nobel Prize people baited a nice juicy trap for the S. U. into which they fell like a ton of bricks. Needless to say, no one had read the book . . .

Most of her political activity was local, involving work for the East Bay Civil Rights Congress (CRC) on numerous cases of police brutality perpetrated by the Oakland police department. Despite subpoenas received and passports denied, Mitford sustained an overall feeling of comfort among Americans, whose "lack of bleakness" contrasted with so much of what remained back home in England. "Could it be," she wrote her mother with some amazement in 1951, "that I am, after all, the only one who is really settled down, as they say?"

Of all the sisters, she probably made the happiest marriage. Treuhaft, himself a fine wit, is "Darling Old Bob" in decades' worth of salutations to her letters, whose domestic subject matter proceeds from pablum ("a kind of sawdust which they mix with water & feed to children here") to housekeeping (four-year-old Dinky shows her how to clean the stove properly) to a phase in which the children are old enough to pass out leaflets and make do with sandwiches on days of heightened political activity. The Treuhafts' worst sorrow—the death of their first son, run over by a bus in 1955—makes scant appearance in the letters; in Mitford's memoirs she could not bear to write of it at all.

Otherwise, death became her.

Led to the subject by Treuhaft, who was doing legal work for a Bay area co-op promoting inexpensive burials, Mitford soon beheld the American funeral industry as a high-pressure game of grotesque profiteering, not to mention a paradise of macabre euphemism and fantastic technique: "If [the corpse] should be bucktoothed, his teeth are cleaned with Bon Ami and coated with colorless nail polish," she wrote in what became the bestselling *American Way of Death* (1963). "His eyes, meanwhile, are closed with flesh-tinted eye caps and eye cement."

It all left her "roaring" (a favorite word). A muckraker had been born, one whose spirits would forever be as high as her dudgeon. Magazines began calling with story ideas, and she soon had "masses of things ½ cooking." The tastiest results included her takedown of Elizabeth Arden's exorbitantly ineffectual Maine Chance beauty spa in Arizona, and her assembled letters show that writing home was sometimes a way of making notes for her articles: "I have cased the visitors book," she tells Treuhaft from Maine Chance in November of 1965. "Part of it reads like a list of products advertised in the daily press (Heinz, Ford, Fleishmann etc)." Retaining a sense of herself as a kind of lucky amateur, Mitford would always be surprised by her success in investigative journalism. She was particularly pleased when her 1970 exposé of the Famous Writers School, a mail-order fraud that had grown fat with promises to the aspirant scribbler, forced the operation out of business.

The onetime revolutionary was actually a born meliorist, shining her gleeful light upon the venal and phony, even if she never again found quite so glorious a target as the funeral industry. Her largest other subject was the U.S. prison system, whose Advanced Han-Ball Tear Gas Grenade, seen by Mitford at a corrections convention, was a kind of counterpart to the embalmer's Flextone preparation. But the prison book that she produced, *Kind and Usual Punishment* (1973), while full of fine stuff on matters like abusive medical experimentation, ends up feeling too much of a downer for the author's natural talents. In *The American Way of Death*, the corpse, well out of it but all made up, seems often to be as amused as the reader; not so, of course, the wretched convict.

The prologue to her memoir *Daughters and Rebels* includes the confession (odd in a memoirist) that "Looking backward is not much in my nature." Even so, the second half of Mitford's life was often spent coming to terms with the first. She traveled several times to Lady Redesdale's home on Inch Kenneth, a Hebridean island in which Decca herself had received, from her only brother, a one-sixth share. (An attempt to donate her portion to the Communist Party of Great Britain proved unsuccessful.) By 1960, her gradual reconciliation with Muv had become a source of deep pleasure.

Her sisters were a more intractable matter. Unity, who died in 1948 from the aftereffects of her suicide attempt, would come to Mitford in dreams that reflected Decca's own enduring and horrified love: "well there's no forgiveness possible (nor would it have been sought by that feckless, unregenerate soul)." In the 1970s, a willingness to help Unity's biographer, David Pryce-Jones, get to the whole truth about his subject, nearly ended Mitford's relationship with Debo, now the duchess of Devonshire.

With Diana there had long since been nothing left to sunder. Mitford disliked not being on communicative terms—"writers" or "speakers"—with almost anyone, but at the close of a letter to Muv would send love to relations "with the usual exceptions." She was prepared to go to great lengths to avoid seeing the Mosleys during a 1959 visit to Paris, where not only Nancy but Diana's family would be: "We envisage scenes as in corny French bedroom farces, the Mosleys popping out of one room, down an oubliette, [the

Treuhafts] hiding in the stove, etc. As I pointed out to Nancy, just their chosen place for us anyway."

Nancy Mitford—the most brilliant and personally cruel of the sisters—remained the one whose approval Decca most desired, the only one for whom she could become a "doormat" time and again. Lady Redesdale once pointed out that Nancy's letters "usually contain a skillfully hidden dagger pointed straight at one's heart," but compared to Decca's, the letters collected in *Love from Nancy* come across as grating little performances, falsely shrewd and oddly fluttering, self-congratulatory even when self-critical. The contentment they proclaim, over even Nancy's long and manifestly unfulfilling affair with a married French colonel, isn't the least bit convincing. If Decca, so badly teased and knocked off balance by her oldest sister, had been interested in the last laugh, she could have had it.

Her own letters are so full of comic set pieces, vivid narrative and wonderfully replicated speech (a whole page of parodic Southern palaver written out during a 1961 visit to the Durrs) that one wonders why Mitford never tried writing a novel. Fear of imitating Nancy, already so successful in the genre, may have been a factor; Decca even worried that the British title of her first memoir, *Hons and Rebels*, might cause the older sister, famous for her "U" and "non-U" speech distinctions, to "think it's cashing in on her stuff." One suspects, however, a more fundamental reason, namely, that the novel would have seemed too precious and artificial a form to such a lover of real-life rumpus and corrective action.

Letter writing, by contrast, always retained its element of practical urgency, even as it allowed Mitford to roar and entertain and sketch verbal equivalents of the faces she liked to make at the lectern in front of flesh-and-blood crowds. If she sometimes overindulged tendencies toward the crude and the cute, these resulted only in small blots upon her contributions to a genre that was never—one has to remind oneself, Madame de Sévigné aside—designed for artistic perfection. Mitford's letters are a smashing, buoyant accumulation; they ride what one hopes is not the last wave of a literary form soon to be as dead as one of her Flextoned corpses. During the fax's brief moment between the post and e-mail, Mitford corresponded with Miss Manners over the etiquette governing the new machine and managed to adapt at least one old epistolary convention to the world's new instantaneousness: "Yrs of 9:54 from Chatsworth just rec'd," she informed Debo.

Mitford preferred gadgets to greenery ("Nature, nature, how I hate yer") and believed that keeping fit was only likely to prolong the miseries of whatever cancerous affliction got one in the end. Nursing homes would have been a marvelous subject for her, better than her late exploration of obstetrics; she described herself as going "from the Grave to the Cradle" with *The American Way of Birth* in 1992. She did, after a bad fall, give up drinking, but backslid from efforts to quit smoking, which included her husband's attempt at aversion therapy: "Bob collected a ton of disgusting butts & ashes, & all I did was to breathe in deeply & say 'HOW divine.'" Their marriage survived an affair of Treuhaft's in the mid-1980s, and they soon returned to "all the old feelings of pleasantness & fun" between the two of them.

As friends died off, Mitford realized that she missed the arrival of their letters more than the people themselves: "Oh for the writing on the env!" In the middle of the night, two weeks before she died, she wrote a splendidly matter-of-fact farewell to Treuhaft: "Bob—it's so ODD to be dying, so I must just jot a few thoughts." Those mostly concerned the good fortune they'd had together, but Mitford moved on to giving her husband some advice: "you'll need someone—I mean you've got all those household skills, cooking etc., pity to waste don't you agree? Be thinking of someone agreeable. You won't have to as they'll come flocking I bet. I do have some ideas but fear to mention for fear of annoying or being intrusive, none of my business you'll say." She concluded with an expression of avidity for the next simple thing: "By the way—do go to that film this evening [and] dinner . . . I long to hear all about it . . . Should be v. innaresting." Once she was gone, on July 23, 1996, her cremation cost $475.

Mitford assessed herself, accurately, as being "not a specially introspective type." She "never felt 'let down'" by anyone, and for all that she took to America, considered the "pursuit of happiness" to be "an absurd idea." Nonetheless, she found it, in the knockabout company of enemies and friends alike. To those who had assured her that a week at Maine Chance spa would leave her feeling wonderful, she later reported: "As I always feel perfectly OK anyhow, I haven't noted the difference." A week spent with her letters makes everybody else seem a bore. One wonders how *she* stood it, and with such fine gusto.

BUT WHAT OF THOSE who had Mitford's nerve and still lacked money for the voyage of escape? Earlier emigrants from England, short even the price of steerage, ran into one of the crueler conundrums that face the penniless striver: it costs money to start alleviating one's poverty. The enterprising poor of the nineteenth century needed someone to stake them toward a newer world, and in 1850, the Family Colonisation Loan Society set about raising money for just that purpose. Mrs. Caroline Chisholm (soon, alas, to be caricatured in *Bleak House* as Mrs. Jellyby) pressed Charles Dickens, that champion of the poor, into promoting the Society's idea. She provided the novelist with emigrant success stories in the form of letters from Australia, hoping that, once Dickens worked them into an article for his new *Household Words* magazine, citizens would loosen their pursestrings to help more of the downtrodden find better lives away from home.

In our own day, Dickens's publicist might have given Mrs. Chisholm a slogan: AUSTRALIA—IT'S NOT JUST FOR CONVICTS ANYMORE! In the event, Dickens presented a brief selection of the letters with some supportive, if not quite impassioned, personal commentary. He imagined clusters of successful new Aussies reeling in poor souls who still suffered in smoky, overpopulated England. In one of the letters, a man from Sydney tells his brother: "Send me word in your next what progress you are making toward finding your way out here do not stop there to staarve [*sic*] for as bad as Sydney is no one that is willing to work need want." Another writer marvels at how some ex-Londoners have taken to the farmwork Down Under more easily than emigrants from the English countryside have managed to. And yet, lest anyone think Australia a panacea, the writer informs his brother and sister that the drunkard wife who followed him here has not been able to mend her ways: "I gave her another trial and I expended about £20 but all to no purpose therefore I have left her about four months since."

The letters' power comes in part, Dickens knows, from their originally having been "written for no eyes but those to which they were addressed." Their unexpected second life gives a jolt to readers—the feeling of having blundered in on someone else's private business—that not even Dickens's novels can always provide.

Half a century later, and half a world between England and Australia, a less powerful and famous voice put out her own call for emigration—of the pioneering, internal-American kind. "When I read of the hard times among the Denver poor," writes Elinore Pruitt Stewart, from Wyoming, on January 23, 1913, "I feel like urging them every one to get out and file on land . . . To me, homesteading is the solution of all poverty's problems, but I realize that temperament has much to do with success in any undertaking, and persons afraid of coyotes and work and loneliness had better let ranching alone."

She has found that ranching suits her own temperament down to the big open grassy ground. Raised in the Oklahoma Indian Territory and orphaned at fourteen, Elinore Pruitt Rupert moved to Denver in her early thirties, around 1908, with a baby daughter; scholarly opinion differs as to whether she was widowed or divorced from Harry Rupert. Either way, once in Denver she began fending for herself and her little girl, Jerrine, as a nurse and laundress. Then, in 1909, she took a job keeping house for Clyde Stewart in Burnt Fork, Wyoming, though what she really wanted to do was stake her own claim to some land close by his. Mr. Stewart seems to have been happy enough about that—even after their marriage, which took place shortly after Elinore's arrival.

Elinore Stewart imparts her adventures, most of them amusing, in letters to a Mrs. Coney, who had been one of her bosses back in Denver. In fact, she'll sometimes sign herself "Your ex-Washlady," with lighthearted pride in how far her gumption has now taken her. So keen is she on presenting her triumph that for some time she delays letting Mrs. Coney know about her marriage: "It was such an inconsistent thing to do that I was ashamed to tell you." She would prefer to keep looking like the fearless single person she was when riding the stagecoach to Wyoming with a Mormon driver: He was "so handsome . . . I was not a bit offended when he insisted on making love all the way . . . But, of course, as I had no chaperone I looked very fierce (not that that was very difficult with the wind and mud as allies) and told him my actual opinion of Mormons in general and particular."

Once she files her claim, she presents herself as "a bloated landowner" whose new propertied status doesn't save her from having to cut hay, milk seven cows and "put up thirty pints of jelly and the same amount of jam." Still worried that her quick alliance with Mr. Stewart will make Mrs. Coney regard her as "a Becky Sharp of a person," she reassures her correspondent with the news that "although I married in haste, I have no cause to repent. That is very fortunate because I have never had one bit of leisure to repent in." So constant are the chores, at Mr. Stewart's house and on her own piece of land, that she reports forgetting even to remove her apron before the justice of the peace began the wedding ceremony. Her husband—born in Pennsylvania, but quoted with a thick Scottish accent in the letters—is a fine fellow whom she won't allow "to do anything toward improving my [own] place, for I want the fun and experience myself." After a few years she can tell Mrs. Coney: "I have tried every kind of work this ranch affords, and I can do any of it."

Mrs. Stewart coats understandable self-regard with pleasing self-deprecation, and she knows the value of a little concealment too: "long ago I learned that the quickest way to get what I want is not to want it, outwardly, at least." She usually *does* get what she wants, but her new contentment is hedged with risks and privations: "Out here where we can get no physician we have to dope ourselves," and when both Mr. Stewart and Jerrine get the grippe, Elinore adds nursing to the rest of her tasks. "The magazines were much appreciated," she writes Mrs. Coney. "They relieved some weary night-watches."

Still, she's in no greater difficulty than her neighbors in this can-do, cooperative culture she's joined. A reader learns how, in order to save a hired man from gangrene, her neighbor Mrs. O'Shaughnessy tricked him into putting "his finger on the chopping-block and before he could bat his eye she had chopped off the black, swollen finger." Journeying toward a gathering of friends, Mr. and Mrs. Stewart and their companions reach a rock wall with the black-lettered legend: DICK FELL OFF THIS HERE CLIFT AND DIED. A snowslide then imperils the party, after they've gone twenty-five miles; they'll be guided to safety by a bugler, a Mexican man who along with his wife offers them food and shelter. Such kindness requires no literary embellishment from Elinore: "Poor Carlota Juanita!" she writes. "Perhaps you think she was some slender, limpid-eyed, olive-cheeked beauty. She was fat and forty, but not fair."

Not that Elinore is against romance, of either the literary or amorous kind. She throws herself into the wedding of Bishey Bennet and "Miss Em'ly," the sweetheart who took twenty-five years to follow him West from New York State. The bride arrives "a very travel-stained little woman, down whose dust-covered cheeks tears had left their sign." But all is well once Miss Em'ly is taken charge of by Elinore Stewart, her brisk, self-appointed matron of honor.

The letters convey, sometimes sentimentally but more often like cold water from a canteen, the flavor of the frontier's closing hours: the toys made from waste paper and women's hair; the lonesome late-night sadness of a cowpunchers' camp; the rough German tongue of the camp boss's wife, who insults the most timid boy in her employ by insulting his father as well: "he waded the creek vone time und you has had cold feet effer since."

Mrs. Stewart had sent her first letter to Mrs. Coney in order to reassure her ("Are you thinking I am lost, like the Babes in the Wood? Well, I am not"), but the ones that followed from the Burnt Fork post office, a two-mile gallop from the house, are written as much for the sender as the recipient, to help fill up the new vastness that surrounds their author: "I know this is an inexcusably long letter, but it is snowing so hard and you know how I like to talk." As every letter writer and diarist learns, Stewart can relive her pleasures by writing them down, so long as she's willing to pay the forfeit when the time comes to recount her pains. It takes her more than two years to admit to Mrs. Coney that the little boy whose funeral she described was actually her and Mr. Stewart's firstborn son.

Letters are the trade winds and storehouse of her emotional life, and she expects them to be that for everyone else as well. After finding out that her illiterate seventy-nine-year-old friend Zebulon Pike Parker has never been able to exchange letters with the relatives he left back East decades before, Stewart jumps in and corrects the situation, writing to Parker's youngest sister and then reciting to him the replies that start arriving.

If Mrs. Stewart sometimes seems to high-hat her own chief correspondent ("I am so glad when I can bring a little of this big, clean, beautiful outdoors into your apartment for you to enjoy"), Mrs. Coney does not appear to have taken offense. She eventually helped get the letters printed in magazine and book form. In 1914, their hardcover publisher insisted on their genuineness, assuring readers that they were being "printed as written, except for occasional omissions and the alteration of some of the names." Such editorial fidelity doesn't, of course, rule out bits of embroidery having been performed during the original writing. Elinore Stewart, who also wrote some pieces for *The Kansas City Star*, shows herself a dab, deliberate hand at dialect, narrative shapeliness and literary allusion: references to Shakespeare, Dickens and James Fenimore Cooper find their way into her letters, along with an occasional straining after lyricism: "I saw the moon come up and hang for a while over the mountain as if it were discouraged with the prospect, and the big white stars flirted shamelessly with the hills."

But all of this conscious composition only highlights the writer's regard for letter writing itself. Mrs. Stewart dismisses one of her own briefer efforts as a mere "reply," not to be counted with what she typically tries to produce. Not just length but *detail* is required if letters are to do what they have to do in these days before the easy enclosure of sharp color photographs; it's the same thing Dickens's novels had to do before movie cameras could pan all the kingdoms and rooms a reader would never set foot in himself. "I feel just like visiting to-night," Mrs. Stewart writes to Mrs. Coney on December 1, 1911, "so I am going to 'play like' you have come. It is so good to have you to chat with. Please be seated in this low rocker." She then invites her imagined guest to look, paragraph after paragraph, at every object and rug in her home.

According to a local-history website, the Stewart house is these days pretty much a shambles and tenanted by animals. But it's all as it was in its former mistress's irreverent letters. In them a reader can even now see, hanging on the wall, a match-holder given by Mrs. Coney and described by Mrs. Stewart. "It is the heads of two fisher-folk. The man has lost his nose, but the old lady still thrusts out her tongue."

"EVERY DAY HAS ITS REVELATIONS," writes Lafcadio Hearn on October 11, 1893, though the geography of his life has been so exotic that any new experience must be fresh indeed to rise to such a level. At the age of forty-three, three and a half years after his arrival in Japan, Hearn is on his third continent. Born in the Greek Islands, raised in Ireland and educated, at least for a time, in England, he landed hard in America at the age of nineteen, settling and then nearly starving in Cincinnati, whose poorest residents he began writing about for two different newspapers. A subsequent decade in New Orleans made Hearn's literary reputation as a chronicler of that city's human and culinary gumbo; another two years in the West Indies kept his feet off anything that might come to feel like home ground.

He goes to Japan hoping that "several years' soujourn" there will allow him to produce magazine articles and "a good book," but he also needs to find a teaching job, if only to help him learn the language and the "emotional nature" of the Japanese people. A letter of self-introduction to Basil Hall Chamberlain, a British professor of Japanese at Tokyo Imperial University, helps him to land his first position, in Matsue; he will begin a second, longer stint in Kumamoto the following year. While living and working in both places, he continues to write, voluminously, to Chamberlain, imparting a record of cultural discoveries to a man who had already made most of them, on his own, decades before. No matter: over the course of four years, until his teaching life gives way to a newspaper job in Kobe, Hearn is vivid, astute, preposterous and contradictory in all he notices and feels and pours upon the page. He declares that good letter-writers make bad chess players—spontaneity aiding the one and strategy the other—and explains to his correspondent: "my letters are too prolix and gushy, I know; but if I stopped to polish them, I would never get through, nor would I feel quite honest."

Much of what he sends does, in fact, suggest careful composition, but the ink on even those letters seems erasable, so prone is their author to revising his first impressions. Early in his stay, he heartily assents to Percival Lowell's belief that "the Japanese are the happiest people in the world"; he seems convinced that their serenity derives from "the very absence of the Individuality" that forces Westerners to hustle and assert. Within two years, however, Hearn will repeal both pronouncements, having by then seen instances of the native sensitivity being taken to suicidal extremes and having realized that his own cook "wears the mask of happiness as an etiquette."

All that's before him shifts and feints; he never feels confident that he's getting things right. "Paralyzed for lack of certainties" about what he should write—he's not even "sure of [the] position" he's taking in a philosophical article on jiujitsu—his mood oscillates perpetually between contentment and loneliness.

His most consistent perspective is a kind of frustrated fascination. *The Atlantic Monthly* will probably never get the kind of material it would like from him, he decides, because real cross-cultural intimacy is impossible here: "If I speak, I am saluted," he tells Chamberlain. "If I ask a question, I am politely snubbed or evaded." A foreign teacher in the government schools "is trusted only as an intellectual machine. His moral notions, his sympathies, his intuitions, his educational ideas are not trusted at all." Still, Hearn manages to get a hangover after drinking sake with his students, and he allows himself to hope that they might be fonder of him than he's imagined. More often, though, he entertains Chamberlain with samples of their fractured English and laments the regimentation of their natural impulses.

He rarely finds humor among the Japanese and remains ever struck by their premium on emotional restraint. He swears he's even observed "a difference between the Western and the Japanese dog! How different the gaze, the intuition, the memory! And how utterly deficient the Japanese dog in gratitude! And how indifferent to the question of who owns him!" The training of a young geisha, audible just beyond Hearn's garden, is a source of moral and emotional distress: "The child is very young; but she is obliged to sing nearly seven hours every day. I can tell what time it is by the tone of weariness in her voice. Sometimes she breaks down and cries to be let alone in vain. They do not beat her—but she must sing." On the other hand, the docility of a Japanese baby creates in Hearn a comic feeling of his own spiritual inferiority: "Sometimes I feel downright afraid of it; it knows infinitely too much; and I strongly suspect that it still remembers all its former births."

His Japanese wife and child, both acquired in fairly short order, provide him with considerable happiness if no permanent immunity from surges of lonesomeness. (Hearn makes no mention to Chamberlain of the African-American wife he had during his Cincinnati days.) The rituals of his current household are described with a tender, appreciative precision that bespeaks, despite the above, at least a *little* susceptibility to geishalike behavior: "always, according to ancient custom, the little wife asks *pardon for being the first to go to sleep*. I once tried to stop the habit—thinking it too humble. But after all it is pretty,—and is so set into the soul that it could not be stopped."

Hearn is a kind of one-man *National Geographic*, replete with observations both pedantic and sharp. He inclines toward the production of theories on just about everything, most of them exuberant, a few of them crackpot. He declares, for instance, that "a man can scientifically triple the assimilating capacity of his stomach," and that he can "read all day without fatigue" by lying on the floor and holding a book above his head.

Published in 1910, his letters to Chamberlain give us only one side of what a reader suspects was a one-sided exchange to begin with. We get discourses on the nature of parody; musings upon Wordsworth (for all his coldness "we have to love him"); a consideration of when to use foreign expressions in one's writing. Hearn is all for it: "I write for beloved friends who can see colour in words, can smell the perfume of syllables in blossom." His greatest literary love—to the point of near-constant evangelism—is Kipling, though enthusiasm is his natural readerly condition ("Oh! I love Heine") and overstatement his favorite rhetorical mode ("one of the most touching things in all literature").

The riddle of Japan—its willful impenetrability, signified by the way its people wear their European-style clothes "only outside the house"—remains his chief subject and bafflement. And yet, for all that he would like to be let in on its secret, he seems to concede that he shouldn't even be prying into it. He judges the opening of Japan by Commodore Perry, less than fifty years before, to be on balance "a crime." The West is infecting the new Japan with "the frank selfishness, the apathetic vanity, the shallow vulgar scepticism" that have the country's former charm and gentleness "evaporating more rapidly than ether from an uncorked bottle." Hearn would prefer the old reverence for the emperor and the former (quite ungentle) "military spirit"; he wishes for a "return to autocracy" as the antidote to "Beastly modernization!"

The most corrupting Western import is Christianity, whose missionaries are Hearn's recurring villains. Someone needs to write the truth about them, or better yet, he tells Chamberlain, put them "on a small ship" that can be "scuttled at a reasonable distance of one thousand miles from shore." Hearn admits to being "rabid" on the subject—the Jesuits did a nasty job on him when he was young—but even so, he dislikes "*shallow atheists*"; he admits the underlying metaphysics of all material fact, and acknowledges the religious longings of "that much bescratched thing called my soul." Early in his stay, Hearn sees the old Japan's virtues embodied in Shinto, though as time goes on its appeals "to tradition and race feeling" seem less attractive than Buddhism's "appeal to the human heart."

Setting aside his approval of militarism, Hearn tells Chamberlain that he is "not altogether in sympathy with the worship of Force in our century." At times, in fact, he sounds like his born-too-late American contemporary, Henry Adams, as he laments the absence of "angels and demons and gods" in a new world of "electricity, steam, mathematics." And yet, he also misses the modern West from which he's currently absent, "a world charged with spirit, like a dynamo with lightning," and he startles the contemporary reader's eye with this 115-year-old postscript: "I wish it were 1994,—don't you?"

While we read the letters, our own knowledge of the future, necessarily greater than his, is a kind of deadly superiority ("Nagasaki is the prettiest seaport I ever saw," he writes on July 22, 1893), but Hearn's mind is nothing if not fearless in its own forays far ahead, as when he predicts the demise of the gluttonous white race: "There is something very sinister in the fact that the cost of life to an Englishman is just about twenty times the cost of life to an Oriental." Hearn is in fact willing to push things toward the longest and gloomiest planetary view: "What is even the use of the life of a solar system—evolution, dissolution,—re-evolution, re-dissolution, forever more?" Buddhism, he supposes, can help a little.

One enjoys Hearn most, however, when he pulls back from the infinite and grandiose and takes a look at what's in front of him: the light of today, August 28, 1893, when "the shadows are sharp as the edge of a knife"; the Japanese eyelid, whose superior beauty he explains in a brilliant piece of physiognomic observation; or the national variant of archery that involves "shooting at a paper lantern at night." His wife remains a partial mystery, but he notes her clever and agreeable behavior, including the shrewdness she displays in hiding, rather than mailing, an envelope he handed her in a bad mood.

His views are forever proclaiming and then disowning themselves. Hearn was indeed made for letter writing instead of chess, at which he would probably try to play both black and white. Four years after arriving in Japan, he calls himself "a disillusioned enthusiast," regretting the way he once "described horrible places as gardens of paradise, and horrid people as angels and divinities." But the angels and devils never cease switching sides. Hearn changes his mind about his students; declares that even in the slick new Japan "the Japanese are still the best people in the world to live among"; finds that in some respects Shinto may be preferable to Buddhism after all; and successively decides that the Japanese won't, will, won't be able to resist foreign influence.

When making the occasional delicate apology to Chamberlain ("I am sorry to have praised to you stories you do not like"), Hearn can sound almost Japanese himself. But when he scolds himself for allowing a letter to go on too long, it's ourselves we recognize, since the only epistolary apology more familiar than this is the one we make for having taken so long to write in the first place. In Hearn's own case, the mass production of words is necessary to a mind always having its own ideas "reconstructed, repaired, renovated, and decorated"—a mind locked in a jiujitsu match with itself.

THE PRINCIPAL REQUIREMENT for homesickness is having a home to begin with. Hearn was so rootless and peripatetic that he can't really be said to meet the condition. The letters we best know him by are not to his nearest and dearest but to a professional acquaintance, and as such they stand apart from the sort of letters—written with longing, memory, sheer need—by which we typically come to understand any person who's had to write when far from home.

We wouldn't—would we?—go to William Faulkner for that kind of letter. What would a writer so elusive and opaque offer in the way of such simple, familiar feelings? As it happens, after opening the letters he sent home from his youthful Northern travels, a reader amasses enough evidence—as if performing what the legal profession charmingly calls "discovery"—to make a case for Faulkner's callowness and ordinary vulnerability. There he is, during and after the First World War, up in Connecticut and New York and Canada, telling his parents all that's happening, but writing letters mostly to receive them, as the homesick have always done.

On April 5, 1918, after a long stretch of newsy chatter from New

Haven, where he's just arrived, he bursts out with a single-sentence confession of need ("I'm terribly lonesome") before signing off "Love, Billy" and no doubt running to post the letter before he becomes embarrassed and changes his mind. A day later he assures his parents that he "shan't starve"; the restaurants are clean, and he can get coffee, toast and eggs for a quarter. Still, this twenty-year-old fellow needs mothering: "As regards sending me clothes—shirts—shirts—shirts. And please, Mother dear, make them with *one* button instead of 2 at the collar."

For the next couple of months he's a peculiar outsider, a literary young man working ordinary jobs in a town where other young men are strutting toward their gentlemen's Cs within the gates of Yale. There are times here, one realizes, that Faulkner must have felt more set apart than Quentin Compson, who in *The Sound and the Fury* would at least be a registered student at Harvard.

In the middle of 1918, seeking opportunity for the quickest advancement, Faulkner entered the British military instead of the American, training for the RAF in Canada. The editor of his letters from this particular period judges them more confident than homesick, but to most readers the new airman will still seem to be in short pants rather than a white scarf. Though he hates to ask for it, Faulkner could use ten dollars from his folks; he doesn't even have money for stamps. The senior men he describes seem just as marvelous and remote to *him* as they must to his parents back in Mississippi: "I wish you could see some of these flight sergeants and mechanics—fierce mustaches and waists like corset models and tiny caps and swagger sticks." During the flu epidemic, Faulkner drinks a lot of milk, remaining healthy but then having to face the sudden end of the war, which makes his months of training moot: "They have started dismantling the 'planes and putting them away, a job that has been most magnanimously given to us."

Throughout his young adulthood, Faulkner seems less a harbinger of modernism than a figure out of Booth Tarkington. His humor and style remain a boy's. In the letters addressed to her, Mrs. M. C. Falkner (the "u" would be her son's later affectation) is sometimes "Mother," sometimes "Moms," and sometimes "Momsey."

Billy sends candy home to his little brother, Dean, and wants to be remembered to his "Mammy," Caroline Barr. During his first stint in New Haven, he delightedly conveys to his mother the humor of Ray Noon, the Irish housemate who has "just wandered in and said—'Give her my love, Bill'—taking it that I was writing to a flapper. I told him it was you, and he said—'Then be sure and send my message, and tell her we have only had to get you out of jail twice.'" Mrs. Falkner sends cakes to her son for years, and he guards them when his pals crowd in like "vultures." Billy insists that being "naturally rather unapproachable" helps to fend the others off, but he's tenderhearted enough to buy a "pink ice-cream soda" for a newsboy who reminds him of Dean, whom he misses so much "I almost dream about him every night."

When Faulkner returns to New Haven a few years after the war, a racial and regional smugness have settled over him. He blows hard to his mother, refusing to believe that Northern "niggers are as happy and contented as ours are, all this freedom does is to make them miserable because they are not white." It will serve him right, a month later in New York, when he has to write that "the other dishwashers, Greeks and one Irish, thought I was a wop, and looked down on me." His first subway ride proves repellent: "The experience showed me that we are not descended from monkeys, as some say, but from lice." Struggling to break into magazines, he finds that he's got competition throughout Greenwich Village: "all Oshkosh is here with portfolios of strange verse and stranger pictures under one arm." He lands a job at Lord & Taylor, but the department store's management proves so unfriendly he has to tell his mother not to "send any more mail to the store."

The young Faulkner is an appealingly self-conscious letter-writer, curious about epistolary form, the way it both mirrors and distorts human action. He can be "having such a hurried life that all [his] letters sound disjointed," but on the other hand, mail from home takes so long to reach him that "things happen and then unhappen by the time I hear of them." Faulkner will complain of being unable to remember what he intended to write once he finally gets the chance to pick up a pen, though a few weeks earlier he'd scolded himself for allowing a moderately long letter written at different sittings to turn into something more like a diary. After realizing that his awful penmanship is causing some of his letters to get lost in the mail, he vows to start putting a return address on the envelope. Mixing sweetness and strut during his RAF days, he tells his mother that every time one of his letters does make it through, "I feel a certain pleasurable glow of exultation, as though I had downed a Hun machine."

By 1925, during a productive half-year in New Orleans that will have him metamorphosing from poet to novelist, Faulkner keenly begins to feel himself a writer. (Indeed, he sometimes Writes as determinedly as Elinore Stewart: "Sky all full of fat white clouds like little girls dressed up and going to a party.") Along with verse and fiction, he's turning out newspaper sketches that are almost literally potboilers: "They want some short things," he explains to his mother, "about 200 words with a kick at the end. I can knock off one of them while I'm waiting for my teakettle to boil." The longer ones, he believes, are fit for a scrapbook, and his work is provoking fan letters from "strange females" who've seen the author's picture in *The Times-Picayune*. A new bumptiousness infuses his correspondence; he pronounces his novel-in-progress "very good" and boasts of having put down "7000 words in one day this week." By the summer of '25 he can tell his mother that writing letters has become a busman's holiday.

Actually, it was the three years between his days in New York and his time in New Orleans that really dimmed the luster of letter writing. Back home during that period, Faulkner supported himself as the University of Mississippi's postmaster, playing cards and writing on the job and sometimes throwing away letters before they could be delivered. "I reckon I'll be at the beck and call of folks with money all my life," he declared after being fired, "but thank God I won't ever again have to be at the beck and call of every son of a bitch who's got two cents to buy a stamp."

THE MODERN TRAVELER's iPhone will begin pulling e-mail down from the sky the moment his plane has landed in Ulan Bator, whereas little more than half a century ago, while studying and traveling abroad, the young V. S. Naipaul could write to his family back in Trinidad and say, almost believably: "I have been in Paris for a week and have only just come across a post office." Before Xerox and the SEND ALL button, dispatching the same news to multiple recipients also required considerable labor from a novelist on the make; as Naipaul explains to Kamla, his sister studying in India: "Writing two copies of a letter is pretty tiring. To write home and then to write to you about the same thing is a heavy task."

Like the letters Faulkner sent home from New Orleans, the ones Naipaul mails from Oxford show him quickly gaining traction as a writer and fast coming into a sense of his own superiority, though he seems to have been inclined to that almost from birth. As the family prince, its great hope for distinction, "Vido" reports on his social navigation through the university—his attendance at bottle parties, his need for dance lessons—as well as his decidedly unimpressed view of the competition: "There are asses in droves here," he writes just months after arriving. He has every reason to believe that he "can beat them at their own language."

The hauteur of this fellow, still a teenager, who likes being called "sir" and believes Jane Austen's books to be "mere gossip," makes him scorn fellow passengers on a train as well as the offspring of an uncle who resides in England ("The children nauseate me"). He finds it difficult to be polite, and can't even beg his family's pardon for the bad typing in one of his letters without adding: "I have no time nor the desire to correct." As his sister's birthday approaches, he tells her: "I shan't send a card, but I offer my best wishes."

All the salient personal features of the Nobel Prize winner are on display fifty years before he takes the stage in Stockholm. Misogyny is everywhere in the letters. Patricia Ann Hale, the wife he will make miserable for decades, occasions a premarital assessment, written for his family, that seems in spots more like literary criticism than love: "She is a member of the university, not unintelligent, nor altogether unattractive . . . About her character: she is good, and simple. Perhaps a bit too idealistic, and this I find on occasion rather irritating." The Naipaul who will come to dismiss entire civilizations that have offended his intelligence or nose, is up and running even before he leaves Trinidad. On November 24, 1949, he writes to Kamla, already in India: "My thesis is that the world is dying—Asia today is only a primitive manifestation of a long-dead culture; Europe is battered into a primitivism by material circumstances; America is an abortion."

But between the broadest brushstrokes one sees a corresponding love of precision and cool: "This is my last day in Paris. I have not been having a wonderful time, as all good postcard-writers say. I have been having a quiet, agreeable stay." The young man who "hate[s] writing badly, at any time" speaks of "the process of my emergence" and reports from Oxford that "when I do write an essay it turns out to be a really excellent one. This is not boasting; for my tutor is truly impressed." Any doubts he may have about a paper he's to deliver to his college's literary society are dispelled as soon as it's been given: "This morning someone told me that my paper was by far the brightest he had ever heard at the society. So it appears that I still retain some of the old fire." He is nineteen years old.

But the rejection of his novel seems to unleash the full force of suppressed loneliness, and early in 1952, Naipaul suffers what even he is not too proud to call a nervous breakdown. He pleads with the family back in Trinidad ("My love to all, and don't forget me"), though it is only to Kamla that he can make himself truly vulnerable. She urges him not to hold back: "Tell me everything and, believe me, I'll understand." Even before the breakdown, Naipaul had beseeched her: "Please keep me alive with letters." Their epistolary relationship can be stormy, scolding, interrupted by the sort of regrets that can cost extra postage. As Naipaul explains to those back home: "Just last night I tore up a letter that I had written to Kamla—on an air-letter form too. I get into certain moods and write things which, when read the following morning, read badly and are usually disgustingly maudlin."

In a collection of the Naipaul family's correspondence, a reader sees Kamla, during the years of her own university exile, becoming not so much older and wiser as a little harder and sadder. She at one point advances to her brother the theory that it's "best to marry the person who is mad after you—almost worships you—than marry one you love." It is difficult for her and Naipaul to have any relationship that exists outside the vexed and loving context of the family that remains far away on a third continent entirely. Letters from one Naipaul to another often involve a kind of emotional triangulation, at once delicate and manipulative. During one bad misunderstanding, Vido receives this request from his father: "Please explain to [Kamla] and say we love her and want her home for her own sake and not for any money she may have to give to us."

There is always a novel's worth of news and complication and worry coming from Port-of-Spain. The elder Mr. Naipaul seeks the advice of his precocious son on how to handle Deo and Phoolo, two young female cousins who are living under the family's roof: "I had never realised, until about three weeks ago, how shockingly 'advanced' these girls have become . . . so ultra-modern that they make no distinction between Negroes, Mussulmans or any other people." While Vido is grateful for his parents' affection and sacrifice ("Frankly, whenever I think about you and Pa, I think that you have been noble"), his letters also make plain that his own home will finally have to be somewhere else. Running into an old Trinidadian friend after three years in England throws him into a xenophobic snit about his own country: "Two days ago I met Solomon Lutchman. I never realised the man was so utterly ugly, so utterly crass—his low forehead, square, fat face, thick lips, wavy hair combed straight back. Now S. L. is an educated man. Yet to me he appears uncultured. The gulf that I felt between people and myself at home—people called me conceited, you remember—has grown wider. Take Lutchman. Narrow, insular, still looking upon Trinidad as the source of all effulgence."

Naipaul may miss his home island's climate, but his longing for distinction—and even luxury—will keep him in the midst of England's chills and damp: "I discover in myself all types of aristocratic traits, without, you know too well, the means to keep them alive." Right now he must endure ordinary student poverty, a condition that his always-tender father tries to alleviate in ways large and small. In July 1951, Mr. Naipaul sends Vido a ten-dollar money order. "It will help you see a patch or two of France. It's such a flea-bite, but I'd feel brutal if I didn't send anything at all." The following March, thinking bigger, he makes a pledge as touching as it is implausible: "I want you to have that chance which I have never had: somebody to support me and mine while I write. Two or three years of this should be enough. If by then you have not arrived, then it will be time enough for you to see about getting a job. Think over this thing. I mean every word of it."

"Pa," with his own thwarted literary aspirations—a writing life sacrificed to the production of inconsequential newspaper features—is, even beyond Kamla, the central figure in both Vido's psyche and the family letters, which would eventually be published in the United States as *Between Father and Son.* As gentle as his son is imperious, the senior Naipaul again and again counsels Vido against depression and anxiety, sounding like a man who has been battered by both: "Be cheerful . . . Home is bright and gay. Plush carpets and so on. Next week I might have the outside of the house painted. We never forget you for a day." Though he claims to believe in the power of mind over matter, Mr. Naipaul's troubles forever mount. At one point he feels forced to make an embarrassed confession to the humorless Vido: "This will pain you: but your Ma will be having a baby—in September or October . . . I know it's a mess, but there we are."

For all their difference in temperament, father and son share a host of mannerisms and seem, even an ocean apart, to be on the same somatic wavelength, experiencing similar eye trouble, the same indigestion, shared sleep patterns, even the same mechanical problems: "My typewriter, too," writes Pa, "is behaving badly, n & g sticking, the v not typing." But their father-son relation isn't leveled into fraternity so much as simply reversed. In any number of matters, but especially literary ones, Vido parents his own Pa, criticizing the older man's use of the apostrophe, holding up the late-blooming Joyce Cary as an example to him, and taking advantage of his own malfunctioning keyboard to hector Mr. Naipaul with the following advice: YOU HAVE ENOUGH MATERIAL FOR A HUNDRED STORIES. FOR HEAVEN'S SAKE START WRITING THEM. YOU CAN WRITE AND YOU KNOW IT. STOP MAKING EXCUSES. But the marching orders seem to leave Pa crumpled instead of invigorated. In his next letter to Vido, he demurs: "Go on writing, for progress' sake, and don't mind me. I am all right. I just want to see you do the thing . . . I am going in for orchid-collecting—in a small way."

And yet, more embarrassing than the new baby, Pa's dream of publishing his fiction persists. Late in 1952, he tells Vido that he wants to send him the manuscript of a newly fattened story collection, hoping it "will not interfere too much with your studies. Exams are near. Can you manage taking it to two or three publishers during the Christmas vacation?" Within a few months, Mr. Naipaul will have suffered a heart attack, leaving his wife and daughter convinced that only publication of the book will allow for his recovery. Kamla lays down the law in a letter to Vido: "Write now to Pa. See about his stories. Write me saying what you have done. Carelessness about these means Pa's death."

Mr. Naipaul himself becomes increasingly desperate in his urgings ("I don't want you to delay over this business"). Even his job at the newspaper is gone: "the *Guardian* no longer wants me, nobody wants me," he writes on September 24, 1953. A few weeks after sending this last, terrible letter, he is dead. Upon hearing the news, Vido sends a telegram home, the all-caps conveying, this time, not only commands but grief: HE WAS THE BEST MAN I KNEW STOP EVERYTHING I OWE TO HIM BE BRAVE MY LOVES TRUST ME.

The next cable printed in *Between Father and Son* was sent two years later, when Vido could tell the family back in Port-of-Spain: NOVEL ACCEPTED. He was on his way, in bitter, baleful flight, ever farther away from the gentle hand that had sent him aloft.

CHAPTER TWO *Friendship*

> *Sir, more than kisses, letters mingle souls;*
> *For, thus friends absent speak.*
>
> John Donne, verse letter
> to Sir Henry Wotton

UNLIKE DONNE—and he was, to say the least—Milton wrote few letters. Those he did compose were often in Latin, and so far as we know not one of them to a woman. Toward the end of his life he authorized their publication (*Epistolarum Familiarium*) along with his youthful *Prolusions;* the printer, in a note to the reader, acknowledged the "paucity" of the letters by themselves. Indeed, Milton's laxness as a correspondent is one of his own themes. On March 26, 1625, he responds to Thomas Young's complaint about the shortness and infrequency of his letters, admitting that the only thing to recommend them is "their rarity."

And yet, in this same letter to his former tutor, the still-teenaged Milton comes up with what may be the most self-serving, and charming, rationale ever made for the epistolary neglect of a friend:

> as that most vehement desire after you which I feel makes me always fancy you with me, and speak to you and behold you as if you were present, and so (as generally happens in love) soothe my grief by a certain vain imagination of your presence, it is in truth my fear that, as soon as I should meditate a letter to be sent you, it should suddenly come into my mind by what an interval of

> earth you are distant from me, and so the grief of your absence, already nearly lulled, should grow fresh, and break up my sweet dream.

What letter could compete with this excuse for one?

The man who in his epic poem would justify the ways of God to man usually seeks, in his letters, to explain his own silence. In 1628, again apologizing to Young, he can say only that he "preferred writing little, and that in a rather slovenly manner, to not writing at all," and nearly a decade later, to Charles Diodati, the greatest friend of his youth, he makes the excuse that he is "one by nature slow and lazy to write." Unlike Diodati, he teases, he cannot take epistolary breaks from scholarly effort: "my genius is such that no delay, no rest, no care or thought almost of anything, holds me aside until I reach the end I am making for."

In the young Milton's letters, we can glimpse the competing moods of both "L'Allegro" and "Il Penseroso," the so-called "twin poems" of gaiety and contemplativeness. But it's mostly the peaceful, melancholic atmosphere of the latter that Milton endorses to his friends. His letter to Young of March 26, 1625, is "written in London amid city distractions, and not, as usual, surrounded by books: if, therefore, anything in this epistle shall please you less than might be, and disappoint your expectation, it shall be made up for by another more elaborate one as soon as I have returned to the haunts of the Muses." Writing from Cambridge to Alexander Gill, he looks forward to a summertime of "deeply literary leisure, and a period of hiding." The pensive mood asserts itself yet again when he accepts an invitation from Young in July of 1628, glad to "withdraw myself from the din of town for a while" to the rural spot where Young peacefully resides in "triumph over riches, ambition, pomp, luxury, and whatever the herd of men admire and are amazed by."

The playfulness in Milton's youthful letters to friends—another part of the above-quoted RSVP swells with a mock-heroic pileup of classical allusion—surprises and supplements our usual idea of the poet. Decades later, by the time Milton has stiffened into Cromwell's theocrat and become literally blind to much that once delighted him, it will be too late for us to seek frivolity or fellowship in his company. In the meantime, it's to Diodati that Milton makes his most fervent expressions of affection. Late in 1637, he tells him that "when it had been fallaciously reported to me in London by some one that you were in town, straightway and as if by storm I dashed to your crib; but 'twas the vision of a shadow! for nowhere did you appear." He longs to see Diodati, needs to know when he will. This letter of longing is enthusiastic, flirtatious, more like the production of an undergraduate than the twenty-eight-year-old that Milton is when he writes it. A few weeks later, when he outlines some musings upon immortality and the nature of the beautiful, Milton tells Diodati:

> I would not have true friendship turn on balances of letters and salutations, all which may be false, but that it should rest on both sides in the deep roots of the mind and sustain itself there, and that, once begun on sincere and sacred grounds, it should, though mutual good offices should cease, yet be free from suspicion and blame all life long. For fostering such a friendship as this what is wanted is not so much written correspondence as a loving recollection of virtues on both sides.

English literature's most august and terrifying adherent to convention here criticizes, if not letter writing itself, then rote epistolary expression, almost as if he were Whitman trying to liberate a genre from the overused forms that are crushing the emotions it's supposed to convey.

IF FRIENDSHIP DEPENDS on the endurance of similarities—not the combustibility of opposites that passion requires—then George Sand and Flaubert should have enjoyed a torrid fling. And yet, despite wildly disparate temperaments, they sustained a close epistolary companionship over the last decade of Sand's seventy-two years. "I don't think there can be two workers in the world more different from one another than we are," she writes to the much younger but already middle-aged Flaubert in January of 1869. There he is, she imagines, "confined to the solitary splendour of the rabid artist," struggling for the mot juste and "scorning the pleasures of this world," while she goes on gobbling them up, never allowing the production of mere literature to keep her from the delights of the table or the garden or the bedroom.

Their correspondence begins in 1863, at a moment when Flaubert is critically friendless. Against the contempt of other reviewers, Sand rises in print to defend his *Salammbô.* He writes to thank her, suppressing the revulsion he's often felt toward her own crowd-pleasing and message-laden books. Three years later, once their exchange gets going in earnest, Sand sends him her complete oeuvre, with a warning that "There's lots of it."

In the time he takes to finish a chapter, she can usually complete a book, barely noticing she's done it amid the rest of her life in the country: "every day I pitch myself into an icy brook that shakes me up and makes me sleep like a top. How comfortable one is here, with the two little girls [her granddaughters] laughing and chattering like birds from morn till night, and how foolish one is to go writing and putting on *fictions* when reality is so easy and good!" When Flaubert reports feeling nauseated over the last corrections he's making to *L'Éducation sentimentale,* Sand confesses that, when it comes to reading her own proofs, "I always scamp it, but I don't set myself up as an example." Early in their friendship she's abashed by his exacting artistry ("When I see the trouble my vieux goes to to write a novel I'm depressed at my own facility and tell myself my work is only botched stuff"), but as the years pass she relaxes into a kind of amusement about the contrast: "We're not literary enough for you here, I know, but we love, and that gives life a purpose."

Admitting to the "mania of Perfection," Flaubert says he can only remain the way he is, "living absolutely like an oyster," his novel "the rock I'm attached to." He won't so much as attend the christening of Sand's grandchildren, lest witnessing such an event inflict too much life upon his art: "My poor brain would be filled with real pictures instead of the fictive ones I'm at such pains to invent; and my house of cards would crumble to dust." The reader can picture Sand throwing up her hands over this; she responds with a request that Flaubert at least admit the pleasure his aesthetic hair-shirt gives him. Ten days later he owns up to it—more or less: "As to my mania for work, I'll compare it to a rash. I keep scratching myself and yelling as I scratch. It's pleasure and torture combined."

There are real rashes, too—a nervous eczema, as well as grippe, a facial boil, morbid sensitivity to noise and capacious self-pity. Living with his frail and ever-more-deaf mother, Flaubert complains—no more convincingly than when he curses his creative burdens—about the "terrible solitude" of his "arid" existence. He is probably at his most considerate and least self-absorbed when he concedes to Sand, "I must be boring you with my eternal jeremiads." On one occasion she does lose patience with him, but confides the irritation only to her son: "I've had enough of my young friend. I'm very fond of him, but he gives me a splitting headache. He doesn't like noise, but he doesn't mind the din he makes himself."

Aside from displacing himself into his novels ("Madame Bovary, c'est moi"), Flaubert's chief means for getting out of himself is to flay the rest of mankind, whose "irremediable wretchedness has embittered me ever since my youth." Sand's belief in socialist progress can't tempt him away from a loathing for the whole political spectrum from royalists to Communards. He would do away with politics and religion both, replacing them with objective science. Sand refuses to despair of France or humanity and suggests that, at a minimum, they try to "die without cursing [their] own species!" Even during the atrocious Franco-Prussian War, she would have the two of them go on loving life: "We need these harsh lessons in order to realize our own foolishness, and we must make good use of them." But her heartfelt gropings are met with mere wit. Flaubert replies that "The vile things I witnessed in the capital are enough to add years to a man's life."

Sand calmly answers what she calls "weighty" arguments with "sincere" ones, and she would prefer that emotion trump analysis: "Je t'aime—that's how all my dissertations end." Flaubert, by contrast, declares himself to be "choking on gall." In 1875, as Sand's death approaches, he will express envy of her condition, hope that there is no hereafter, and sign himself "St Polycarp."

Can his endlessly forbearing correspondent really be the pants-wearing sorceress who once devoured Chopin like a truffle and whose long amatory life was a kind of intermissionless opera both grand and bouffe? Yes, in however measured and mellowed a way. One of Sand's biographers, Benita Eisler, points out that the erotic and maternal were almost always conflated within her, and Sand's adoption of Flaubert is not without its own avidity and passion. Within months of their friendship's real beginning, she would be proclaiming that she had come to love him with all her heart. She finds Flaubert "a very special and mysterious being, and yet as meek as a lamb."

Whatever joking attempts the two of them make to erase the difference in their sex and years—he calls her a "fine fellow," and they both claim the title of "old troubadour"—Flaubert and Sand are always male and female, a prescriptive mother and her stroppy son. She steadily sets an example of ease and self-sufficiency, telling him of her "rude health," of how well she's sleeping, about how enjoyable even winter can be. He should lead a more varied life, she says; he should exercise. Sand had often made her romances into projects, not just passions, and Flaubert is there in this late part of her life to be straightened out and smothered with solicitude.

"Your Strength charms and amazes me," he writes a half dozen years into their friendship. "I mean the Strength of your entire person, not only your brain." It's doubtful he ever thought much of the latter, but when it came to this capitalized Strength, he was able not just to admire but also to derive a portion of it—as Sand intended—for himself. Francis Steegmuller, the editor of their letters, points out that Flaubert, after a visit from Sand in 1868, reported to one friend as follows: "Such character! Such strength! And at the same time there is no one whose company is more soothing. Her serenity is contagious."

In considering the relationship she and Flaubert had constructed, Sand could liken and contrast it, in a single sentence, to love: "our real discussions must remain between ourselves, like lovers' caresses, only more delightful, since friendship has its own mysteries, untroubled by the storms of personality." Even Flaubert could contemplate their closeness with a certain sentimental swelling. "You know, chere maître," he writes in January 1869, "it's very nice about the two of us—writing to each other simultaneously on New Year's Eve. There is clearly some strong bond between us."

It was a bond forged from appreciating a disparity that Sand expected to widen even further beyond the grave. "My ambition has never flown as high as yours," she tells Flaubert late in 1872. "You want to write for all time; I think *I* shall be completely forgotten, perhaps severely denigrated, in fifty years' time. That's the natural fate of things that are not of the highest order." She would not have stopped to think that her letters to Flaubert, productions even hastier than her novels, might have a kind of incidental, lasting greatness.

BETWEEN MARY McCARTHY and Hannah Arendt it was love at first slight. At the end of World War II, McCarthy was an intellectually racy novelist and *Partisan Review*'s ferocious theatre critic, Arendt a political philosopher who had taken refuge from Nazi Germany in New York. They were acquaintances, a bit fascinated with each other, but the possibility of friendship seemed lost when McCarthy made a foolish witticism about Hitler and Arendt protested with an exaggeration of her personal sufferings at his hands. The two women steered clear of each other for the next few years, until finally Arendt approached McCarthy on a subway platform: "Let's end this nonsense. We think so much alike."

So much so that, where they're concerned, the word "correspondence" seems to speak more to intellectual affinities than the actual letters that passed between them for twenty-six years. Each a believer in individual moral responsibility and the values of what used to be called the "democratic left," both of them skeptical of cant and technology and mass culture, they admitted few impediments to the marriage of their minds. After making up on that subway platform, they tested the waters of epistolary friendship with two fan letters (one for McCarthy's satirical novel *The Oasis*, the other for Arendt's *The Origins of Totalitarianism*), after which McCarthy pressed forward like a suitor determined to prove herself worthy of Arendt's formidable mind and ethics.

The philosopher embodies a seriousness to which the novelist will constantly aspire. In her letters McCarthy declares the older woman an inspiration, calling Arendt's replies gifts that she doesn't deserve. "The sensation of being honored" by Hannah's praise "doesn't diminish with familiarity." Arendt inspires McCarthy toward a certain restraint ("My novel [*A Charmed Life*] is going ahead, but I have you horribly on my conscience every time sex appears"), while McCarthy nudges her toward a greater gaiety in return: "I bought the dress," Arendt reports after dutifully following McCarthy's suggestion that she treat herself to something new for an awards ceremony.

It is McCarthy's geographical displacement, as voluntary as Arendt's was enforced, that allows the correspondence to flourish. In the 1950s, she begins spending long periods in Europe to work on books like *The Stones of Florence*. Arendt's letters are sources of advice and calm, whether McCarthy is dealing with an unexpected pregnancy, an extramarital affair with a chronic liar ("Their charm," Arendt explains, "is that they with all their lies are somehow more truthful than all the philistines who don't lie") or, back home, *The New Yorker*'s fact-checking department. McCarthy, who can be as self-critical as she is merciless toward others, complains: "A normal person cooperates with the checkers or uses them as a convenience, but I cannot help competing with them." Arendt reassures her that institutionalized verification is only "one of the many forms in which the would-be writers persecute the writer."

What makes their letters so pleasurable, sometimes even thrilling, is a consistent mixture of the abstract and concrete, of world politics and personal foibles. Along with meditations on the nature of will and the problems of equality, one finds literary gossip ("this is the second mad girl [Raymond Aron] has been involved with; the first tried to commit suicide to embarrass him"); sharp dismissals ("Dame Rebecca [West] is a good talker and cracked . . . she imagines that various authors are alluding to her and all her relatives under disguises in their books"); and quick character sketches that rise above comic specificity toward some larger insight. It's inevitable that most of the letters' sparkle, including the quotations above, comes from McCarthy. Her eye for misbehavior was unerringly avid, and linguistically she stood on native ground—though Arendt's malapropisms ("ends and odds") have their charm.

The greatest romantic drama of McCarthy's life comes at the beginning of the 1960s, when she finds herself "totally, entirely in love" with the man who will become her fourth husband, the American diplomat James West. The complications are formidable. West's current wife seems ready to use their children as a weapon against him, while he and McCarthy, trying to secure divorces, conduct their affair behind the backs of West's State Department bosses and within earshot of the Communist authorities in Warsaw, where he is posted: "we've come to look on my hideous [hotel] room with flowered bedspreads and curtains decorated with Red stars and the listening device in the lighting fixture as a tenderly loved home and refuge. As though we were living a peculiar modern idyl: intense love in extreme conditions, to be transcribed by the Secret Police."

McCarthy typically views her experience in such literary categories, a tendency not shared by Arendt. But both of them, however they may conduct their own lives, like to exhibit an almost frilly antifeminism. When reporting to McCarthy on an honorary degree she has received with "Margaret Mead, a monster, and Marianne Moore, an angel," Arendt decides to call Mead "by her second name, not because she is a man, but because she certainly is not a woman." McCarthy and Arendt each display something like a protective crush on their buccaneering publisher, William Jovanovich, who did much to secure a measure of commercial success for their less saleable work.

In 1963, by which time McCarthy has settled in Paris with James West, both she and Arendt find themselves caught up in far greater literary celebrity than they have previously enjoyed, or endured. *The Group* brings McCarthy real fame and money—"That is the right thing for you, dear, enjoy it and be happy!" Arendt reassures her, perhaps a bit condescendingly—while *Eichmann in Jerusalem*, with its characterization of the "banality" of Nazi evil, earns Arendt a torrent of vicious criticism. The attacks excite McCarthy to a vigorous defense of her friend: "I want to help you in some way and not simply by being an ear. What can be done about this Eichmann business, which is assuming the proportions of a pogrom?" McCarthy's public riposte on Arendt's behalf (an essay called "The Hue and Cry") satisfies her aggressive streak, which sometimes surfaces with a life of its own inside the correspondence: "I think I've been longing to get into a fight with someone."

Away in Paris, where she has "no real friends," McCarthy depends on Arendt as a link to America, even while the philosopher is beginning to be overwhelmed by widowhood, sickness, and what she calls the "relentless defoliation" of friends. As the years pass and technology improves (the almost Luddite McCarthy would hate to see that last noun ever accorded such a verb), phone calls become more frequent, but the women never abandon the exchange of letters. If much of their correspondence seems to come from another age (McCarthy arguing with a postal clerk about regulations governing scotch tape; asking for the return of newspaper clippings instead of sending Xeroxes), that's because it does. The small hardships of letter writing—having to think a moment longer before completing utterance; remaining in suspense while awaiting reply; having one's urgent letters cross in the mail—are the things that enrich it, emotionally and rhetorically.

The remoteness of each writer from the other provokes both of them into a kind of telepathy. On April 2, 1965, Arendt asks: "Do you ever see Lippman's [*sic*] columns about Vietnam?" The same day McCarthy, in Paris, is writing: "I am in a state of doubt and dismay about Vietnam . . . I read with slight relief the *New York Times* editorials and Walter Lippmann." The rituals of letter writing, with its non-instant gratification, excite and regulate the emotions. "Here is the 'Arrived safe' letter," McCarthy writes upon reaching Rome in 1960, some months before Arendt sighs: "Oh Mary, how I wish you were here and how tired I am of this letter writing. I somehow had the feeling during the last week or so that you would suddenly stand in the door."

When it comes to their work, the two women learn to exchange not only admiration but concrete suggestions and editorial help. Still, it is the independent operation of their intellects, rather than the cooperation, that most entertains a reader. A week after rhapsodizing to Arendt over Nabokov's *Pale Fire*, McCarthy gets a response: "There is something vulgar in his refinement," Arendt believes. McCarthy finds that "in Rome even the weather seems to belong intimately to the Romans, while in Paris it is just a pleasant fact," but Arendt sees the latter capital differently: "it is like a house . . . the whole city really is, with many many rooms; but you feel never exposed, you are always 'housed,' protected, an entirely different spatial feeling from all other big cities I know."

McCarthy, early on, protests that she is "a frightful correspondent," but for a reason that actually makes her a good one: she's "never learned to communicate in a brief style." There is an amplitude, a long steady narrative drive, to both women's letters. Only one instance of wounded feelings occurs in the whole quarter-century-long exchange, in 1974, when McCarthy sees Arendt off after a visit and is left to worry: "It was sad to watch you go through the gate at the airport without turning back. Something is happening or has happened to our friendship . . . The least I can conjecture is that I have got on your nerves." Arendt's reply is an immediate, exasperated reassurance: "For heaven's sake, Mary, stop it, please." It says something about the authenticity of their connection that a reader is moved by this little blip of misunderstanding, fearful the friendship might come, disastrously, full circle. As it is, their love and letters carried on, the harmonic convergence of a woman Norman Mailer once dubbed our "lit arbiter, our broadsword," with somebody McCarthy herself described as the only person she had ever watched thinking.

IN READING THE LETTERS of Rebecca Primus and Addie Brown, two young African-American women living through the middle of the nineteenth century, one imagines occasions when Addie must have watched Rebecca not just thinking but also setting her mind to act on whatever conclusion she had reached.

According to Farah Jasmine Griffin, the letters' editor, Addie Brown (born 1841) and Rebecca Primus (born 1836) may have met when Addie moved to Hartford from Philadelphia sometime in the 1850s and began boarding with the Primus family, whose middle-class members included a clerk, a seamstress and a future portrait painter—Rebecca's brother, Nelson Primus. The two women write to each other while Addie spends the early part of the Civil War in New York, but the heart of their correspondence comes with Reconstruction, when Addie has returned to Hartford and Rebecca moved to Royal Oak, Maryland, in order to build and run a school for the local black population.

We have to follow the exchange obliquely. Addie's letters to Rebecca survive, but those Rebecca wrote directly to her have so far not been discovered. (Since they're alluded to in Addie's own letters, Professor Griffin remains hopeful.) It is only through the letters she sends to her own family—letters that almost surely reached Addie's eyes, too—that we hear her urgent, zealous voice.

Addie gives us sharp-eyed glimpses of her life as a servant, including her short-lived stay with the family of Reverend Huntington, a Trinity College professor whose wife, Addie knows from the start, will be hard to get along with. Addie does not believe she should have to take Mrs. Huntington's white son to church—and don't get her started on the stairs. As she explains to Rebecca just after putting the Huntington children to bed: "yesterday I counted how many times I went up and down before breakfast six time you can judge for yourself there is a hundred & seven steps when it time for me to go to bed my limbs ache like the tooth ache." Miss Porter's School soon proves a more congenial place to work: the money is good; Addie is allowed to use the library; and on cold days the girls keep her company in the kitchen. She can't, alas, say much for their dancing ("not many of them graceful").

Addie reports to Rebecca on her efforts toward self-improvement—reading Frederick Douglass's autobiography, hearing a speech by Henry Ward Beecher—and she's not entirely without political opinions: she'd rather see Andrew Johnson shot than impeached. But the letters she sends to Rebecca mostly fizz with gossip and mischief; they're alive with the natural letter-writer's lack of proportion. The drama of Aunt Emily's broken butter dish equals, in length and intensity, a local murder that Addie also describes, and while she won't lose any sleep over a big meteor shower that's expected, she loves making a sarcastic report of someone's unexpected pregnancy: "I heard yesterday a young girl in New Haven went from there go south to teach her health was miserable so her Mother sent for her to come home since her return she present her Mother with a grand child. That is a new method of teaching."

One can feel this story being customized for Rebecca, who has herself, after all, gone South to teach, but one can't imagine the recipient having more than a moment to smile over it (and even then a bit disapprovingly). The pressures facing Rebecca Primus in Royal Oak, vividly enumerated in her letters home, often seem unendurable. The struggle for "something like justice" is conducted amid everything from the underpayment of blacks by "Secesh" employers to a violent "unprovoked assault" on young black men by the "low white fellows in St. Michaels." Rebecca reassures her family, and herself, with the thought that she is in "the hands of the same Supreme Being that has the charge of us all everywhere."

Her focus remains the schoolhouse: finding land for it; getting it built; keeping it running. She will not accept the freedmen's own excuses for going slowly: "Their invariable plea is we're all poor, just out of bondage and times are hard with us etc." With a sarcasm worthy of Addie—who reports to her on the success of a fundraiser for the school back in Hartford—Rebecca mentions her failure to obtain the land. The owner, who at first "gave every reason to believe that we should have it," has proved to be "a hard-headed old Negro-hating secessionist" who "looks like an angry bulldog in the face—which is his most pleasant facial appearance."

Will Rebecca have to bear what Miss Dickson went through a month ago in Trappe? Her colleague was "stoned by white children & repeatedly subjected to insults from white men." Whatever her fears, Rebecca persists, expressing optimism whenever she sees a reason for it: some trees for the schoolhouse eventually come "from southern rights men, which I think shows they have no real hostile feelings toward the col'd. school." And once that school is in session, woe betide those who act up in Miss Primus's class. The pupils generally "behave very well," she writes on February 23, 1867, "but now & then an evil spirit rises among them, and I introduce different methods of punishment to quell it."

Addie hears all of this in letters that Rebecca usually writes on Saturday mornings, compositions she calls a "home weeklie." Despite her modest protest against the idea, Rebecca must have expected the letters to be passed around outside her immediate family. They would have been read with interest by everyone, but their chronicling aspect would not long have satisfied Addie's disposition toward intimacy.

It seems likely that she and Rebecca had had a physical romance in the earliest days of their acquaintance. Certainly Addie's ardor could still blaze up during her friend's distant, preoccupying mission in Maryland. "O why have you left me alone no one to love me an give me a fond imbrace how I long for yours," she laments in an unpunctuated rush during November 1865, not long after Rebecca's departure from Hartford. Addie signs herself "your loving Affectionate Adopted Sister" and makes a point of telling Rebecca that she rereads her letters and appreciates their smell, even if they can never substitute for her presence. She may even be trying to provoke Rebecca's jealousy when she mentions another servant girl at Miss Porter's: "She is a fine looking girl, quite tall. She take hold of my hands and look at me and hug me so tight she hurt me." And yet, for all this, Addie remains a cheerful realist, amused by and finally receptive to the affections of Mr. Joseph Tines ("I do love him but not fasinated"), whom she will marry, after some hestiation and postponement, in 1868.

Rebecca worries when she doesn't hear from Addie, whose letters must have appealed to the softer portions of her own nature, the ones she had to keep armored against all the hostility and danger in Royal Oak. Receiving and writing letters seems generally to have relaxed Rebecca, whether she was getting them from her students ("They are very amusing & in some respects contain very sensible expressions") or writing them to Jim, the cat she loved back home: "I know you can not be beaten in the whole U.S. Tis too bad poor Major & Kittie Smith had no Thanksgiving, and I don't believe you gave them a very strong invitation to partake with you."

Rebecca returned to Hartford some time after the school she founded was renamed the Primus Institute. Back in Connecticut, she married, taught Sunday school and lived to be ninety-five. We know as much as we do of her early life, and of Addie Brown's short one—Addie died at the age of twenty-eight, less than two years after her marriage to Mr. Tines—because Rebecca Primus stood her ground against Royal Oak's "poor old secesh Post-master." Late in 1866, he seemed bent on interfering with her mail, and to protect it she wrote to the man's counterpart in Easton, asking that he "take charge of all my papers & letters hereafter." Within three months, the Royal Oak postmaster and his wife appeared to learn a lesson; they became "very particular" about this complaining customer who'd taken her business elsewhere. "I suspect they feel the slight," Rebecca reported to her family back home. "These white people want all the respect shown them by the col'd. people. I give what I rec. & no more."

A CENTURY LATER, the kind of frustrated attraction that Addie felt toward Rebecca may have been what made Tennessee Williams find even his close male friendships "less deeply satisfying than those I have had with a few women." Chief among these female friends was Maria Britneva St. Just, a Russian actress expatriated to England as a baby. Williams met her in 1948, in London, at a party hosted by John Gielgud. "He told me that Chekhov was his favorite playwright," St. Just later recalled. "He'd never met a live Russian before." For the next few decades, she and Williams developed the sort of friendship he preferred to call an *amitié*, a relationship "probably all the deeper because it exists outside and beyond the physical kind of devotion."

St. Just once played Blanche DuBois in a New York revival of *A Streetcar Named Desire*, and in a letter from 1954 about *Cat on a Hot Tin Roof*, one hears Williams telling her: "I think a lot of you has gone into the writing of it." In times to come, St. Just would downplay the comparison of herself and Maggie, but only after drawing attention to it. Over the years, Williams tried to find her work in the theatre; urged her away from self-pity; and reminded her that she at least had two lovely daughters to ease the pain of having been, like him, "so unlucky in love." In advising her on the "condition" of her depressed, titled husband, Williams let out a typical cackle concerning his own state: "[Peter] is simply the victim of an overpowering mother who wants to make him a helpless dependent. Don't believe that stuff about hereditary influences affecting the child. Insanity on all 4 sides of my family, and look at me! A model of mental stability if ever there was one."

What St. Just does for Williams is listen to his troubles; these include the moods and, eventually, cancer of his lover Frank Merlo ("Must seal this letter at once as Frank is returning from the barber's"), as well as Williams's difficulties managing his own terrible glooms. "Of course I have been through periods somewhat like this before, when the sky cracked and fell and brained me," he writes St. Just in 1957, "but this time I seem less able to struggle out of the debris." She remains his confidante during what he calls "these nightmare years"—far worse ones would be coming—and Williams counts on her "wonderfully sweet, funny letters" to bring him "back to life and to something closer to sanity."

Alas, as with Addie and Rebecca, only his side of the correspondence survives. It's an irony that besets epistolary relationships: the letters of the disorderly person or the wanderer (Addie changed residences a great deal in her short life) wind up being saved and filed and organized; what's written by the correspondent with regular habits disappears into the other person's chaos.

Or else, who knows? Williams may have jettisoned St. Just's letters in an angry mood. In 1977, he writes to a third party: "I sometimes suspect this friendship and concern for me is all a myth that she has constructed. However, this is a suspicion that I'd love to dismiss [discuss?] as there's no one else whom I can look to in times of emotional stress." Eight months later, he writes to St. Just herself: "I guess that you are the only person whose loyal friendship I have never doubted."

Williams insists he's "not at all clever about people unless they're people of my own invention," but his letters are painfully alert to his own and others' natures. "My heart and my life hang suspended when I don't have a play," he declares. A sense of the vocation that was fulfilled early and then cruelly thwarted suffuses the letters, along with an impression of real kindness, that quality for which Blanche could depend only on strangers. Williams is generous with money and sympathy; hopes for the best in return; rarely gets it. He remains inspired by the "brave, patient" heart of his grandfather, the Rev. Dakin, as well as the gently mad and mysterious behavior of his sister, Rose, confined to an asylum and "the greatest person I have ever known." When, according to the letters' editor, a reporter in London asks him for his "definition of happiness," Williams replies with casual brilliance: "Insensitivity, I guess."

In 1955, from Key West, he diagnoses Carson McCullers's troubles with the same mordant tenderness he gives his own. McCullers, whom he called Choppers, is at that point drinking and "dreaming herself away." Williams has paid for her visit to Florida, but tells Maria: "It is much easier to give money than love. Choppers needs love but I am not the Baa-Baa Black Sheep with three bags full for Choppers. I don't even have any for the Master or the Dame or the Little Boy Down the Lane . . . life makes many demands, and these decimal offerings of the heart are never sufficient."

When work goes well, he's too tired to answer letters; when it doesn't, he's too depressed to write them. When he finds the sweet spot, he can be surprisingly meticulous, composing rough drafts and making sure, on one occasion, that St. Just knows his shaky handwriting results not from alcohol but the lurchings of a boat. He is happy when she ends an "epistolary hiatus" but declares that "when people have been friends for so long, an unbroken succession of letters is not that important." It's something she will need to keep in mind during the 1960s, what Williams called his "stoned age." As an editorial note reminds the reader: "They were years of few letters, although he kept in constant touch with Maria by phone." Their written exchange regained frequency in the 1970s, during which we see Williams acknowledging one of modern life's odd accelerations: "No doubt we'll be talking before you get this."

St. Just sympathizes with the particular nature of Williams's tormenting decline, a normal falling-off in power that was lethally exacerbated by the refusal of producers and critics even to consider that he might still compose something good. "I feel so deeply what you are going through as an artist," she writes in a 1974 letter, a rare survival of her side of the correspondence, composed midflight on British Airways letterhead: "no one minds trying and being turned down, but not being allowed to try—God!"

Williams at one point writes that he doesn't want his complaints to be "a waste of this beautiful stationery," but how can he avoid mentioning the up-and-coming young man who says to him, "Here I am, a yet-to-be actor with a has-been playwright!" Sometimes angry to the point of despair, he ceases to worry that he'll embarrass himself. "You'll think I'm starkers, but, honey, I've had it in aces and spades for 10 years," he writes St. Just from New Orleans in 1972, the year he turns sixty. Soon after, on his way to Japan, he observes that the "venom, the vindictiveness, the betrayals and callousness of this world incline one at times almost to anticipation of the oblivion to come." Even so, he'd rather close with a bang: "This is not the honk of a dying duck in a thunderstorm, honey, but the howl of an enraged beast at bay!"

When cries like these come through a telephone, they tend to fall on ears that turn self-protectively deaf. On paper, they are actually harder to ignore, curtain lines that even now hang in the air.

WITH THEIR occupational inclination toward zingers and backbiting, theatre people often find that the compulsion to entertain, and compete, extends to their letter writing. What they send to friends must be shapely and sharp; in fact, a letter should feel like its own enclosure, the bright on-purpose prose dancing out of the envelope like photos or cash.

Late in life, Groucho Marx responded to a publisher's proposal to collect his letters with the following telegram: YOUR LETTER RECEIVED AND PROMPTLY BURNED. I PREFER NOT TO HAVE STRANGERS PRYING INTO MY MAIL. WOULD DISCUSS THIS IN DETAIL BUT MY SECRETARY HAS A DATE IN FIVE MINUTES—WITH

ME. Once he relented, a section of the book was called "Friends Abroad." Its contents show Groucho doing a star turn for each of his correspondents, and all of them trying to top him in his own style.

In 1959, for example, Groucho informs his friend and collaborator Harry Kurnitz, over in England: "If you will tell me precisely when you are coming to Hollywood, I will arrange a party, something small but select, for your degenerate friends . . . at the moment, I'm leaving the food up in the air—where I'm sure it will be after you eat it." Five years later, by then in Paris, Kurnitz reports experiencing a surge of nostalgia for Groucho: "a plastic tear which I carry for just such occasions welled up in my eye."

Some of what looks like imitation is actually the real thing, since so many of Groucho's latter-day correspondents are the screenwriters who helped make him into himself. Two decades after creating dialogue for *Monkey Business, Horse Feathers* and *Duck Soup*, Arthur Sheekman is still more or less writing it in letters to Groucho: "People ask me if you are as amusing off-screen as on and I—please forgive me—tell them the truth." Groucho answers Sheekman, also abroad, with the same sort of invitation he gave Kurnitz: "If you ever get back, and would like to have dinner sometime, just say the word and I'll be at your house . . ." Like all shrewd entertainers, he professes a wariness of overexposure, even through the mails: "Since you make your living as a writer," Groucho tells Norman Krasna in March of 1960, "I deliberately have waited two months before answering you. I don't want to burden you with the Damocles' sword of a steady correspondence. The next letter you get from me will be three years from now."

Alexander Woollcott, the *New Yorker* writer and Round Table wit who touted Groucho to the highbrows, was so fat it seems wrong to call him brittle. But brittleness was his trademark mode, so much so that a reader of Woollcott's letters will be rather stunned by the thoughtfulness of one that he wrote in 1928, at the age of forty-one, to a close friend of his sister, who had just died. He wants to make Julie Woollcott Taber's deathbed as consolingly vivid as he can for the friend, Lucy Christie Drage, who was unable to be at it. Woollcott's descriptive success is extraordinary:

> She just lay there at rest in a room that somehow began to look like her, with the yellow roses on the table and the blue silk shawl thrown across the foot of her bed. Day by day the years seemed to fall away from her, cast off like garments she no longer needed . . . If you bent close, you could hear her say "Sweet, sweet." The lines went out of her face, the gray out of her hair, the pain out of her eyes . . . One of her last commissions to me was to write you the birthday letter for which she could no longer hold a pen.

Even in his prime—let alone our fading memory of him—Woollcott's enormous person had been swallowed by his even larger persona, the acerbic reviewer and know-it-all broadcaster who inspired the title character in *The Man Who Came to Dinner* and then went onstage to play it himself. If Groucho's epistolary stock-in-trade was the seemingly inadvertent insult, Woollcott's was mock rage: "Listen, you contumacious rat" is how he begins a letter to Ira Gershwin when they're having a dispute over the proper use of the word "disinterested."

Woollcott strongly preferred typed letters to handwritten ones, and generally dictated to a stenographer. Filtration was part of the fun. At his remote country place in Vermont, he explained, "I get news of the outside world in the form of telegrams which are telephoned from Rutland to a boatman living on the shore who takes them down in a firm Spencerian hand and gives them to his son to bring over to me in a motor boat. This makes my favorite occupation guessing what the sender really intended to say."

Compliments were best applied with a backhanded slap to the face. In January 1940, while gloomy over England's wartime plight, he sent this inverted tribute to Beatrice Kaufman: "From sundry sources I hear an echo of your reproaches about my shortcomings as a correspondent. On this subject I never want to hear a peep out of you again. In times like these it is quite impossible for me to write a letter to anyone to whom I have so much to say. So shut your trap, dear, and let me hear no more from you." A few years later, following Woollcott's death from a heart attack suffered in mid-broadcast, Kaufman would be co-editing his letters. While he was alive, any burst of tenderness they contained had to be packed in the ice of exasperation: "I can't believe I've known you less than thirteen months," Woollcott wrote to Dr. Gustav Eckstein in November 1937. "It's ridiculous."

Back in this period when popular culture actually had some, Noël Coward seemed to create about half of it. He put his own lyrics to his own music, and on the London stage sometimes acted the lead in the comedies he'd written. In gossip columns and on the town, he was so much the apex of sophisticated wit that not having been to "a party where they honored Noël Coward" was one reason, according to Rodgers and Hart, that the lady is a tramp. And yet, Coward's sophisticated wit had a peculiar come-join-us quality. Even when heard from the second balcony, the high-life repartee of *Design for Living* made the listener feel he was third-row center—and actually belonged there.

Any chance to unpack what Coward described as his "fluffy little mind" reveals, beneath all the brightly colored excelsior, an assortment of sharp and steely tools, a first-rate intelligence that received only the peculiar education to be had while touring the English provinces as a child actor before the Great War. His glamorous adult success sprang from excellent theatrical instincts and a lot of bloody hard work. If love really were all—well, then there wouldn't have been time for so much of everything else. Coward generally kept his romantic affairs and disappointments within the well-regulated limits he set for his plays, and built up a devoted, long-serving "family" of secretaries and majordomos who kept his spirits high and his show going decade after decade, through the chromium brilliance of the thirties (*Private Lives*), the butched-up patriotism of World War II (*In Which We Serve*) and the mixture of hits and nostalgia-soaked flops from his long last act, which ended only with his death in 1973, three years after a scandalously delayed knighthood.

Coming after many volumes of his diaries and autobiography, *The Letters of Noël Coward* turned out to be a bit of a swindle, containing as it did about as many letters to the maestro as from him. Such an arrangement may have biographical potential, but the results can be a terrible jumble; the star seems thrown into a revue that needs lots of cutting and clearer direction. Still, time and again Coward steals back the scene, whether he's assessing a performance by Deanna Durbin ("she sang 'There'll Always Be an England' with tears rolling down her face as though she were bitterly depressed at the thought"); asking his new fan and correspondent, T. E. Lawrence, Aircraftman #338171, "May I call you 338?"; or defending his latter-day tax exile to a fatuously scolding Laurence Olivier: "I also know, darling, that the best way I can serve my country is not by sitting in it with a head cold grumbling at the climate and the telephone service . . ."

For all his verve, Coward's chief epistolary gift turns out to be for careful truth-telling, for giving actors and intimates the firm correction they require, in a manner that risks, but almost always retains, their affections. His audience for this human and literary artfulness includes a deludedly grand Mary Martin: "Please believe that your future career depends on your throwing away your, and above all [your husband's] exaggerated and grotesque conception of 'Stardom' and concentrating on learning, diligently and painstakingly, to be the fine artiste your potential talent entitles you to be." Marlene Dietrich, lovesick over Yul Brynner, comes in for the same combination of velvet and sandpaper—"Stop wasting yourself on someone who only really says tender things to you when he's drunk"—and John Gielgud, upbraided by Coward for "overacting badly and using voice tones and elaborate emotional effects," takes it like a man: "I think it was like you to write like that and I do appreciate it."

This talent to disabuse is in large part the obverse of Coward's capacity for shrewd self-assessment. He had a firm sense of his professional skills ("my facility for writing adroit swift dialogue and hitting unimportant but popular nails on the head") and usually took care not to overreach with them. The letter-writing showman sometimes gets his best effects playing against type, as when in the midst of an ill-fated musical adaptation of *Lady Windermere's Fan*, he reports to Alfred Lunt and Lynn Fontanne that the voice of the leading lady "to coin a phrase, sounds like someone fucking the cat.

I know that your sense of the urbane, sophisticated Coward wit will appreciate this simile."

It was always important to make an impression and then get off. He wrote his biggest hits very quickly (*Hay Fever*, in three days), and he liked them played the same way; in his correspondence, he sometimes reminds one of Balanchine, wishing that the wretched actors and directors and mixed-up friends would take things faster, faster. When he crossed the Atlantic on the *Queen Elizabeth* in 1932, the ship's bandmaster delighted him by playing only songs composed by the most famous passenger on board. Even so, Coward borrowed the baton and upped the tempo.

FITTINGLY ENOUGH, on this side of the Atlantic, much of Coward's epoch was presided over by a president whose cigarette holder often clicked against the stem of his champagne glass. A brilliant radio performer, Franklin Roosevelt, during one first-term broadcast, asked his New Deal constituents to write him with their troubles—a suggestion that wound up sorely taxing the White House mail room, which took to measuring the results with a yardstick. The president's love-him-or-hate-him personality assured a yield as varied as it was voluminous. One White House secretary culled a list of thirty-one different salutations from the arriving letters. They ranged from "Franklin Dillinger Roosevelt" to "My Pal!"

The variety contrasts with FDR's own consistency of tone. His policies may have made him a traitor to his class, but his epistolary style betrays only his birthright. Nearly every one of his letters, no matter the recipient, brims with the effervescent serenity of the country gentleman and clubman. In May of 1943, when the time has come to arrange a face-to-face encounter with Stalin, Roosevelt suggests they meet "either on your side or my side of Bering Straits." Instead of being ranted over in the Jeffersonian manner that we'll see a couple of chapters from now, enemies are merely diminished, into "that Goering person," and the "silly Congress," and, in the case of Thomas E. Dewey, "the little man." Critics, even the most tormenting, are responded to with an understanding, seigneurial scold: "So, my dear friend," he writes America First's General Robert E. Wood, "stop being disturbed and get both of your feet back on the ground." It helps that the domestic enemy is what his own set would call "people like us." When a Mr. Alexander Forbes writes *The Boston Herald* to recommend evasion of taxes earmarked for New Deal boondoggles, Roosevelt remonstrates: "My dear cousin and old classmate, that being your belief, I do not hesitate to brand you as one of the worst anarchists in the United States."

But he would prefer to congratulate, buck up and enthuse. "Thrilled" and "grand" are favorite words, the exclamation point as much his characteristic punctuation as the question mark was Lincoln's. If that predecessor's self-deprecation often has the feel of sincere self-appraisal, Roosevelt's put-downs of himself are a pick-me-up, a delightful little dividend atop the day's cocktail of events. He mocks his own "well known voice—the voice that Wall Street uses to inculcate fear in the breasts of their little grandchildren," and complains to James Farley, the postmaster general, that if recovery depends on women like the overly robust one on the NRA stamp, then "I am agin recovery." (Even so, "it is a grand stamp," probably worthy of inclusion in a collection he's "tickled to death" to be offered by a voter.)

Ever the squire, while in office he continues his interest in the activities of the Dutchess County Historical Society and the landscaping to be done at Warm Springs, Georgia. Roosevelt has the outlook of the generalist, which is what he seeks in others. In appointing a reluctant James Couzens to the Maritime Commission, he assures him that "One of the many good reasons that makes me want you for Chairman is that you do not know the first thing about water shipping, naval construction or design!" Whatever self-doubt he had at the beginning, and whatever weariness toward the end, the written evidence of all the long years in between points to a man who enjoyed being president more than anyone except perhaps his distant cousin, Theodore.

Unlike TR, who could get rather monomaniacal in what he called the "arena," one part of FDR always seems to be smiling from the box seats at this fellow so busily engaged below. His correspondence offers fewer surprises, fewer contradictions to the popular image, than any other important president's. Hidden depths and dark corners are so absent that his enjoyment of the job becomes, like his indiscriminate cheer, something dubious. There are moments when his presidency seems to be an avocation, the desktop puttering of the same gentleman hobbyist collecting stamps.

In his memoirs, de Gaulle referred to Roosevelt as "this artist, this seducer." The quick note was his means of turning on the charm. In talking Harold D. Smith out of quitting as budget director, Roosevelt tells him: "I would no more accept your resignation than fly by jumping off a roof." He convinces Harold Ickes not to leave the administration by saying that they have been "married 'for better or worse' for too long to get a divorce or for you to break up the home." Such cozy expressions give a kind of rhetorical ballast to all his snazzy epistolary sailboats.

Beyond the immediate demands of the in-basket, Roosevelt likes to maintain genuine, ongoing correspondences: with his old Groton headmaster, Endicott Peabody; his childhood friend, now Canadian prime minister, Mackenzie King; and his new close associate, Winston Churchill, to whom letters, before mixing business with pleasure, sometimes begin "Former Naval Person." If the president's faceless bonhomie toward Stalin looks naïve or just plain silly, Roosevelt's natural informality acts, in the case of Churchill, as a sort of wartime crash-construction program, speeding up the relationship's development at a pace beyond the natural. As the editors of their correspondence note, "the two leaders did not really know each other at all at the time the war broke out." Their single meeting, which Churchill could not even remember, had been at a London dinner in 1918, which FDR had attended as Woodrow Wilson's assistant secretary of the Navy.

Before they meet again, in the North Atlantic during the summer of '41, Roosevelt's side of their exchange has a tentative feel to it. "I wish much that I could talk things over with you in person," he writes early in 1940; a year later he is dispatching Harry Hopkins to London to "talk to Churchill like an Iowa farmer," and sending another letter via the just-defeated and newly cooperative

Wendell Willkie. Only after their own face-to-face encounter does Roosevelt rise to his usual full epistolary gusto, one ingredient of which is the chance to talk about third parties behind their back. Sizing up de Gaulle and his Free French rival General Henri Giraud, Roosevelt confides to Churchill his "very distinct feelings that we should not send further equipment or munitions to the French Army in North Africa if our prima donna is to seize control of it from the old gentleman." The casualness of such letters, which did their bit to save the world, can be regarded as one more species of wartime deception.

When Roosevelt writes to Churchill, a connoisseur of language is addressing one of its princes. In one unsent letter he tries to deflate the prime minister's interest in Basic English ("I wonder what the course of history would have been if in May 1940 you had been able to offer the British people only 'blood, work, eye water and face water,' which I understand is the best that Basic English can do with five famous words"), and he learns to ration his own broadcasting partly because he has seen the diminishing returns from "too much personal leadership" by Churchill.

The president writes a good many letters to European royalty just before and during the war; the recipients are the only people in the world who can leave him a little starstruck. He offers shelter to several sets of royal offspring, and the Nazi invasion of the Low Countries makes him even more conscious of his Dutch ancestry than he had been. There is a familial feel to the letters being sent Princess Juliana ("Affectionately" from "your old uncle") and her mother, Queen Wilhelmina. With the monarchs of Europe he could now play knight chevalier, and after years of noblesse oblige toward destitute Americans, his fealty must have been a relief. "You do not know it," he writes Wilhelmina in 1939, "but the only time I have seen you was when we were both children—and you were driving in one of the parks at The Hague." When five years later things are reaching their victorious conclusion, he expresses a wish to the exiled Grand Duchess Charlotte of Luxemburg ("Dear Lottie") that he "could stand on the street corner to welcome you back to the city."

The state of others' health always offers Roosevelt a chance to display some cheering, if passionless, affection. (Ira Smith, the White House mails chief, never found "anything particularly personal" in Roosevelt's "almost professional attitude of good-fellowship," and a reader of his letters may not either.) When any appointee is under the weather, he approaches them as "special consulting physician" with a tip-top bedside manner. In the summer of '35, ambassador to Italy Breckinridge Long is ordered to "Watch out for that tummy!" while over in Moscow, Ambassador Bullitt is reassured that "the small growth on [his] spine will develop eventually into wings!" One would have thought he was a perfectly well man himself. Writing these letters may have given him the intermittent illusion that he was.

Roosevelt liked to remember himself as a young assistant secretary, made for merriment and fast on his feet. If years later, as president, he tried micromanaging any part of the government, it was the Navy. Two days after Pearl Harbor, he would be writing Captain John R. Beardall about plans for a ship called the *Sea Cloud:* "I incline to her use as a weather patrol ship, that her four lower masts be retained and that she be rigged on these masts with two jibs and four trisails." The *Sea Cloud* was a yacht, undergoing conversion, as he had so long ago, to more serious uses.

IN THE LETTERS of Whittaker Chambers, Alger Hiss is often "Alger," not "Hiss," for a reason beyond the two men's having once (pace Hiss) known each other. After Chambers left the Communist party, even after he exposed Hiss and brought about his imprisonment for perjury, the two men had something fundamental in common, a peculiar position in the world that made them into familiars. Both were creatures of faith, their "case" an article of belief to supporters on each side of it. As Chambers puts it, both men were pursuing "a mystery in the religious sense."

Following Hiss's conviction, Chambers had little taste for combat of any kind. He preferred to remain on his Maryland farm, nursing his deep glooms and "almost incurable wound." In June 1952, he writes to his fervent supporter, the conservative journalist

Ralph de Toledano, about passing "hours of bitterness which can only be called crippling. While they last, and they come unexpectedly and last for long times, half a day, a whole day, I am unfit for any good use. I woke at dawn the other morning, and, half asleep, felt a sense of pain and distress, and slowly realized, as I wakened more, that it's because I was sorry that another day had come and that I must live through it."

This cry is uttered at an especially hard time, during the liberal press's predictably negative reviews of Chambers's memoir *Witness*, but it's not terribly different from much of what's spoken before and later. Immediately after telling de Toledano of "an effort to spare you the darker moods of the last few months," Chambers asks him: "Do you think I care whether I get out of this bed again or not?" Reserving suicide as an option, he considers the convenient weapon he carries inside his body, a heart so damaged by disease that any overexertion will kill him: "God has given me one out of infinite mercy. It is in my left side. I have only to run upstairs to use it."

The man whom FBI agents called "Uncle Whit" relies on de Toledano and his wife, Nora, for practical assistance with the foreign editions, dramatic adaptations and lawsuits growing out of *Witness*, as well as for considerable help to Chambers's son. In return, Chambers dispenses a wisdom that de Toledano seems almost worshipfully eager to hear. Politically marginalized at *Newsweek*, the younger man listens to Chambers's pleas to hang on there, such as this one offered shortly after Republicans have recaptured the White House in 1953: "these jobs on the established journals . . . offer the best base from which the Right may utilize the changed climate to infiltrate and practice a little cell fission."

There is no doubting the strength of the bond between the two men. "When I was alone, you walked beside me," writes Chambers. "And when I was without a roof, you sheltered me." Inclined to second-guess his own letters, and destroy them before they can make it into the mail, Chambers writes to few others ("The bile is better kept within"). With de Toledano, he is tripped up by the unconscious telepathy that runs between sympathetic letter-writers:

"I can't remember whether I wrote to say, of course come when you can get away. If I didn't, it was simply because that was what I thought when I read your letter."

However nourishing it may be to correspondents, mutual admiration is not very satisfying to later readers. In *Notes from the Underground: The Whittaker Chambers–Ralph de Toledano Letters*, the younger man never quite loses an acolyte's reverence; when he attempts to trim a British edition of *Witness*, it feels as if he's "cutting living flesh." A sonorous morbidity dominates both sides of the exchange, each man outdoing the other with fortissimo chords. "In this tremendous room," writes de Toledano, "even a whisper has the sound of doom." Their literary range is rich—the two talk of Rilke, Shakespeare and Cervantes—but even on this ground there are signs of self-consciousness and strain.

Only in the late 1950s does de Toledano seem to have raised the possibility of one day publishing "our noble correspondence," but the letters' stentorian quality makes one feel that he and Chambers had this idea in the back of their minds from the beginning. A reader must struggle—in considerable fascination—with the way the book's dual protagonists, as well as the United States, simply cannot win. The truth may eventually have given Chambers his Medal of Freedom (in 1984, no less), but it never set him free. In fact, if he had lived to accept the honor from Ronald Reagan's hand, it is doubtful he would have felt much triumph. Publishing the letters in 1997, de Toledano made plain that, despite everything since 1989, Chambers would see no reason to retract his famously pessimistic declaration, in *Witness*, about having left the winning for the losing side. The Soviet empire's demise, de Toledano argued, "did not demonstrate the strength of the West but a viral infection which the sapping of the world's immune system could not fight."

Chambers already saw, in 1956, a growing resemblance between the United States and the USSR. Technology was socializing the West, and its capitalists were killing souls just as surely as the commissars were:

> I, for one, have never envied a capitalist in my life. Quite the contrary.

> They, their minds, their notions, and ways of life, fill me with nothing so much as an irrepressible desire to keep as far away from anything like that as possible. They fill me not with envy, but with abhorrence tempered by compassion. I do not want to liquidate them; I want to get away from them. They seem to me the death of the mind and the spirit.

This comes from Chambers in rural Maryland, but it sounds like Solzhenitsyn, twenty-two years later, delivering his jeremiad against the West in Harvard Yard. For anyone who ever admired the jut of Barry Goldwater's jaw, or the goofy grace of Ronald Reagan's smile, the Chambers–de Toledano letters amount to the strangest sort of anti-anti-Communism, a fraternal echo chamber of high regard and dankest despair.

LIKE "SISTER CITIES" and Esperanto, the "pen pal" phenomenon—not quite a movement, but a venerable twentieth-century activity, especially for the well-intentioned young—made its own small contribution toward piercing the long international darkness that enveloped Chambers and de Toledano. At the phenomenon's apogee, many thousands of American students were matched with new epistolary friends, both foreign and domestic, by a giant, boxy computer inside the Parker Pen Pavilion at the 1964–1965 New York World's Fair. Most of the pairings lasted no longer than a summer romance, but some, here and there, endured for decades.

In 2001, an American named Caren Gottesman and an Englishwoman named Carol Clarke could look back on a thirty-seven-year-long exchange that was now being reported on by a magazine writer who'd gone along to witness the pen pals' first face-to-face meeting, in London. Clarke, by then a forty-seven-year-old receptionist and the divorced mother of four, explained: "Because Caren is so far away, I knew she would never tell anyone else. So I told her lots." Inside Clarke's home the women gave each other presents, one of which, amidst the charm bracelet and the necklace and the flowers, must have struck a forward-looking but slightly sad note: Gottesman presented Clarke with a laptop. One guesses that their correspondence is now instant and electronic, the visit having broken the long air-mail exchange as if it were an enchantment needing to be lifted.

"Snail Mail Lives!" cries the homepage of The Letter Exchange, a cozy twenty-seven-year-old enterprise that makes use of the Web mostly to advertise its thrice-yearly print magazine for people in search of old-fashioned papery fellowship. A subscriber can respond to—or submit—one of the anonymous, numbered requests for mail that the publication carries, such as "4035. I enjoy baseball, music, Monty Python . . . movies, history, comic strips—the list goes on. Please feed my mailbox." From its home in North Oaks, Minnesota, The Letter Exchange forwards any initial replies to an ad; after a connection has been made, correspondents may write each other directly. "No prisoners or singles ads," the website gently warns, though it does encourage fantasizing: "Ghost Letters let you write in character as historical or fictional people (or whatever!)" From the look of the Ghost Letter listings in one old issue, "whatever" seems to include a lot of movie characters: "Red Sonja, Where are you? Miss you very much.—Conan."

Any actual meeting between Conan and Sonja seems so certain to guarantee anticlimax that we can be pretty sure these two role-players never intended to proceed from missives to mattress. And yet, probably one defining circumstance of every friendship-by-mail is the desire of its participants to move, like Caren Gottesman and Carol Clarke, toward a moment when both parties step from behind the curtain. No matter how sincere or formal, long-term epistolary relationships always have an element of the tease, a should-we-or-shouldn't-we subtext that only complex logistics and insufficient funds may keep from being directly discussed.

The most famous postal friendship of modern times may be the twenty-year exchange begun in 1949 by Miss Helene Hanff of New York City and the employees of Marks & Co., London booksellers at 84 Charing Cross Road. The first letter from Miss Hanff—as her principal correspondent, Frank Doel, will call her for quite some time—is a response to the firm's ad in the *Saturday Review:* "The phrase 'antiquarian booksellers' scares me somewhat, as I equate 'antique' with expensive. I am a poor writer with an antiquarian taste in books and all the things I want are impossible to get over here except in very expensive rare editions, or in Barnes & Noble's grimy, marked-up schoolboy copies." Hanff encloses a list of her "most pressing problems," two of which are soon alleviated by the delivery of essay collections by Hazlitt and Robert Louis Stevenson.

After a bit of coaxing, Frank Doel emerges from the initials he's been concealing himself with, and he is soon learning more than he would ever himself ask about his new customer and correspondent. Miss Hanff, in her early thirties, works out of an underheated brownstone in the East Nineties, reading scripts and also writing them, for the new black-and-white television *Adventures of Ellery Queen.* Thanks to her comma-spliced wisecracks and his clerkly fastidiousness, the Hanff-Doel letters become a winning vaudeville of American sass and British reserve. Her mock scoldings about the slow pace of Marks & Co.'s commerce ("Dear Speed—You dizzy me, rushing Leigh Hunt and the Vulgate over here whizbang like that . . . it's hardly more than two years since I ordered them"), or against the shop's disgraceful use of old book pages for wrapping paper, are always met with his muted forbearance: "please don't worry about us using old books such as Clarendon's Rebellion for wrapping. In this particular case they were just two odd volumes with the covers detached and nobody in their right senses would have given us a shilling for them." After eight years have passed, one can hear Doel finally acquiring a bit of Hanff's mischief, when he tells her about a crush of American tourists who've been visiting the shop, "including hundreds of lawyers who march around with a large card pinned to their clothes stating their home town and name."

Hanff's own liveliness extends to a penchant for personifying whatever books make the trip across the ocean: "SAM PEPYS . . . says to tell you he's OVERJOYED to be here, he was previously owned by a slob who never even bothered to cut the pages." Not having the money to finish college, Hanff had derived her literary tastes from reading the criticism of Sir Arthur Quiller-Couch, "whom I fell over in a library when I was 17." She prefers old books to new; antique prose to the revised-standard sort; frankness to expurgation; and nonfiction to novels. She would rather read Chaucer's diary, if he'd written one, than *The Canterbury Tales.* Only Jane Austen makes a temporary dent in her bias toward reality: "went out of my mind over *Pride & Prejudice* which I can't bring myself to take back to the library till you find me a copy of my own."

The letters between New York and London lack nothing in the way of plot. Their referential weave—replies alluding to letters just received, or to ones far back in the exchange—makes for a natural storytelling that most novelists, vexing themselves with the creation of a narrative arc, can only envy. Once Hanff begins sending food parcels to the still-rationed Londoners who work in the shop, there are questions to be settled (next time, fresh eggs or powdered?) and an expanding cast of characters wanting to get in on the epistolary act. Cecily Farr ("I do hope you don't mind my writing. Please don't mention it when you write to Frank") says she's decided that Miss Hanff must be "young and very sophisticated and smart-looking," a series of inferences Miss Hanff quickly corrects: "I'm about as smart-looking as a Broadway panhandler. I live in moth-eaten sweaters and wool slacks."

Within a couple of years, even Frank's wife is writing.

The underlying drama is, of course, whether Helene and Frank will ever lay eyes on each other. By 1952, she has an open invitation to come to England, and she gives it careful thought, confiding both her desire and reluctance to a friend: "I write them the most outrageous letters from a safe 3,000 miles away. I'll probably walk in there one day and walk right out again without telling them who I am." The possibility of going over for the queen's coronation is soon dashed by dental bills: "Elizabeth will have to ascend the throne without me," she tells Frank; "teeth are all I'm going to see crowned for the next couple of years." In 1956, the owners of her brownstone are making renovations and evicting the tenants, and she needs to put what savings she has toward a new apartment.

The years pass, references to Churchill giving way to mention of the Beatles, whom Frank "rather" likes, if only "the fans just wouldn't scream so." In September 1968, Hanff opens a letter with:

"Still alive, are we?" and the two of them appear ready to settle into a new phase of gentle complaints about growing older but no richer. As it turns out, within three months of the joking salutation, Frank Doel is suddenly dead, from peritonitis that follows a ruptured appendix. Hanff receives word from the shop secretary—somebody new, one feels sure—who closes by asking: "Do you still wish us to try and obtain the Austens for you?"

By the time she at last travels to England, the shop itself has closed for good. Its sign will find a new home in Helene Hanff's apartment, once it's filched for her by a fan of the letters that she published, in 1970, as *84, Charing Cross Road.*

CHAPTER THREE *Advice*

LORD GORING: *I always pass on good advice. It is the only thing to do with it. It is never of any use to oneself.*

Oscar Wilde, *An Ideal Husband*

EPISTOLARY COUNSEL operates with a number of advantages over the face-to-face variety. Its written form betokens a certain effort—and hence, perhaps, sincerity—that oral persuasion may lack. If spoken advice is one's "two cents," the inked kind now costs at least forty-four. Paper permits no interruption and preserves advice for purposes of reinforcement, unless of course the recipient chooses to rip it up, a gesture that can be as satisfying as stabbing Polonius behind the arras.

In letters, as in person, advice is often offered with its own prefatory suggestion—advice about the advice—that the recipient should "feel free to take it or leave it." The admonition relieves the advisee of pressure and the advisor of potential embarrassment: if the advice is rejected, no matter; its extension was never a matter of consequence. How awful, by contrast, to have been in the position of the Archbishop François de Salignac de la Mothe Fénelon, a tutor to young seventeenth-century noblemen who wrote letters to his star charge as if the fate of all France lay in the balance.

The author of *Télémaque* (1699), an instructive romance on politics and world affairs, Fénelon gradually fell into the role of epistolary advisor to any number of wellborn scions: "Fulfill your vocation—" he writes the duc de Chaulnes in 1713; "mine is to torment you!" Indeed, his letters to the young and the noble are exacting little syllabi of good sense. The Vidame d'Amiens, something of a wastrel, gets lectures against ambition; in favor of piety; against flattery; for charity. He is told to "eschew melancholy, folly, and false modesty; be neither proud nor pliant," and advised, dispiritingly enough, to put aside pleasure until such time as "the passion is gone out of it."

Fénelon's highest and most tricky responsibility is the duc de Bourgogne, grandson of the aging Louis XIV and second in line to the throne. The duke is told, repeatedly, to model himself on Saint Louis, who before canonization had been the merely royal Louis IX: "Before you inherit his crown see to it that you inherit his virtues." Less remotely, Fénelon points to the current pretender to the English throne, the would-be James III, as a fit, if unexciting, subject for emulation: "He is very self-possessed, good-tempered, and with no quirks of character, does not possess a great deal of imagination and acts at all times by the light of reason."

When need be, Fénelon's mentoring can move from the pious to the politic. In 1708, he tells the duke to remain at the head of the armies around Lille, even if French forces fighting the War of the Spanish Succession can't lift the siege of the city; sticking it out will give him political credit he can draw on later. The pupil, when requesting counsel, can get equally specific: "I would take this opportunity of asking you whether you think it is right that I should have my headquarters in a convent as is the case at present."

Fénelon is a bit besieged himself. Out of favor at court—thanks to *Télémaque* and for promoting heresy—he is forbidden to speak with the duc de Bourgogne without a third person there to hear the conversation. He must send his letters of advice through another tutor, the duc de Beauvilliers, and take care not to put the duc de Bourgogne's name on the envelope. Grateful for the royal heir's loyalty, Fénelon calls him "our dear Prince" in letters to the go-between, who becomes one more recipient of Fénelon's counsel. "Take care of your health," the archbishop writes Beauvilliers; "no medicines but a rest occasionally, freedom and high spirits." He adds advice on how to advise: "Concern yourself with the inner rather than with the outer life of Monsieur le Duc de Bourgogne." So compulsively, in fact, does Fénelon counsel change and correction and proactivity that it becomes difficult for a reader of the letters to remember that the heresy with which the author had been associated was the passive, soul-surrendering doctrine of "quietism."

His theology can't stop him from fretting over his protégé, or from worrying about himself. In 1712, the duke—not yet thirty and by now the dauphin—suddenly dies. The seventy-three-year-old Sun King, having outlived his son and grandson, remains on the throne, and Fénelon must now nervously write to the duc de Chevreuse about what he long ago transmitted in those unmarked envelopes:

> Was there not, among our dear Prince's papers, an article of mine and some letters which I wrote to him during the siege of Lille? Was there not also a gold reliquary containing a piece of the jawbone of St. Louis which I once gave him? Are all his papers now in the possession of the King? . . .

One usually finds this level of anxiety operating in the retrieval of love letters, not packets of mail that so often, along with so many other suggestions, counseled the avoidance of love's snares.

ON OCCASION one side of a published correspondence will make for better reading than two. After all, in replying to a letter, the writer will often make verbatim reference to some of its contents, trying to remind the first sender of what he wrote some time ago. But these are the same words that a latter-day reader, if both sides of the exchange have been published, will have read just half a page and a minute ago.

One-sidedness also offers the pleasures of inference, the intellectual labor it takes to surmise what the other party said and was like. After James Agee's premature death in 1955, his letters to Father James Harold Flye were published by themselves, without his lifelong advisor's half of their thirty-year correspondence. The teacher had outlived his pupil, and whatever counsel the Episcopal priest gave to Agee—from the time the boy left St. Andrew's School in Tennessee, all through his attempts to balance serious work and slick journalism, and beyond the success of *A Death in the Family*—was to remain mute, the unheard half of a conversation on which we're now trying to eavesdrop. What we get is all Agee, and the general effect is that of a long, hesitant recessional. As he grows up and older, the author's handwriting shrinks; he switches from definite ink to impermanent pencil; flares to a brief fulfillment and then keeps backing away from his oldest friend and his own better self.

From Exeter in the late 1920s, Agee reports that the Dreiser he is reading is "horribly obvious, and has no humor," though the novelist's "dullness is a relief from the heady brilliance of Dos Passos or Lewis." (Agee is also reading Anita Loos, on Flye's surprisingly hip recommendation.) The boy's own writing shows the exuberant strain of someone realizing he's got what it takes. A girl he's met has an "unobstreperous intelligence, tinged with a charming limeadish sarcasm"—a description self-conscious enough to make the young Agee follow it with an amiable retraction: "Well, I'll cease to make a jackass of myself." He's performing for Flye and delighted by his own showing off.

It's a wonder to see how fast he becomes genuinely good: "'Through pull' with an Irish Politician, I got to see the [Boston] Morgue and the Jail, neither of which were what I'd expected, but rather worse, in a clammy, metallic way. I had a taste in my mouth as if I'd been licking an old sardine can." By the time he's ready to go off to Harvard, he's the one recommending writers to Flye, though as soon as he's done so ("Don't you think [Housman's] beautiful stuff?"), he remembers his manners and who's supposed to be mentoring whom: "Probably you know it—even have the books in the house."

Precocity doomed him. His letters resemble no one's so much as those of Rupert Brooke, who also, in style and psychology, became at a very early age not just all he would ever be but all he could ever have become, however long he lived. At twenty-eight, a dozen years after leaving home, Agee is a paunchy, anguished Peter Pan, unable to stop singing in an adolescent tremolo: "The world (and my self) seem to me this morning, in light of recent context, evil, exhausting and hopeless, not to mention nauseating and infuriating and incurable, yet I am thoroughly glad I am in it and alive." He never sheds the self-importance of youth. One sees it mutating, as he embarks upon *Let Us Now Praise Famous Men*, into a kind of grandiose humility: "If I could make it what it ought to be made I would not be human." Once the book is done and Flye has praised it, Agee's mea culpa is more megalomaniacal than self-critical: "What you write of the book needless to say is good to hear to the point of shaming me—for it is a sinful book at least in all degrees of 'falling short of the mark' and I think in more corrupt ways as well." In 1940, he continues to fly a teenager's banner ("I never in all my life want to feel respect for a half-good"), and ten years after that he's still taking birthdays hard.

From his own point of view, the worst compromises are the ones he must negotiate between his literary ambition, honestly confessed to Flye, and the need to make a living. Having famously parodied *Time* for the *Harvard Advocate*, he lets Henry Luce's magazine empire co-opt him with a job offer from *Fortune*, the acceptance of which he ceaselessly bemoans. When, in 1937, he decides never to take another staff position, it's with a brass band of renunciation: "I will work for money only when I have it and think security and solidity and respect for these hopeless and murderous traps and delusions."

Drinking floats his "enormously strong drive . . . toward self-destruction," and yet it's only when he's at least half-drunk that he can write a letter less about himself than his concern for Father Flye. Twenty times more often it's his own spiritual sloth that goes into the mail, styled in a self-pity that Agee is well aware of himself. "I am in most possible kinds of pain," he writes on October 30, 1934, ashamed of this letter he still won't stop himself from sending. He apologizes for posting near-suicide notes, but even when a terrible mood lifts mid-letter, he goes ahead and burdens Flye with the whole thing he's written. On one occasion, he retracts responsibility below the signature: "P.S. This is now several days later. If this seems bad, annoying, ill-tempered or otherwise no good please forgive it."

Having begun to teach his second wife to play the piano, he can discourse to Flye upon "some funny and tricky things about teaching"—without ever seeming to realize that Flye may already have discovered one or two of them for himself in a lifetime at the job. The impending birth of Agee's child has him passing out cigars to himself: "On that I feel such complications of hope, fear, joy, sorrow, life, death, foreboding, interest, and a dozen other true emotions on which the copyright has expired, that I am not qualified to try to touch them now." He knows that Flye is endlessly willing to listen and respond, and that their correspondence has, finally, only one subject: "So I want to write, as I would talk if we could, only of the few most urgent things you have written of—all to do with me."

One can sometimes guess Flye's specific recommendations from Agee's responses: "You used to tell me what to do—that is about relaxing my mind and body—when things tied up in knots. I didn't really know what you meant, but I do now." Most of what the older man said, however, could not have been as important as his letting Agee vent; if Agee is using the priest, this seems to be no more than what Flye desires. In one instance, Agee directly solicits spiritual guidance, receiving back the single, quite beautiful, letter from Flye that its author allowed to be printed (as an almost apologetic footnote) in this whole book of those he got from Agee: "You are naturally religious . . . There are those who are bored by what is clean, sweet, beautiful, tender, reverent. As between the high and the low, they will choose the low. There are those who disapproved of Christ and those who laughed and jeered at Him as He hung on the cross. I know that you are of those who love the highest when they see it; *anima naturaliter Christiana*, as the old expression was. As between Christ and those against Him, there is no doubt to which side you are drawn. The way to make this allegiance open will I think become clearer to you."

As the volume ends, with Agee dying in his forties of heart disease, illness makes the author approachable. The pompous self-appraisal drops away in favor of concrete realities and sincere feeling. Even so, these letters are not art by Agee's own definition (an "attempt to state things as they seem to be, minus personal opinion of any sort"). In fact, Agee deliberately excludes them from that realm: "this is a lousy letter, a mouthful of sweet potato," he writes Flye on February 12, 1953. "I've said virtually nothing about myself. Maybe that is a virtue in the Art of Letter-writing, but between friends it seems a vice . . ." He more than once derides letters as a poor substitute for face-to-face conversation, and yet, when a chance to see Flye presents itself, he seems reluctant to take it. Agee doesn't visit him on a trip South, and appears tentative when the priest has the chance to come to New York—as if the prospect of talk, which would require some self-interruption, had become suddenly unattractive.

James Harold Flye remained a faithful listener until the end, taking Agee's last letter ("I feel, in general, as if I were dying") from the writer's living-room mantel, where it had been placed, addressed and stamped and waiting to be mailed.

THE ONLY REALLY DIFFICULT thing about giving advice, epistolary or otherwise, is getting people to take it. In the early 1930s, already an object of aesthetic veneration, Frank Lloyd Wright set about making sure he would have a long string of disciples by setting up a fellowship for apprentice architects at his Taliesin studios, first in Wisconsin and, later, Arizona. For two decades, past his eightieth birthday, he kept his own administrative hands on the enterprise. The letters he wrote for an hour or two each morning show him more in the role of a dean than a deity: begging donations; dunning tuition; scaring up the right mix of cello players and carpenters among the applicants. He also wrote their acceptance letters: "Come along and get to work." Time and again, not wholly trusting a brochure to do the job, he explained the fellowship, right down to what the recipient should pack: "Strictly formal clothes are no[t] essential. Bring your own bedding: sheets, blankets, etc., and if you happen to have sleeping bags bring them with you."

His great theme is the superiority of Taliesin's "culture" to education, the kind provided at Yale and leading to "a scrap of paper" called a diploma. "No academic preparation is necessary to enter Taliesin"; in fact, the best time to join is before corruption by schooling. Besides, "a letter of recommendation from this office is of more value than a degree of architecture from any college of Architecture in the world." Over the years, throughout an era when "degeneracy looms," Wright pours it on against "the scholasticism that has manufactured parasitic white collarites by the million."

More gently—reluctant to bite the hands feeding his community—he writes to the fellows' parents. Sometimes the news is bad ("your son Willets . . . with a pint of whiskey got dead drunk and messed the place up rather nastily"), and in one case where it's good, Wright must ask a thriving boy's father to "give us some explanation of your sudden resolve to take [your son] out of here and throw him back into the stagnant city pool." Woe betide the student who fails to resist such parental retraction: "I may invest Taliesin and myself in a likely boy like yourself and then have him ditch both Taliesin and myself when both need him most to help 'ma' and 'pa.' I didn't foresee that. But I see it now and do not find it good."

In perpetuating its founder's architectural gospel of romantic form and individualism, Taliesin could not avoid a certain cultishness. Wright warns one prospective fellow, in 1947, that "as a fountain head we are not for all and sundry," quoting, perhaps unconsciously, Ayn Rand. It's hard to imagine that ego-hymning objectivist, whose dirtiest word was altruism, as anyone's acolyte, but her fiction's one memorable hero came out of her own prolonged hero-worship of Wright. *The Fountainhead*'s Howard Roark was not meant to resemble Wright biographically but to fight his fight for a modern expressionist architecture against the pack of Beaux-Arts Philistines.

Her novel, she writes him in 1937, while still researching it, will be "a monument to you . . . to the spirit in you and in your great work." She has contacted Wright to obtain an interview, employing the sort of blaring overstatement that she would use in the book itself: "you can understand why it seems to me that of all men on earth you are the one I must see." Still, this first letter to him contains as much posturing as prostration: "I do not suppose that you have heard my name, since I am not that famous—as yet."

She would have her fame, and it would bedazzle her into a delusion of uniqueness: "The success of other books was always due in large measure to big-scale publicity, organized pushing, book-club-wholesaling. My book is the only one that rose, unhelped, through sheer, genuine popular response." Wright, who never sat down with Rand until after this supposedly unheard-of phenomenon had occurred, eventually wrote her a sort of fan letter, to which she replied "Gratefully—and always reverently," without letting him get away with a single reservation about her book: "Am I really 'sensationalizing' my material? If I am, I think it is in the same way in which your buildings are 'sensationalized.' "

Her ordinary fans—many of them far more worshipful than Wright's most enraptured apprentice—got away with even less. Rand didn't usually like their letters, but if she detected seriousness, she could gratify it with lengthy, even generous, advice, as when she addresses the vocational anxieties of a gifted sixteen-year-old: "don't expect any outside circumstance or observation to give you a desire for a particular career. That desire comes from your own convictions about life, its purpose, what you want to do with it, and in what form you want to express it." More typically she rewards compliments with lectures, scoldings and corrections; letters written to two different fans on March 6, 1965, both have paragraphs that begin: "You are mistaken."

A long, early reply to Nathan Blumenthal—who as Nathaniel Branden would become her public expositor and secret lover—whips him into philosophical shape: "now let *me* ask *you* a question: Do you really know what Capitalism is?" More casual correspondents must "earn" responses—like one sent to the hapless Raymond B. Young, Jr., who apparently had kind things to say about Rand's intellectual archenemy, Plato. The practical difficulties of authorial celebrity keep her guard up—but so, no doubt, does the memory of long ago having tried to earn that interview with Wright. "May I come?" her first letter to him had ended—before she was denied.

The seriousness with which she could take her fans reflected, more than anything else, the colossal seriousness with which she took herself. She speaks of Howard Roark as if he were really alive, and refers to "the author of *The Fountainhead*" in a manner less detached than awestruck. Possessed of an extreme literary intentionalism, she seems never happier than when megaphoning exactly what she means by her elephantine allegories: "Much later in my novel I will have a very long speech by the hero in which I will summarize the entire philosophy of the story and cover all the important details of the free-enterprise system."

Any novelist learns that enjoyment of his own work in progress should be taken as a warning light, a sign that he's tarrying in his own fantasy world instead of creating one that will be intelligible to his readers; but Rand's self-delight throughout the years and reams of paper required by *Atlas Shrugged* borders on the autoerotic: "it is moving well, and I love it, and it is much better than I expected it to be." The filming of *The Fountainhead*—that "atom bomb of the movie industry"—seems "even more miraculous" than the book's sui generis triumph. Rand directs any admiration she has left over toward pop-cultural tough guys like Mickey Spillane and Robert Stack, both of whom can turn her all girly and giggling: "If you want me to be a 'Spillane Hunter'—take this as part of the pursuit." The objects of these crushes are spared the chilling tone of the liquidator, the Stalinist rhetoric that elsewhere comes so naturally to this fierce anti-Stalinist.

The ugly, pile-driving clarity of Rand's writing was, in fact, sometimes suited to the giving of advice, at least in those instances when the requestor needed someone else's certainty to pulverize hesitation. When Rand's niece asked to borrow twenty-five dollars for a dress, the repayment terms that were offered must have made the young woman consider running to a convent instead of a boutique:

> I want you to understand right now that I will not accept any excuse—except a serious illness. If you become ill, then I will give you an extension of time—*but for no other reason.* If, when the debt

> becomes due, you tell me that you can't pay me because you needed a new pair of shoes or a new coat or you gave the money to somebody in the family who needed it more than I do—then I will consider you as an embezzler. No, I won't send a policeman after you, but I will write you off as a rotten person and I will never speak or write to you again.

This is just Aunt Ayn, trying to save her niece from the evil altruists and hoping "that this will be the beginning of a real friendship between us." Perhaps less attracted to the dress than to the letter's crazy definiteness, the niece took the deal.

STAGE-FRIGHTENED TEACHERS and tentative physicians do not make the best purveyors of wisdom, and yet at least one book of counsel by an underconfident master has remained—through eras during which Hermann Hesse, Anaïs Nin and Kahlil Gibran have come and gone—a staple of support to the artistically inclined young. The *Letters to a Young Poet* that Rainer Maria Rilke wrote between 1903 and 1908 provide an odd spectacle of encouragement in which the nervous mentor seems to preach as much to himself as his disciple: "Do not believe that he who seeks to comfort you lives untroubled among the simple and quiet words that sometimes do you good." Rilke's correspondent is Franz Xaver Kappus, who, while enduring the same sort of military schooling that once traumatized Rilke, sends the twenty-seven-year-old poet his own verses—under "a covering letter in which I unreservedly laid bare my heart"—and forces Rilke into a role he seems scarcely strong enough to perform.

Rilke's prescriptions for writing are more or less firm. Kappus must avoid reading criticism and look for validation only within himself. He must honor sadness and not overvalue irony. He must respect the difficult and learn to love questions more than answers. He must cultivate a ripeness-is-all patience that will bring forth works of art made inevitable by their own necessity. The boy must avoid "unreal, half-artistic professions," such as journalism, in favor of one that "will make you independent and set you entirely on your own in every sense."

During much of this period, however, Rilke himself lacks any compelling artistic project. Poverty forces him into the reviewing and article writing he so dislikes, and keeps him from sending Kappus any more than the titles of the books he has managed to publish. Already married and a father, Rilke nonetheless imparts the most ethereal sort of sexual advice: "most people misuse and squander this experience and apply it as a stimulant at the tired spots of their lives and as distraction instead of a rallying toward exalted moments." Depressed by springtime whenever it arrives, he recommends solitude, muses on the chance for a new androgyny in the world and talks about a state of mutual regard between lovers that sounds like D. H. Lawrence's "star-equilibrium" without the preliminary fun: "this more human love (that will fulfill itself, infinitely considerate and gentle, and kind and clear in binding and releasing) will resemble that which we are preparing with struggle and toil, the love that consists in this, that two solitudes protect and border and salute each other." In fact, Rilke's imagined lovers appear as if they'll always be exchanging letters instead of kisses.

Letter writing was one more thing that came to him with difficulty. From Rome, in October 1903, he apologizes to Kappus for the delay in answering his last communication: "Forgive this dilatoriness—but I do not like writing letters while traveling, because I need more for letter-writing than the most necessary implements: some quiet and solitude and a not too incidental hour." (There is also, he pleads, the state of Italian mail delivery to consider.) Even when in the mood to address Kappus's tribulations, he will demur that he "can say almost nothing that is helpful, hardly anything useful." As he's told him before: "for one person to be able to advise or even help another, a lot must happen, a lot must go well, a whole constellation of things must come right in order once to succeed." What he really has in mind here is the advice he requires, not dispenses. His great lessons about work are still coming from the man he sometimes serves as a private secretary, Auguste Rodin, and few things can upset him more than a break in the sculptor's letters.

IF RILKE HAS an erotic and self-confident opposite, it is probably Henry Miller, whose letters to New Directions publisher James Laughlin are so bumptious and bullying that there's frequent confusion in a reader's mind as to who's working for whom. In 1936, before they begin the business association that Ezra Pound has been urging, Miller writes: "I am thinking, Laughlin, me boy, that you're the guy I must count on over there. I was thinking about it all night. Shit, you're a *Gentile*, which counts tremendously, in the first place, and you're dogged (I can see that from your mug), and you don't give a shit, and well, a lot of things combined."

Laughlin *is* a boy—a Harvard alumnus not yet twenty-five—and Miller makes no bones about his own pissed-off, middle-aged poverty, or his unwillingness to stop writing dirty, if literary, books. Nearly two years after their negotiation begins, Miller finally decides that the whole thing won't work:

> I don't think I'll be sending you any script after all. What I'd like to see published you either can't or won't take—so what's the use? . . .
>
> You're thinking now about your public, your buyers, your family etcetera etcetera. And I think only of what I want done. Deadlock . . . Why should I compromise? To please America? Or to please *you*? I don't see it. I'm playing my hand for all it's worth. Winner takes all—that's always been my motto.

When Laughlin offers some unexpectedly good terms, the author sends back a hymn of thanks ("You are the Jesus Christ of the publishing world!"), but Miller takes care not to sing it too long. He's soon warning the young publisher that Laughlin will be the one, not the printers, to catch Miller's ire if there's any bowdlerization of *Tropic of Capricorn;* and Laughlin must "never ask . . . if I am in need—I am and will be for a long time." After Laughlin turns down the author's Greek travel book (*The Colossus of Maroussi*), the only letter he'll get from Miller for the next three years is an open one in *The New Republic*, attacking him for timidity in the face of censors.

After they've reconciled, Miller insists, for the next few decades, that Laughlin do more to stimulate American demand for his books. He sounds rude even when he's trying to be polite: "You don't need to feel *obliged* to bring the book out. I'm writing to you first because you are entitled to first choice." For his part in this up-and-down correspondence, Laughlin gently keeps Miller aware of practicalities—the need, for example, to have a new book from him now that backlist sales are slowing down, and the importance of distinguishing "the literary crowd" from "the non-academic reader." But Laughlin himself—for a while the fiancé of that other literary sounding-board, Maria Britneva (St. Just)—can't quite make up his mind about where Miller belongs: "I have never thought of you as a highbrow writer," he declares in 1951. "To my mind, you belong in the great popular tradition of Cervantes, Rabelais and Balzac." Seven years later he's pronouncing his volatile correspondent "an important thinker as well as a brilliant writer of fiction."

Laughlin realizes that his own moodiness allows him to understand and put up with Miller's, but over the course of thirty years his letters—so many of them written in the teeth of Miller's temper and presumption—never lose a feeling of distance, even formality. "All in all," he writes in 1961, "it sounds as though you are having a marvelous time over there, and exerting a very stimulating effect on the European literary scene." His signature "JL" or "J" can sometimes freeze back into "With best wishes, as ever, James Laughlin."

The fluctuation was probably deliberate. When you have a reader who is likely to blow up over any letter's content, formality can be an instrument of peacekeeping. Miller would have been *impossible* with e-mail, which has made the telegram's instant high dudgeon affordable to all. One imagines him hitting the "Send" key three or four times a day, retracting and re-releasing sentiments with the same dosage of overstatement used in their initial dispatch. In the low-tech event, there was probably more than one occasion when he cooled down while rummaging for a stamp.

Maxwell Perkins, that earlier Harvard graduate come to Publishers' Row, usually dealt with a more mainstream, though often no less high-maintenance, run of author than Laughlin had in Henry Miller. If Perkins were alive in today's publishing culture, his colleagues would probably be approaching him to do a book on management style, given the deftness of his letters not only to the writers on his list but also to the occasionally ruffled purchasers of Scribner books.

He was a master of the passive-aggressive. "I detest argument," Perkins assures Scott Fitzgerald in 1926, and it's no wonder. He knows how to win one before it gets started. His general epistolary strategy toward authors is common enough—start off with some praise and then get to the problems—but Perkins has a knack for making his essential demands seem incidental to everything else. At times he comes off more Southern than Yankee, layers of subjunction and subordination ballooning up like petticoats: "I don't like to say . . . But I do think . . . Just the same . . . And I am inclined to think . . . But I should say"—all these phrases occur in one paragraph of a letter that advises its recipient to "trust your own instinct," while making clear that this author should abandon his current subject and start another book entirely. The warmth with which Perkins declines an unsolicited manuscript matches the tact with which he rejects a commissioned one. The diffident pose, so elaborate and constant ("I don't advance this view with much confidence"), always distracts from the cocking of the gun. He pretends to cede the whole field while securing the only square foot of it that counts.

His most famous challenge was the novelist Thomas Wolfe, who needed praise and reassurance and, above all, cutting. Perkins wrote by hand, his own posthumous editor informs us, "where the situation was delicate." With Wolfe it often was. "It seems rather futile to write this letter," Perkins admits on September 10, 1930, "in view of your having stopped all communications." Wolfe is in despair over reviews of *Look Homeward, Angel*—a "few unfavorable" ones, Perkins reminds him, as opposed to "the overwhelming number of extremely and excitedly enthusiastic" ones. A few years later, in a letter to Hemingway, one finds Perkins outlining his and Wolfe's continuing efforts on *Of Time and the River:*

> We have got a good system now. We work every evening from 8:30 (or as near as Tom can come to it) until 10:30 or 11:00, and Tom does actual writing at times, and does it well, where pieces have to be joined up . . . but his impulse is all away from the hard detailed revision. He is mighty ingenious at times, when it comes to the organization of material. The scheme is pretty clear in his own head, but he shrinks from the sacrifices, which are really cruel often.

When they were through, Wolfe would offer Perkins the novel's dedication; Perkins would refuse; and Wolfe would insist, thus commemorating what Perkins called "the most interesting episode of my editorial life"—one that didn't end with the book's publication. Perhaps inevitably, Wolfe went on to pour out long, private complaints to Perkins, biting the hand that had blue-pencilled him toward finishing a book he would otherwise never have completed. Perkins's replies display a patience that sometimes seems more paternal, even psychiatric, than editorial:

> I don't see why you should have hesitated to write me as you did, or rather to send the letter. There was mighty little of it that I did not wholly accept, and what I did not, I perfectly well understood. There were places in it that made me angry, but it was a fine letter.

Perkins's epistolary manners took years to develop. A letter on the general subject of competition, written to Van Wyck Brooks in 1914, when Perkins was still in the Scribner's advertising department, is by his own admission verbose ("I have not been able to say it fully or well, and now my pencil is used up entirely"), a far cry from the plain, perfect reassurances he would eventually learn to offer writers like Marjorie Kinnan Rawlings ("It is all simple, not complicated—don't let anything make it complicated to you") and James Jones: "Let me know occasionally how things go."

In 1921, Perkins wrote to John Galsworthy about a young American novelist who "needs steering." The editor had begun the effort to direct Scott Fitzgerald's talents two years earlier, when Scribner's acquired *This Side of Paradise* and Perkins outlined publishing's seasonal rhythms to the young author, explaining why "it would damage your book exceedingly to try to rush it out before Christmas." When it comes time to help Fitzgerald revise *The Beautiful and Damned*, Perkins has very specific ideas about one of the novel's crucial speeches, but opens his critique, typically, with some advice against advice: "Don't ever *defer* to my judgment." He claims no desire to control Fitzgerald the way William Dean Howells controlled Mark Twain.

Perkins recognizes *The Great Gatsby* as a novel of such near-perfection that in his editorial comments of November 20, 1924, he's "ashamed" to make even the few suggestions he has about the best way for Fitzgerald to acquaint the reader with Gatsby's past. In this letter, praise is not strategic prologue but the main agenda; Perkins is only too pleased to enumerate "such things [in the book] as make a man famous . . . You once told me you were not a *natural* writer—my God!"

Sixteen years later, only seven months before Fitzgerald's death, Perkins would be writing to the novelist in Hollywood, invoking his great long-ago success in an effort to hoist him up from his current low point. "I never see an editor or writer, hardly, but they ask about you. It shows what you did, for think of all the writers who were thought to be notable, and whose output has been much larger, who have simply vanished without a trace. But we know the 'Gatsby' was a truly great book . . . You know that you are in almost all the school anthologies." Three paragraphs later, at the close of the letter, Perkins seems to realize that this sort of praise might make a man of forty-three feel more depressed than encouraged, and so he decides, with lovely matter-of-fact courtesy, to sign off by looking not toward the golden past but to the active, if uncertain, future: "At the 'sales conference' about the fall books, the salesmen were all anxious to know what you were doing."

FITZGERALD WAS more naturally a taker of advice than its giver, but he had to assume the second role when his daughter reached adolescence. Deprived of her mother (by then in a sanatorium) and of her "golden childhood," Scottie Fitzgerald watched her father become a stern parent whose hard written admonitions could melt like ice cubes in the swirl of his own alcoholic behavior. At Christmastime in 1936, for instance, Fitzgerald insists on a hurdy-gurdy instead of a swing orchestra for the tea dance he's giving his daughter, and he specifies exactly how the invitations to her friends should be written. On the day of the dance he winds up getting drunk in front of them all.

Many of his letters are mailed from Hollywood, where he is trying to earn money, to Scottie's boarding school or college. He tells his "Dearest Pie" to stay away from fluff ("What purpose is served in teaching that second-rate Noel Coward at Vassar?") and to concentrate on the Romantic poets who helped lyricize and sometimes even title his own novels: "For awhile after you quit Keats all other poetry seems to be only whistling or humming." He is honest about her own literary possibilities ("I do not believe that so far you are a 'natural'") and confident of his artistic marching orders: "the above is really good advice, Pie, in a line where I know my stuff." He proposes for her a regimen not unlike the young Gatsby's self-improving daily schedule: "If you will trust my scheme of making a mental habit of doing the hard thing first, when you are absolutely fresh, and I mean doing the *hardest* thing *first* at the *exact moment that you feel yourself fit for doing anything* in any particular period, morning, afternoon or evening, you will go a long way toward mastering the principle of concentration."

He lectures Scottie on self-confidence; cautions her against whining (in a letter where he whines a bit about the loneliness of writing); and tells her he "never believe[s] much in happiness." He urges the tragic view of life instead, though the stratagems he recommends for achieving it are often the eternal tricks of comedy: "A great social success is a pretty girl who plays her cards as carefully as if she were plain." Such maxims read like the sayings in his notebooks, where he stored observations and overheard remarks for eventual use in his fiction. His view of Scottie's life is actually more aesthetic than tragic. In the fall of '38, he goes so far as to offer, in a long, cruel paragraph, a sort of predictive plotline: "Knowing your character, here's about the way things will go in the next month . . ."

He presents himself and her mother as negative examples ("Just do everything we didn't do and you will be perfectly safe") and regulates the letters through which Zelda now must relate to them both. He urges Scottie to write her but not to spend much vacation time in her presence: "I think the pull of an afflicted person upon a normal one is at all times downward, depressing and eventually somewhat paralyzing." Zelda's letters are "tragically brilliant on all matters except those of central importance," while his own, he knows, reveal too much of the latter. A postscript to Scottie just months before his death in 1940 tells her to "Be careful about showing my letters—I mean to your mother for instance. I write very freely."

It seems that Scottie will survive only with constant dire warnings. Fitzgerald speaks of "dreamy people like you and me," whose "danger is imagining that we have resources—material and moral—which we haven't got." Incessant red flags against early drinking and early sex and failure to study read less like advice from a father to a daughter than loud slaps to the face of a drunk one is walking to keep awake. Fitzgerald claims to dislike the role of scolding parent, but he plays it to the girl's most vulnerable spots, splashing contempt upon her first love and declaring that Vassar shouldn't even admit her. "Don't answer this, justifying yourself," he shouts: "of *course* I know you're doing the best you 'can.'" He can only "wish to God I wasn't so right usually about you."

In a postscript whose sarcasm was surely lost on a teenager, Fitzgerald reminds her that "At the *Saturday Evening Post* rate this letter is worth $4000. Since it is for you only and there are so many points, won't you read it twice?" He is, in fact, constantly setting his advice against his own published work and vanished world ("The Bachelors' Cotillion simply doesn't mean what it did twenty years ago—or even ten") and, above all, his own killing mistakes: "This is the most completely experienced advice I've ever given you." Scottie Fitzgerald points out how Malcolm Cowley went so far as to say that her father "wasn't writing those letters to his daughter at Vassar; he was writing them to himself at Princeton." Fitzgerald himself knew, in one of the letters' most shrewdly loving moments, that Scottie's world wouldn't bother to distinguish between the two: "people will be quick to deck you out with my sins . . . would like to be able to say, and would say on the slightest provocation: 'There she goes—just like her papa and mama.'"

Actually, he's sending many of these letters neither to Princeton nor to Vassar, but to the Hollywood hotel room in which they're being written. Fitzgerald is trying to keep himself, one final time, on the straight and narrow—"You don't realize that what I am doing here is the last tired effort of a man who once did something finer and better"—and if he can't keep doing it, he will be finished for good. "If I hear of you taking a drink before you're twenty," he writes Scottie, "I shall feel entitled to begin my last and greatest non-stop binge."

Scottie later recalled being too rebellious and self-protective to bear this onslaught, with its clear evidence of her father's pain. When "these gorgeous letters, these absolute pearls of wisdom and literary style" arrived in her mailbox, she'd "simply examine them for checks and news, then stick them in [her] lower right-hand drawer." In at least one of them, her father mentioned that he was keeping a carbon, so he'd be able to check whether or not her reply touches "on *every point*" he has made. But the copy's real job was to keep those points, especially the last one—"Please work—work with your best hours"—faceup and available to the man still struggling in the Garden of Allah Hotel.

ON THE MORNING of his resignation, during a rambling and sometimes mawkish farewell to White House staffers, Richard Nixon quoted the young Theodore Roosevelt's grief-shattered reflection upon the death of his first wife: "And when my heart's dearest died, the light went from my life forever." This portion of Nixon's remarks is usually regarded as downright dissociative—equating the loss of a wife with the end of a mere presidency. Actually, the comparison had the sort of raw sincerity that Nixon-haters always judged the man incapable of demonstrating; he used the quotation as evidence of things being never as dark as they seem. Nixon was already plotting his comeback, a reputational one this time, and his model only happened to be a politician. In the twenty-five-year-old Roosevelt, he had a spectacular model of personal renewal, a man whose painfully restarted pursuit of happiness turned into a gaudy shower of familial joy.

The whole TR story—asthmatic childhood; gym regimen; widowing; flight to the Dakota; big second family and Sagamore Hill; all of this before Rough-Riding and trust-busting—used to be better known to children than it is now. Perhaps it's just too remote, or maybe polio and PT boats make for better legends. But once it really gets going, nothing rivals Teddy Roosevelt's story for speed. In the space of three years he went from San Juan Hill to the White House, with time enough to be governor of New York and vice president of the United States in between.

When he moved his six children into the Executive Mansion, they ranged in age from three to seventeen. His fatherly letter writing was made necessary by the boys' absences at school or his own presidential progresses. For all that he dismisses his traveling routine ("I had the usual experience in such cases, made the usual speech, held the usual reception, went to the usual lunch, etc., etc."), it doesn't seem that he resisted it much. In her long and admiring introduction to *A Bully Father*, her selection of the paterfamilas's correspondence, Joan Paterson Kerr quotes Roosevelt's daughter, Alice: "Father always wanted to be the corpse at every funeral, the bride at every wedding and the baby at every christening."

He was also the most popular attraction in a self-assembled zoo. Throughout his letters he is either pampering animals ("I am acting as nurse to two wee guinea pigs") or slaughtering them ("P.S.—I have just killed a bear"). The children's pets—terriers, macaws, flying squirrels, kangaroo rats—seem to have outnumbered the live humans and mounted taxidermy around them, and their father proved a sharp and entertaining observer of the creatures' ways. He observes that a guinea pig (another one, not the two above) is "squirming and kicking and looking exactly like Admiral Dewey," and solemnly reports to Archie on a new dog: "The kitchen cat and he have strained relations but have not yet come to open hostility."

"Cunning" is a favorite word of Roosevelt's for pets and children alike; in fact, any line between the human species and the rest of them is barely detectable. Roosevelt calls his offspring "bunnies," and plays "bear" to them with such terrifying gusto that his wife demands the activity no longer be conducted after supper. There are pillow fights and "scrambles," all part of a need to be treated by his children "as a friend and playmate." Mrs. Kerr points out the observation of Cecil Spring Rice, a British diplomat: "You must always remember that the President is about six."

Modern theorists of "parenting" would applaud the way in which the roughhousing paternal grizzly could so easily metamorphose into something distinctly feminine. Quentin is "Quenty-Quee," and Archibald, in the year he turns ten, "Blessed Archie-kins." Their father likes a good game of "tickley," and adopts the title "vice-mother" when the First Lady is away. On occasion he seems more like auntie: "Doctor Riley is along, and is a perfect dear, as always."

Parental instruction of the epistolary kind is often a starchy, backfiring affair. There are those famous, awful letters from the earl of Chesterfield to his son, excruciating in their self-regard and sheer obviousness: "Do you use yourself to carve ADROITLY and genteelly, without hacking half an hour across a bone; without bespattering the company with the sauce; and without overturning the glasses into your neighbor's pockets?" Chesterfield complains about his boy's "exceedingly laconic" communications, recommends the letters of Madame de Sévigné as models and urges that he write as if "conversing freely with me by the fireside." Ah, what a relaxed hearth *that* must have been, considering how the previous summer the lord had written his Grand-Touring boy with "fair warning, that at Leipsig I shall have an hundred invisible spies about you; and shall be exactly informed of everything that you do, and of almost everything that you say."

By contrast, Roosevelt proceeds via gentle indirection, telling one of the boys how he's had to discipline another. To Kermit: "I have just had to descend with severity upon Quentin because he put the unfortunate Tom [a kitten] into the bathtub and then turned on the water. He didn't really mean harm." To Archie: "I have just had to give [Quentin] and three of his associates a dressing down—one of the three being Charlie Taft." (They'd put spitballs on some White House portraits.) He raises the children with the same cheerful definiteness he used in steering those "turbulent little half-caste civilizations." The sea bores him; the past is overrated; discouragement is the enemy: "Don't worry about the lessons, old boy. I know you are studying hard. Don't get cast down. Sometimes in life, both at school and afterwards, fortune will go against any one, but if he just keeps pegging away and doesn't lose his courage things always take a turn for the better in the end."

Character must trump intellect and athletics. Roosevelt's limited enthusiasm for school sports is a frequent theme, though one has to remember that an apostle of the strenuous life is bound to have an exceptional notion of what *not* overdoing it means. To Ted at Groton: "To have you play football as well as you do, and make a good name in boxing and wrestling, and be cox of your second crew, and stand second or third in your class in the studies, is all right."

He seems to have viewed the presidency as an opportunity for personal development, a chance to mix it up with Japanese wrestlers and contemporary poets. He enjoys the job ("I like to do the work and have my hand on the lever") but appears to work no harder at it than Ronald Reagan did:

> We almost always take our breakfast on the south portico now, Mother looking very pretty and dainty in her summer dresses. Then we stroll about the garden for fifteen or twenty minutes, looking at the flowers and the fountain and admiring the trees. Then I work until between four and five, usually having some official people to lunch—now a couple of Senators, now a couple of Ambassadors, now a literary man, now a capitalist or a labor leader, or a scientist, or a big-game hunter. If Mother wants to ride, we then spend a couple of hours on horseback.

He can worry over "attack and misrepresentation," and seek comfort in Lincoln's letters, but by and large there is no awesome burden; no malaise; no funk. He may not have liked "kodak creatures" or the press, but he took pleasure in the White House (its usher had the prescient name Ike Hoover), and he enjoyed Washington itself. He succeeded by making people adapt to his manner, instead of the other way around. There was no reason he couldn't meet with legislators while watching the boys in their sandbox, and none that the Speaker couldn't deal with the leg-grabbing of a kitten: "Mr. Cannon . . . eyed him with iron calm and not one particle of surprise."

Roosevelt's human preoccupations almost certainly made him a better president. Probably no one who's held the job before or since has left behind a more spontaneous bundle of correspondence—with the possible exception of Woodrow Wilson, who for months on end would neglect his job to type besotted love notes (we'll get to them in Chapter 5) to a woman across town. Both men lived in the last hours of a civilization that used letter writing not just to record the private life, but to conduct it. There are 126 letters in Joan Paterson Kerr's selection; Theodore Roosevelt died at the age of sixty after having written 150,000 others.

JUST AS THE private life began losing letters to the telephone, letters began losing a bit of their own privacy. Great numbers of early-twentieth-century magazines and newspapers started featuring advice columnists who would offer mass-circulation responses to the intimate, if pseudonymous, woes of their correspondents.

The phenomenon of the "agony" column is mordantly dramatized by Nathanael West's *Miss Lonelyhearts*, in which the despairing son of a Baptist preacher—assured by his editor that advice columnists are "the priests of twentieth-century America"—must answer harrowing mail from such correspondents as the woman afraid she'll die if her husband forces her to have another child; the sister of a deaf-and-dumb girl who has been raped; and the lovelorn girl born without a nose, who ends her communication with the straightforward query: "Ought I commit suicide?" "Miss Lonelyhearts" will wind up recommending just that course to another letter writer, in the hope that it will get him fired. But his editor is only moderately upset: "Remember, please, that your job is to increase the circulation of our paper. Suicide, it is only reasonable to think, must defeat this purpose."

By the 1950s, advice columns began moving, along with much else in journalism, in a professional direction. The admirable Ann Landers (Eppie Lederer) started her half-century syndicated run in a voice that was equal parts Midwestern clubwoman, Jewish mother and Rosalind Russell–style dame: "I think when a boy is old enough to ask for a redheaded baby-sitter, he is old enough to stay home alone." All three parts were her real-life components, not just personae. Briskly certain of her chance to do good, Lederer played things down the middle, loosening up the country when it came to divorce and homosexuality, keeping it on the straight and narrow over drugs and drink. She employed scads of assistants; sought information from a mighty Rolodex of doctors, clergy and lawyers; and received much abuse along with requests for help: "I've been told to drop dead, get lost, stop playing God, and quit making up crazy letters," she reminisced in the introduction to one collection of her columns. "I've been called a crummy broad, a square from Iowa, and a broken-down museum piece. The cocktail set insists I am a reformed drunk who is determined to dry up the world. I've been accused of being a public relations agent for the American Medical Association and a mouthpiece for the American Psychiatric Association." She owed her long success to sustained seriousness and a natural American literary style (as recognizable on the page as Will Rogers's), and also to the framework of the letter. Its illusion of intimacy, and the you-asked-for-it nature of epistolary response, always kept her columns free from the sermonizing sound of the editorials going unread a few pages away.

Her successors, a more strident and self-centered bunch, arrived a decade or so ago. Over the last decade, Dan Savage (Savage Love), Paige Stein (The Nuisance Lady) and Mickey Boardman (Ask Mr. Mickey) have generally substituted insult for empathy and spent a lot of time making clear their relief not to be the kind of losers writing to them. Often enough, this seems to be just what the letter writer—not to mention the column reader—is after. In a report on these newer, teardrop-resistant shoulders, William Grimes quoted Robert Levy, the executive editor who used to syndicate Ann Landers for United Features: "The younger generation these columns appeal to is sick of advice. They're almost looking for anti-advice, or the sheer kick of an in-your-face response." The new columns work in "the same way that . . . Letterman is anti-television." The hip authors are too ironic to take their own abusiveness seriously, but they do make public use of the opportunity letter writing has always afforded to those seeing letters as weaponry—slim, sharp instruments of revenge, and even sadism.

Gingerly, and gloved, it's time to open some of those.

CHAPTER FOUR *Complaint*

FUCK YOU. STRONG LETTER TO FOLLOW.

Legendary telegram, Anonymous

WHEN THINGS AT HOME got to be just too much for Sister—when she could no longer bear all the fussing of Stella-Rondo and Mama and Shirley-T. and Papa-Daddy and Uncle Rondo—she remembered her "position as postmistress of China Grove, Mississippi" and went off to live at the P.O.* It might be "the next to smallest P.O. in the entire state of Mississippi," but as Eudora Welty's heroine saw things, that was just the point:

> it's ideal, as I've been saying. You see, I've got everything catercornered, the way I like it. Hear the radio? All the war news. Radio, sewing machine, book ends, ironing board and that great big piano lamp—peace, that's what I like. Butter-bean vines planted all along the front where the strings are.
>
> Of course, there's not much mail.

A blessing, for Sister's sake, since so much of what goes in and out of any post office is filled with the kind of complaint she could find at home.

Sister left her family "on the Fourth of July, or the day after,"

*In homage to the author of this story, one of the largest e-mail programs in the world was named Eudora.

her own declaration of independence, the original of which was authored by a man so contentious that the envelopes he sealed could scarcely contain the din he sometimes dispatched inside them. Thomas Jefferson was a man who could quarrel about anything, the mails included: in an essay he wrote two years before the Declaration, Jefferson asserted that the establishment of a post office in America "seems to have had little connection with British convenience, except that of accommodating his Majesty's ministers and favorites with the sale of a lucrative and easy office."

Diaries have proved unsuitable to all but a handful of American presidents. A readership waiting somewhere in posterity feels too distant, too abstract and unpollable to interest the political animal who would be writing for it. Letters, by contrast, with their actual and immediate audience, offer presidents a kind of flesh to be pressed, recipients who can be wheedled, ordered about, asked for approval, burdened with confidences. Against all this, the diary's effortless candor is a bore.

Between 1801 and 1809, the man who made the "pursuit of happiness" a political entitlement appears almost constantly miserable in his personal correspondence. Having wrested the government from the Federalists ("the enemies hands"), President Thomas Jefferson feels himself to be "the personal object for the hatred of every man." By 1806, the "Hydra" of the opposing party may be down to two heads (Connecticut and Delaware), but some of its members remain candidates "for a mad-house." Along with the Federalists, two budding perennials of presidential grievance—the press and leaks—provoke fits of allergic sneezing from Jefferson. With newspapers constantly displaying their "abandoned prostitution to falsehood," his letter to John Norvell, who wants advice about starting one, must go out with a warning "that this hasty communication may in nowise be permitted to find its way into the public papers."

The archivist who superintends Jefferson's letters in the Library of Congress that he helped to establish will point out to a visitor that our third president saved his own political venom for private correspondence, keeping it out of his above-the-battle public speeches. In fact, the first thing a present-day reader notices in the letters is a contempt for the presidency itself: "I am tired of an office where I can do no more good than many others, who would be glad to be employed in it. To myself, personally, it brings nothing but unceasing drudgery & daily loss of friends." Even the Fourth of July is "always a day of great fatigue"—something he might have thought about before writing his most famous piece.

Forced to maintain neutrality of the seas, he would prefer cultivating his own Virginia lands. He swears that the affairs of Monticello interest him more than the presidency's, and brief trips back to Virginia only make Washington, D.C. "more intolerable" than before. The barely built capital, a burgeoning antithesis of the agrarian society Jefferson has ideally realized at home, is still literally a swamp, full of fever but lacking in ladies and other diversions. Politics is "our only entertainment here," and after five years, the president's "confinement" grows still more "disgusting" by the day. He'd rather be "the hermit of Monticello"—but what choice do "the unlimited calumnies of the federalists" leave him, other than to run for a second term?

Until he can return to them, Jefferson runs the affairs of his family like a government in exile. Over his private realm the founding father is uninhibited by any checks or balances or Tories. When he wants his married daughters to visit Washington, the wishes of their husbands, always "Mr. Randolph" and "Mr. Eppes," are decidedly secondary. Mary Jefferson Eppes, who likes a bit of flattery as much as her father, may protest that she has become too countrified to be comfortable receiving "the civilitys and attentions which as your daughter I should meet with and return," but Jefferson refuses her any left-handed compliments. He replies with some diagnostic advice: "I think I discover in you a willingness to withdraw from society more than is prudent. I am convinced our own happiness requires that we should continue to mix with the world, and to keep pace with it as it goes." There will be no hermiting for her.

The dominant image of Jefferson in the modern citizen's mind is the president as an American da Vinci. This picture of his polymathy was drawn by John F. Kennedy, who famously remarked that a dinner for Nobel Prize winners was "the most extraordinary collection of talent, of human knowledge, that has ever been gathered together at the White House, with the possible exception of when Thomas Jefferson dined alone." And yet, whatever brilliance may lie in Jefferson's letters, the citizen reading them today is disinclined to approach the man's table and pull up a chair.

The president's grandchildren are a whole little colony ripe for rule. He writes to three of Martha Jefferson Randolph's offspring: "the more I perceive that you are all advancing in your learning and improving in good dispositions the more I shall love you, and the more every body will love you." He expects results, and his daughters know it. The following year Martha assures Jefferson that young Ellen is reading during "every lucid interval" of a fever.

Whenever anyone in the family falls ill, Jefferson recommends scientific knowledge, so despised by the Tories' clerical allies, as the proper source of hope. He influences all his progeny toward a graphic frankness about the medical occurrences that are so much a part of their letters. Ellen must be consoled by the immunity-producing benefits of her whooping cough ("You will learn to bear it patiently when you consider you can never have it again"), and at eleven years old she is neither too young nor too ladylike to profit from a clinical description, complete with suppuration, of presidential toothache. Writing of measles to his daughters, or kidney stones to a brother, Jefferson makes concrete knowledge not just the antidote to fear but the instrument of his own power over events. He relishes letters as physical conveyances, kissing the paper he sends his granddaughter and, during a smallpox outbreak, enclosing a "scab of vaccine which I have this moment received from Dr. Worthington." He concerns himself with the speed of his letters' delivery and the implements with which they get written, even helping to develop the "polygraph," a mechanical hand for producing ink copies. In the Library of Congress one can still distinguish its work from Jefferson's originals by the more uniform pressure of the "off pen."

When his grandson Thomas Jefferson Randolph goes to Philadelphia to study medicine, the president offers, along with advice on how to take lecture notes, some admonitions concerning general deportment and the boy's particular position. He lets loose a warning in biblical imagery that's been improved by his own scientific diction: "You will be more exposed than others to have these animals shaking their horns at you, because of the relation in which you stand with me and to hate me as a chief in the antagonist party your presence will be to them what the vomit-grass is to the sick dog a nostrum for producing an ejaculation." A week later, young Thomas thanks him for the advice and postscripts his own warning: "The cover of the letter you inclosed from Mother bore evident marks of having been broken open as likewise several others." Whether enemies and curiosity seekers had tampered with Jefferson's letters—or the president himself had rifled a family communication he was only supposed to be forwarding—remains unclear.

To this grandson, Jefferson recommends a writing style that's "all pith," but this doesn't keep many of his own letters from expanding into loose, ruminative essays on everything from the proper layout of cities to the nature of religion. On political questions, he variously offers a tidy version of manifest destiny ("advancing compactly as we multiply"); thoughts on the possibility of two American confederations, one Atlantic and the other on the Mississippi; musings on African colonization ("Could we procure lands beyond the limits of the US to form a receptacle for these people?"); and a chilling vision of the American Indians' future. He closes his letter on the last subject with a request that the recipient, Governor (and later President) William Henry Harrison, keep it under his cocked hat: "For their interests and their tranquillity it is best [the Indians] should see only the present age of their history."

Much of what he writes in these productions has the hypothetical sweep of present-day "future studies." These essay-letters, which lack the specific marching orders in his family correspondence, offer Jefferson the chance to display a different sort of mastery: the intellectual control that comes with not having to see an idea's executions and consequences. A century and a half after the president's death, another patrician Democrat, Dean Acheson, would judge him greatly gifted, but "as much interested in words as in the reality behind them. The more solid, less glittering qualities of General Washington are what it took to get the country started." Acheson's thoughts were conveyed in a letter to Richard Nixon, a former foe who had gone to the White House and was at the time, 1971, beginning to exhibit, in letters and other media, a distinctly Jeffersonian preoccupation with his enemies.

THE BULK OF Richard Nixon's presidential papers, more or less seized by Congress in 1974, have spent their quarantine inside the National Archives' glassy annex in College Park, Maryland. Even a brief perusal of them makes clear the inseparability of Nixon's personal and official lives.

During World War II, when he was newly married and stationed in the South Pacific, Nixon's letters to his wife Pat had revealed both deep affection and status-conscious insecurity: "You'll never know how proud I was to show [your picture] to all the fellows. Everybody raved—wondered how I happened to rate! (I do too.)" Thirty years later, having so long clawed after the presidency, losing and winning it by a hairsbreadth, he has *earned* it in a way he can never quite make others see. His time in office becomes to some extent *about* his having become president, a dangerously self-referential operation whose most important and personal letters are internal memoranda. He can now deploy his own initials in a message to Pat about office equipment for the White House residence: "with regard to RN's room, what would be most desirable is an end table like the one on the right side of the bed which will accommodate *two* dictaphones as well as a telephone."

His memoranda to desks in the West Wing call frequent attention to "the RN come-back theme" that has brought him to the White House. Even when dispatching some re-election campaign advice to his daughters (members of what he elsewhere calls "the RN family"), he urges them to talk about "the comeback after the defeat in California." The definite articles give a feeling of obsessive rehash. But, unlike Jefferson, Nixon doesn't do his real complaining to his daughters. He saves that for his voluminous memos to his chief of staff, H. R. Haldeman—naked, repetitive displays of self-assertion, authentic cris de coeur, selected by Bruce Oudes for a volume called *From: The President.* On a Sunday in May of 1971, the president tells Haldeman why he'll never attend another dinner of that "disgusting group," the White House Correspondents' Association, some of whose members were that year being honored for anti-administration stories. "I had to sit there for 20 minutes while the drunken audience laughed in derision as the award citations were read . . . What I want everybody to realize is that as we approach the election we are in a fight to the death for the big prize." The third paragraph of the memo's several pages begins "I'm not a bit thin-skinned," but it is Nixon's lack of any skin at all, his agonized translucence, that makes these communications so raw and weirdly moving. Nixon is always talking to Nixon; as soon as the memos are written, they've already been delivered.

To a surprising degree Nixon was, in the parlance of the time he dominated, in touch with his feelings. But the form he gave them was crucial: a memorandum, usually dictated into a machine and then typed up by someone else, offered the illusion that all this was strictly business, not the personal indulgence an ordinary letter might represent, and which "RN" would feel obligated to dismiss as unseemly. Urging Kissinger to speed up construction of the Pan American Highway, Nixon writes, on March 8, 1971: "We will transfer funds from other projects to this one and get this done so that this will be one part of the Nixon legacy (and a very vital project where the country is involved) which we will get accomplished while we are here." No attempt is made to subordinate the embarrassing truth; what's in parentheses is what's parenthetical.

Early in the first term, when constituent mail comes stamped (6¢) with the smiling face of FDR, Nixon displays a lot of interest in the niceties of his presidential operation, requesting first-name salutations on thank-you notes, offering suggestions for redecoration. He declares himself uncomfortable with always being served first by the White House waiters, and sends usher Rex Scouten revised rules to cover a variety of situations: "If it is a mixed dinner, with a guest of honor, the wife of the guest of honor will be served first simultaneously with Mrs. Nixon, and then the guest of honor and I will be served second." The new instructions are "to be followed explicitly from this time forward."

The president's memos often include peremptory warnings that his orders are final: "the decision is not subject to appeal or further discussion unless I bring it up myself"; "There is no appeal from this decision—I've thought it through and have concluded"; "There is no appeal whatever"; "Don't discuss it with me further." These admonitions are less authoritarian than shy, designed to avert face-to-face conflict. In the Archives, the President's Personal Files (PPF) and President's Office Files (POF) remained full of courtesy to subordinates, their dullest policy memos receiving Nixon's enthusiastic compliments. He did not enjoy chewing people out. On November 20, 1972, two weeks after his landslide re-election, Nixon's personal secretary, Rose Mary Woods, sends him a note wondering if he "and the family might want to go to the Eisenhower Theatre (Kennedy Center) to see JOCKEY CLUB STAKES. It is supposed to be a great comedy (British) and is not trying to promote some cause or other." But in RN's emotional makeup, Kennedy trumps Eisenhower, and a handwritten refusal, perhaps to spare Miss Woods's feelings, goes to Haldeman: "I don't want to go to the Center for anything at any time unless it is an event I have to participate in."

The nadir of presidential communication probably arrived with the "recommended-telephone-call" memo—staff suggestions to a president about whom to call, with "talking points" on what to say. "Hope she is feeling better each day" reads point number one in a March 1971 memo recommending a call to Mary Higgins, an administrative assistant on Capitol Hill then terminally ill with cancer. The automatism of the prescribed dialogue is decidedly creepy, and yet Miss Higgins got the call because she had touched Nixon's proudest nerve, the comeback. The "Background" section above the "talking points" explains: "During the years 1960–1968 (when there [were] not too many strong loyalists on the Hill) she had an enormous picture of the President behind her desk and really stood up for him when many people asked why she had a picture up of 'that has been,' etc."

The request for this phone call was put in by Rose Mary Woods, whose lasting fame will rest upon the suspicion that she created the eighteen-and-a-half-minute gap on one of the Watergate tapes. But Miss Woods contributed far more to Nixon's accrual than his deletion: in addition to maintaining the PPF, she was part of a White House system that assembled a voluminous Handwriting File of materials personally annotated by Nixon and retrieved from staffers to whom they'd been sent. Nixon's fountain pen leaves him oddly and more lastingly animate than the typewritten words to which he's reacting. A letter from John H. Dawson, president of Adrian College in Michigan, congratulating him on the Paris peace accords, begins apologetically: "I'm well aware that you are now receiving a veritable deluge of letters from college and university educators . . ." Nixon underlines the sentence and writes a note to pass on to "H & K": "If he only knew—at most a light drizzle—no deluge!"

On occasion, the president would draft an entire reply in the margins of a letter he was reading. Early in 1972, Joyce E. Kozielec, a secretary at the White House, wrote him an emotional, admiring letter of resignation in which she identified herself as "the young lady who clips signature blotters on all materials to be signed by you and follows through on your written requests from the Daily News Summary. As a secretary, I don't believe I could have been closer to your personal thoughts." Nixon's response, "just a note to tell you how deeply I appreciated your letter of February sixteenth," went out to Mrs. Kozielec not in the ink in which he first composed it—but as a typewritten letter, whose carbon copy, along with the presidential handwriting she never received, survives amid so much of the archival material only now being transferred to the Nixon Presidential Library in California.

What handwriting he did send had an odd tendency to slip toward the edge of the paper: as he went farther down the page, the left margin would widen, herding his words toward the right. He seems always in the process of making an exit, even when conducting his last, most personal, campaign, the one for rehabilitation. In March of 1982, he is making himself useful to Ronald Reagan, offering to cheer the president, during a bad polling patch, with a story more in Reagan's style than his own: "Our grandson, Christopher, was three years old yesterday," writes Nixon. "When playing with his dog, they knocked over & broke a vase. He looked up at Tricia and said: 'Don't worry, mommy, Reagan will fix it!'"

It was Nixon himself who broke the presidential inkwell. The installation of the taping system, a device more comprehensively revealing of the presidential mind than any letters or diary could be, ensured, by its discovery, that presidents would never again permit themselves the degree of self-revelation practiced, off and on, by two centuries of White House occupants. The special prosecutor now looms larger than posterity, and the potential "evidence" of a president's letters is a more legal, and less historical, matter than it used to be. (As First Lady, Hillary Clinton explained in all seriousness that she did not keep a diary because of its vulnerability to subpoena.) Nixon chased his successors, not just himself, toward the margin and off the page.

FOR IMMEDIATE, crushing practicalities—not Jefferson's distant hypotheticals—few letter collections can match the angry, agitated stream that Florence Nightingale sent home to England from Scutari at the height of the Crimean War. Dispatches by William Howard Russell to the London *Times* after the Battle of Alma had forced the British public to realize the terrific neglect of its wounded soldiers, and within days of Russell's worst disclosures—still not even sure she could believe them all—Nightingale was organizing a "small private expedition of nurses," and telling Elizabeth Herbert, wife of the secretary of war, just how she was going about it. Her syntax has an urgent brevity quite uncharacteristic of the Victorian lady-epistolarian:

> I take myself out & one Nurse. Lady Maria Forester has given £200 to take out three others. We feed and lodge ourselves there, & are to be no expence whatever to the country.

After a few more clipped sentences like these, she breaks the paragraph and writes "Now to business"—as if she's been anything but.

Her private funding, resented by the army's officers and doctors, hasn't been enough to clear the rats and a Russian general's corpse from some spare rooms in the Barrack Hospital before she and her group of forty-two take up residence there. The casualties Nightingale finds are astronomical—"We now have 4 miles of beds—& not 18 inches apart"—and the conditions so unimaginably mean and filthy that a reader expects nothing but a sustained cry of horror in an early letter she sends home to Dr. William Bowman, a surgeon at King's College Hospital. Instead, the electrified Miss Nightingale marches from sarcasm to humor to lyric affirmation in the course of a single page. From the beginning, she respects the ordinary suffering soldier, reserving her contempt for the complaining officers and whichever of the women prove inadequate to the job they came out to do:

> I can truly say like St. Peter 'it is good for us to be here'—tho' I doubt whether if St. Peter had been here, he would have said so. As I went my night-round among the newly wounded that first night, there was not one murmur, not one groan the strictest discipline, the most absolute silence & quiet prevailed.

She refuses to treat the men as the "brutes" their superiors insist they are. Finding that the soldiers respond not only to kindness but to higher expectations, she secretly sets them to reading and to sending money home for their wives and mothers. She receives, in return, their hearty cheers and shyly proffered nosegays. On the six-month anniversary of her arrival, the wellborn thirty-five-year-old nurse can describe herself as being "in sympathy with God, fulfilling the purpose I came into the world for." She has, in fact, performed a miracle, one that years later will stop even Lytton Strachey in his normally debunking tracks; he can only summarize Miss Nightingale's first days at the Barrack Hospital in the rhetoric and rhythms of a fairy tale:

> With consummate tact, with all the gentleness of supreme strength, she managed at last to impose her personality upon the susceptible, overwrought, discouraged, and helpless group of men

in authority who surrounded her. She stood firm; she was a rock in the angry ocean; with her alone was safety, comfort, life. And so it was that hope dawned at Scutari.

Our enduring image of Florence Nightingale has her walking the ward with a glowing lamp. But she spent at least as much of her time in Scutari wielding a pen, its nib sharpened to a point that could puncture every obstruction and enemy. In the letters, she sizes up each of the women, mocking their trivial complaints—" 'and if I'd known, Ma'am about the Caps, great as was my desire to come out as nurse at Scutari, I wouldn't have come, ma'am' "—and discovering only one sheep for every three or four goats: "About ten of us have done *the whole work.*" Too many of the others have turned to drink and husband hunting for Nightingale to want any more than the forty she has to look after. Some nuns from Bermondsey prove invaluable—she thanks their Mother Superior "gratefully, lovingly, overflowingly"—but she can't bear the Catholic nurses complaining to their priests and being held "scatheless by [them]—through any misconduct."

Her pleadings with distant officialdom are always for more authority and less wasting of her time. The sympathetic correspondent she most frequently assaults is Sidney Herbert, the tactful war secretary who, back in London, presides over what Nightingale tells him is a "grand administrative evil," a Circumlocution Office of paper and red tape that, at her remove, is pitifully irrelevant. Letters from Scutari thrust the conditions she's found under Herbert's eyes and nose:

> Thirty were bathed every night by Dr. MacGrigor's orders in slipper-baths, but this does not do more than include a washing once in eighty days for 2300 men.
>
> The consequences of all this are Fever, Cholera, Gangrene, Lice, Bugs, Fleas—& may be Erysipelas—from the using of one sponge among many wounds.

Hoping to antagonize Herbert toward her own foes, Nightingale lets him know how officials on the scene complain of his administration. Herbert should understand that "these dreadful people" are "refusing, some to tell you the truth, some to know it themselves." But she emphasizes how Herbert must not allow her to look like a government spy and pointedly reminds him to keep her letters confidential. She continues to regale him with horrors—and use him as a back channel—after he's left office in 1855; but his emeritus status earns him no soft soap:

> I received your letter of March 6 yesterday. It is written from Belgrave Square. I write from a Crimean hut. The point of sight is different.

Her letters to Herbert will have to serve as an apologia to all her countrymen—"I wish to leave on record some instance of that which nobody in England will believe or can even imagine"—since others' letters, her enemies', often carry lies. In October of 1855, almost a year after her arrival, Nightingale informs Lady Charlotte Canning "that the correspondence of Miss Salisbury was seized by order of the Commandant here, who thought this step a necessary one—as indeed it proved—& that it laid bare a most conscious system of falsehood, which she had been pursuing in her letters to England. It is so easy for an adventurer of this kind to trade upon people's sympathies in this way."

Tales of "the honorable men who have been our murderers" make even Nightingale's letters to relatives part of the long aggrieved testament she intends to leave behind. However real the agonies staring up at her from the cots, she cannot keep her correspondence free from the tone and style of paranoia. She is sure her uncle Samuel Smith believes she has "a wild imagination," but she promises she can lay everything out for him, chapter and verse, with supporting evidence: "I will give you the slightest, pettiest instance of the hindrance which the pettiest official can make out here, if so minded." Fitfully, in letters to her family, she will allow her guard to drop, making fun of herself as "Poor old Flo steaming up the Bosphorus," and recounting, mock-heroically, her killing of a rat. She will also confess to small, compulsive anxieties all out of proportion to their circumstances. Some five-pound debts she's left at home "torment" her in a paragraph she writes just after one in which she describes an earthquake that's killed thousands.

If she had fewer "interruptions & business of all kinds," she would make her letters shorter, and their indictments tighter, but among all her other duties is the epistolary task of signing condolences to families and kin who don't always deserve them:

> the letters from "heart-broken friends at home" have begun again—friends who want to know whether a man who died in Feb'y (a time when we were never in from the wards till near twelve o'clock) "appeared to have any desire to be saved & left a Savings Bank Book for £20."

She insists to her sister Parthenope that she does "not despair—nor complain. It has been a great cause." But it was the ability to make objective complaint (tinged with a certain messianism, to be sure) that allowed her year and a half's worth of Crimean letters to effect so many systematic reforms and improvements. Not, of course, without some follow-through on her part. When Nightingale arrived home in the summer of 1856, she found herself, according to her latter-day editors, "unable to rest," and so, formulating her prescriptions for change, "she wrote letters," a whole new stream of them, "pursuing Sidney Herbert, on a fishing holiday in Ireland, and Lord Panmure, the [new] Secretary of State for War, shooting grouse in Scotland."

IN HER LATER YEARS, beribboned with honors, Nightingale must sometimes have had to endure the compliments of those trying to forget how they had thwarted her in times of trial and obscurity. She may even have recalled, on such occasions, the most famous thanks-for-nothing letter in English, Samuel Johnson's rejection of praise for his *Dictionary* from Lord Chesterfield, that parental Polonius we fled back in Chapter 3. Johnson reminds Chesterfield that years earlier, seeking assistance for the project, he had "waited in your outward rooms, or was repulsed from your door." Now, rather than accept Chesterfield's bouquets, he prefers to pose a question: "Is not a Patron, my Lord, one who looks with unconcern on a man struggling for life in the water, and, when he has reached ground, encumbers him with help?"

Few anthologies of letters can bring themselves to do without this one, or another that Johnson wrote in reply to a threat from James Macpherson, whose "translations" of a fabricated antique poet named Ossian Johnson had exposed as a fraud. "I received your foolish and impudent note," Johnson wrote. "Whatever insult is offered me I will do my best to repel, and what I cannot do for myself the law will do for me." Just in case his words proved an inadequate shield, Johnson went out and bought an oak club.

Epistolary feuds flourish between professional writers because the breed has difficulty resisting a display of weaponry it can fashion in its own verbal shop. Back in the 1960s, an almost nuclear bout of pedantry and dudgeon broke out between Vladimir Nabokov and Edmund Wilson, when in *The New York Review of Books* the American critic assailed Nabokov's new translation of *Eugene Onegin.* Friends for twenty-five years—"Bunny" and "Volodya" in their salutations—the writers had once been actively supportive of each other. In fact, in 1947, Wilson had used his hardest cudgels on Nabokov's behalf, against *The New Yorker*'s Katharine White:

> It is appalling that Nabokov's little story, so gentle and everyday, should take on the aspect for the *New Yorker* editors of an overdone psychiatric study. (How *can* you people say it is overwritten?) It could only appear so in contrast with the pointless and inane little anecdotes that are turned out by the *New Yorker*'s processing mill and that the reader forgets two minutes after he has read them . . .

And yet, one can find hints of the Wilson-Nabokov explosion in letters that each wrote during the twenty years before it occurred. Neither man had a temperament suited to continual admiration of anyone, including each other, and there are signs of mutual contempt in their letters to third parties. Months after Wilson has praised his novel *The Real Life of Sebastian Knight*, Nabokov writes James Laughlin (still suffering with Henry Miller) that "Bunny Wilson has a very cute but absolutely erroneous theory that 'Sebastian' is composed on the lines of a chess-game." Fourteen years later, he'll be asking a new editor, Jason Epstein, if *Lolita* can go out into the world without a blurb from Wilson: "We are very close friends, I admire and respect him greatly, but it is not a friendship based on a similiarity of opinions and approaches." A few years after that he'll tell one correspondent of his "utter disgust with Edmund's symbolico-social criticism and phoney erudition in regard to DOCTOR ZHIVAGO," and express pleasure at another's behind-the-back "remarks about the Russian language of our dear Edmund." Those remarks, made by Gleb Struve, a Slavic languages professor at Berkeley, came two years after Wilson had expressed to Struve his own surprise at finding "that Vladimir regarded *Lolita* as his most important effort in either Russian or English."

In the years before their open warfare, Wilson becomes increasingly inflated with a sense of his own prowess in Nabokov's language—and more condescending toward Nabokov's command of his: "It may be that neither you nor Mirsky, trained on classic Russian verse, quite realizes what English verse is like." By the mid-fifties Wilson has lost most of his confidence in Volodya's literary opinions: "What I don't like about [*The Death of Ivan Ilyich*]—its not being true to human life—is precisely what enchants him."

In 1964, Pushkin came to shove. Barbara Epstein, wife of Jason, assigned Nabokov's *Onegin* translation to Wilson for review. A first perusal convinced him, he told Epstein in a letter, that it "is full of flat writing, outlandish words, and awkward phrases. And some of the things he says about the Russian language are inaccurate." Nabokov could sense what was coming before the review appeared, and warmed up his public response in a letter to William McGuire: "as I have mentioned before [Wilson's] Russian is primitive, and his knowledge of Russian literature gappy and grotesque. (He is a very old friend of mine, and I do hope our quarter-of-a-century correspondence in the course of which I attempted not quite successfully to explain to him such matters as the mechanism of Russian—and English—verse, will be published some day)." Each has already stopped writing to the other; the mail is now being dispatched to posterity. For the next half-dozen years they speak only in print, using magazine pages the way a divorcing couple do a lawyer's office.

Nabokov's letter to *The New York Review*, where Wilson's Pushkin piece finally appeared on July 15, 1965, takes sarcastic pains to describe his view of their linguistic association: "A patient confidant of his long and hopeless infatuation with the Russian language, I have always done my best to explain to him his mistakes of pronunciation, grammar, and interpretation." He proceeds to list seven of "the ghastly blunders" in the offending review, before saying, with his wellborn courtesy, "Let me stop here." But he can't. A year later he will be telling a professor, "You have a perfect right to quote Edmund Wilson on my contempt for ignoramuses but your readers might have liked to be told that (in my *Encounter* article) I *proved* him to be one." About a year after that, in *The New Statesman*, like a tenor making yet another farewell performance, he takes one more parting shot: "I do not intend to continue my chats with Mr Edmund Wilson, in private or print, but let me humbly concede before ending them, that Pushkin had almost as much English in the 1830s as Mr Edmund Wilson has Russian today. That should satisfy everybody."

How could it? To certain passionate natures the time-consumingness of letter writing offers the chance to cool down (as one imagines Miller doing toward Laughlin), but to disputatious and pedantic people, a letter's slow cooking offers only the chance to make the perfect retort, the irrefutable response. Foes walk away from in-the-flesh encounters thinking, "if only I'd said *this*, or *that*"—this and that being what go into the mail two days later.

Nabokov and Wilson had one last sadly comic personal exchange in March 1971. Volodya wrote that "A few days ago I had the occasion to reread the whole batch (Russ., *vsyu pachku*) of our correspondence. It was such a pleasure to feel again the warmth of your many kindnesses, the various thrills of our friendship, that constant excitement of art and intellectual discovery." A generous overture, yes, but nothing could make him erase that instructive little parenthesis, or keep him from saying "that I have long ceased to bear you a grudge for your incomprehensible incomprehension of Pushkin's and Nabokov's *Onegin.*"

One is sure that Wilson told the truth about his being "very glad" to get this letter. But with equal inevitability, the first personal tiding in his response is the news that "I am just now getting together a volume of my Russian articles. I am correcting my errors in Russian in my piece on Nabokov-Pushkin; but citing a few more of your ineptitudes." Lest one think these two old campaigners are making fun of their inability to give it a rest, there is the announcement, further into Wilson's letter, that he has included a recollection of Nabokov in a forthcoming book (*Upstate*). "I hope it will not again impair our personal relations (it shouldn't)."

In fact, it ended them. Nabokov would find the account "a flow of vulgar and fatuous invention" by—as he told *The New York Times Book Review*—his "former friend." Wilson might by then be ill, but Nabokov argued that "in the struggle between the dictates of compassion and those of personal honor the latter wins." Wilson died seven months later.

WHEN READING THE LETTERS of a chronic and compulsive complainer—let's take a habitual animadverter like H. L. Mencken—one may have trouble differentiating true fits of spleen from that organ's mere pirouettes, rhetorical movements designed to delight both writer and audience. If one drops into just a short span of Mencken's epistolary output, the letters he wrote to a variety of friends and foes in the mid-1930s, one finds him inveighing against sociology, universal suffrage, professional educators, the federal income tax, left-wing book critics, metaphysics, and German red wine—though not German militarism, which the French no doubt deserve. Then again, "All nations as nations are scoundrels."

It's when Mencken goes on about "horrible encounters with lady poets," or sends the greeting "Christmas be damned" to his publisher's wife, that one feels less in the presence of genuine annoyance than trademark style—time-tested bits of vaudeville the recipient probably started to applaud at first sight of the envelope's return address.

Intellectual hatreds may be, as Yeats thought, the worst of all, but one is struck by the cordiality Mencken maintains toward those selling what he judges to be snake oil. Within the same letter he will thrust and sheathe his broadsword, making personal overtures as soon as he's left his opponent in tatters. Dr. Corliss Lamont, for example, is a candidate for his "I Am Not a Communist—But" club:

> It seems to me that the fact that you are not actually a member of the party is immaterial. You are giving aid and encouragement to undoubted Communists, and you are certainly not making very clear the nature of your dissent from their position. Inasmuch as I believe, as I have said, that they are all suspicious characters, intellectually speaking, I simply can't imagine how you can arrive at any alliance with them, however reserved, by a process of reason. I'd as soon enter into an alliance with chiropractors, Methodist bishops, or, indeed, New Deal uplifters.

And yet, knowing that Lamont has a brother nearby, Mencken inquires, "Do you ever come to Baltimore to see him? If so, I hope you let me hear of it the next time. The cooks here have enlightened ideas, and the best beer in America is on tap." When composing that list of allies to be shunned, the particular Methodist bishop he no doubt had in mind is the Rt. Rev. James Cannon, Jr., chairman of the World League Against Alcoholism, but "something close to a friend," as the editor of Mencken's letters puts it. The fact of their pugnacity is more important than the substance of their quarrel. "You and I are men of a certain bellicosity," Mencken writes Cannon on June 29, 1934, "but we seem to have been fortunate enough to get very amiable wives. I often wonder how mine stands my wilder moods and more preposterous enterprises." The letter ends with an invitation to lunch.

Self-mockery combines with self-approval ("I increase in diameter as in wisdom") to put the foam on Mencken's bilious brew, which he sips and serves as refreshment during the pagan spectacles put on by an over-Christianized world: the romance of Edward VIII and Mrs. Simpson, "a highly oxidized double-divorcee," from Baltimore no less, is "the best newspaper story since the Resurrection."

"What a world!" Mencken writes on January 8, 1935, giving out not jeremiad but the sigh of the ordinarily afflicted person. Within months, the amiable wife he praised to Bishop Cannon will be dead of meningitis, and by February of the following year, after the demise of several friends, he will feel himself "surrounded by nothing but death and disaster." When on the train to New York he runs into Heywood Broun, another friendly intellectual enemy ("I must say that, for a friend of the downtrodden, he looked to be extraordinarily well fed"), they have "a long gabble on the horrors of human existence." He's already been at it as "a general assassin" for a quarter century, and he's got another twenty years to go.

One has always scrounged after reasons and excuses for Mencken's anti-Semitism, an explosive incontinence that sometimes gets ascribed to the conventional prejudices of his time, though they can hardly account for the vigor of outbursts that go well beyond the historical "norm" in frequency and intensity. The compulsion does seem less forceful in the letters than in his diaries and posthumous autobiography; indeed, there is enough sorrow and world-weariness in his personal correspondence that a reader is tempted to propose one more probably futile explanation. Was Mencken's horror of Jews (it can't be called anything else, despite his wide, and sometimes close, Jewish acquaintance) a kind of misanthropic strike against his species? Did he recognize the Jew as man most fully human, and therefore most detestable?

Across the ocean and down a few decades, one finds a kind of sallow analog to Mencken in the appallingly entertaining letters of Philip Larkin. Everyone was sure they had him right: as sturdily English as a Burberry bumbershoot, someone whose image belonged on a tin of biscuits. A bachelor poet of highly regarded but comprehensible verse, a top-drawer, unprolific, unbohemian artist, he seemed sedate and reassuring. Even as his literary fame increased, Larkin made his daily living as the University of Hull's librarian. When anyone told Mrs. Grundy that high art and middlebrow convention weren't compatible, she had only to point to Mr. Larkin down the road. Would anyone argue that the author of *The Whitsun Weddings* and *High Windows*, the editor of *The Oxford Book of Twentieth Century English Verse*, had been undeserving of the Queen's Gold Medal for Poetry or the Companion of Literature? Hardly.

There had been some curious utterances from him (that unfortunate first line "They fuck you up, your mum and dad"), but whatever private sorrows his poems might contain or imply, they were precise, even appreciative, evocations of English life. Even in his twenties he was certain he didn't want to fill his verses with "filthy thought or symbols or construction." He could build a poem around "just a man eating a tomato and a bit of cheese and reading a sensitive letter with the sun flooding the earth and feeling bloody fine." He was so *levelheaded*, the opposite of the crazy romantic artist of myth.

Of course, the stupid sods (as he would have said) had it all wrong. "For the last 16 years," he wrote his friend Norman Iles in 1972, "I've lived in the same small flat, washing in the sink, & not having central heating or double glazing or fitted carpets or the other things everyone has, & of course I haven't any biblical things such as wife, children, house, land, cattle, sheep etc. To me I seem very much an outsider, yet I suppose 99% of people wd say I'm very establishment & conventional. Funny, isn't it?" He didn't even have the peace and quiet a miserable bachelor is supposed to. His neighbors below "*bang doors* as if they are perpetually quarrelling or are new to houses with doors. One night I counted 38 such in 2 hours—or an average of almost once every three minutes."

In private, he wasn't so much Britannia's approving bard as a stuffed bull in the English china shop, loathing all its Dickensian pieties. His favorite John O'Hara line was "Christmas stank," and each year he greeted the arrival of that "vile season" with a disgusted sigh: "And now Christmas is coming again, as if we hadn't enough to put up with."

When his *Selected Letters* first appeared in England, Larkin's unvarnished reactionary views seem to have surprised all but those who knew him personally, and they provoked much tut-tutting in the literary chattering classes. Politicized by the sixties, though not in the approved way, Larkin had been revolted by revolution and its "pot-smoking young swine," those "little subsidised socialist sods," and their aging comrades in arms among the Hull faculty: "one hag said she hadn't been so excited since Spain!" He adored Mrs. Thatcher ("The Leaderene") when she came along, but he knew his politics were "really no more than gouts of bile," a tributary of his pleased malcontentment, his chosen unhappiness.

Crimped and crabbed and complainingly pinched into shoes he refused to change, he disapproved of most everything. "Life's colourful pageant is passing me by," he declared, and he insisted it keep moving right along. He judged his own life wasted but "never thought it wd be a dull world if everyone was like me." It is impossible for a reader of his letters to regard them as anything but the strongest possible testimony to the truth of C. P. Snow's observation "What you want is what happens to you."

Jazz was his Dionysian escape, a displacement of his own internal fits. But as the years went by, he listened to it with less and less of an ear. "I sit half-stewed each night," he wrote in July 1957, "while the leaves rustle outside, & the LP platters steadily work their way down the revolving spindle." At some point in the evening, he'd wake with a start, blinking his way out of the bag—expecting to write poetry? "I am quite unable to do anything in the evenings—the notion of expressing sentiments in short lines having similar sounds at their ends seems as remote as mangoes on the moon." The fact is he was always tired, and would have been so even without the booze, or with more self-discipline. His librarianship wasn't some charming sinecure. It was, like most people's jobs, *work*—work that left him "worn to a ravelling" and eventually supervising a hundred employees. He would have preferred an independent income. He envied the few authors, like his closest writer friend, Kingsley Amis, whose books could actually support a life, and he had no trouble resenting the loudly overlauded ("At Ilkley literature festival a woman shrieked and vomited during a Ted Hughes reading. I must say I've never felt like shrieking"). His own need to make a living, long after he was a famous man of letters, left him a "Sunday writer" whose books were few and far between. "Sodding reviewing" was another remunerative distraction (he called a collection of his literary journalism *Required Writing*), and on most weekends it was hard to find the energy to be even a Sunday writer: "My Sunday morning consists of plodding across Pearson Park, past the children's playground, & then on the other side I buy 4 Sunday papers of steep scurrility & vanish into a drab premises called the Queen's Hotel, where in a fireless room I settle on an imitation-leather couch and drink a pint or two of pallid Hull beer, scanning headlines of rare promise ('When the Girl Guide Was Late Home') and sometimes being glowered at by a large yellow cat . . ." Year after year, he wrote in 1958, "the literary life goes on, apart from producing no literature."

He was xenophobic as only a postwar Little Englander could be, despising "filthy abroad," which consisted variously of Wopland, Frogland, Hunland and, most detestably, America. He had a deep-seated need for dreariness, preferring the dry food and mean little gas fires of his native land to any Yank-imitating attempts at flash. He craved sooty windows the way others do bright lights.

Larkin spiked his letters with impotent revenge fantasies, the sort of vicarious violent imaginings indulged in by Lucky Jim Dixon, the character created by his friend Amis. For a fellow worker at the library ("old bagface") the poet had plans: "I speculate on nailing a kipper under her table, privately printing at my own cost a pamphlet proving that her maternal grandmother married a Barbary ape, bribing a corner boy to knock her up at four in the morning." For years his letters were wildly scatological. He was probably more bowel-bound than any writer since Swift, letting shit serve as a sort of anti-Poetry, something with which he could smear and devalue the art he longed to produce and feared he couldn't: "souls are made in the world, not in books, and I must rise up and go—and have a crap." He compared the act of publishing a book to "farting at a party—you have to wait till people stop looking at you before you can behave normally again."

In his letters, he often acts the filthy, disagreeable little boy, and though he cleaned up his mouth as the years went by (and was a perfect gentleman when writing to women), he never stopped making the capitalized Tourette-like outbursts that come mid-sentence in his communications to Amis: "pocking Miss Jane Exall wouldn't be nearly so nice in reality as it is in my imagination WHEN I'M TOSSING MYSELF."

He advertised his misery to friends and took pride in making himself look as awful as he could: "I went to the local Austin Reeds on Saturday and bought some dreary clothes, real chartered-accountant stuff, dead sharp. My duck-green felt hat will slay you: it has a trick of making my neck seem longer & my cheeks more pendulous. I love that." He eventually looked like "an egg sculpted in lard, with goggles on . . ."

Oscar Wilde once claimed to have put only his talent into his work, saving genius for his life. To his own existence, Larkin brought "*self-disgust*, with all my heart . . ." Back in 1993, dismayed American reviewers of Andrew Motion's Larkin biography tended to focus sympathetically on the subject's unhappiness. If this was an improvement upon earlier British excoriations of the letters, it still missed the distinction between happiness and fulfillment. The former may be what one wants, but the latter is what one needs, and as such is much more profound. Philip Larkin's natural temperament was deeply, depressingly fulfilled.

What some people can't forgive about him, more than his unattractive prejudices, is that he was pissed off rather than righteously angry; his letters reveal him to have been less poetic than any poet has a right to be. One American poet writing about the storm over the letters and the Motion biography sighed: "There is no reason that lyric sadness and disappointment cannot be linked to a democratic and progressive social action. It is rare but possible." But as Larkin might have said: so fucking what? The spreading of sweetness and light remains a poet's noblest prerogative, but his first duty is arguably to be himself. The fact is, Larkin had a perfect right to sing, as well as listen to, the blues. The thin volumes of poetry he produced within the cracks of his damp sixty-three years rank with the best of this half century, and his self-pity is better written than most everyone else's passionate cries on others' behalf. The letters of this working writer are bleakly exhilarating, and to his bloated, humbugging shade, one wishes, every year, a very merry Christmas.

NO ONE EVER cracked wiser than he.

S. J. Perelman is known to some film enthusiasts only as a one-time scriptwriter for the Marx Brothers (an identity whose persistence exasperated him), but to better-read legions he was a contributor, for almost fifty years, to *The New Yorker*, a magazine toward which his feelings were also decidedly ambivalent—in part because of "their fussy little changes and pipsqueak variations on my copy."

The truly funny are not often cuddly, and in his letters Perelman oscillates almost exclusively between low and high dudgeon. His "quicksilvery" intelligence and tongue are irritated into action by a reliable roster of dislikes that includes politicians, New York City and most of the exotic stops on his six round-the-world trips. Nothing pricks him more sharply than "that misbegotten flea-pit called Hollywood," whose studio flunkies are a "flock of beetle-brained windsuckers with necks hinged so they can yes Darryl Zanuck." His descriptions of Mike Todd, with whom Perelman worked on *Around the World in 80 Days*, constitute by themselves a wild thesaurus of invective.

When he's talking about friends like Dorothy Parker or his own children, Perelman's letters can seem not just dyspeptic but cruel. Still, if the man is sometimes off-putting, the style he puts on is unfailingly top-drawer. Perelman doesn't just play on words; he plays with, off, against, around and through them. A report from the early lean years of his marriage: "The babe and I have settled down with our schnozzles to the grandstand at 92 Grove Street for the winter and are wondering what's delaying the wolf." A quarter century later, to his daughter away at college studying the classics: "Why don't you take a half hour off from declining irregular Greek verbs—after all, you can't keep declining verbs *forever*; one must eventually suit you."

He cooked up a lingo in his own American melting pot—big-city slang mixed with Ivy League literary allusions and spiced up with Yiddish—and he slung the product with exceptional speed and consistency. After his wife's death in 1970, Perelman, depressed at being alone and disgusted with life in the States, emigrated to England, only to return two years later, when he found himself short of linguistic capital: "I think I need a shot in the arm of Manhattan's violence, filth, disorder, but chiefly our American idiom." All his letters are performances, so dense with the same battery of effects that their recipients tend to blur. Unlike most accomplished letter-writers, complainers or otherwise, he doesn't automatically cultivate a different mood and voice for each correspondent; he lavishes the same dizzy virtuosity on all of them.

Particular circumstances, though, can call forth their own shtick: Betty White Johnston was a young screenwriter at Paramount with him in the early 1930s, and years after she got married and moved to Alabama, Perelman was still innocently drooling proposals for a reunion: "Consider . . . that all this mutual esteem, bottled up over a decade, may erupt like cordite when we finally get within pinching radius of each other. Don't trifle with nature, girl. Be fair to your glands; they've been fair to you." These mash notes are the most charming things Perelman ever put in the mail, lovely enough to make one wonder if she didn't keep postponing the rendezvous just to keep getting the letters.

With less pulchritudinous correspondents, Perelman didn't always relish performing for free. His own incoming mail sometimes consisted, in his nightmare rendition, "of old L. L. Bean catalogues, threats from collection agencies, and vilifying letters from factory girls who claimed I had deflowered them and left them in an interesting condition." His responses to it were often agitated enough to tempt the editor of his selected letters into calling them not *Don't Tread on Me*, their eventual title, but *Jaundice vs. Jaundice* or *Miasma, and Welcome to It.*

BY THE END OF THE eighteenth century, according to the historian Jeremy Black, "the habit of writing to the newspapers was well-developed." Not all the writers were disciplined controversialists; many of their offerings supplied more news than views. Editors had to keep the papers full, especially when, says Black, "the posts from the continent were delayed by wind." Domestic letter writers took up the slack, and in a pinch, the editor might make up some correspondence himself. Eventually, impassioned communications to newspapers—Zola's "J'Accuse" letter to *L'Aurore*—came to nudge history and reform, and epistolary outpourings on different sides of every issue have given signals to both contemporary politicians and latter-day historians.

In the summer of 1868, the London *Daily Telegraph* ran hundreds of letters that were provoked, in a long associative chain, by the story of a poor Belgian seamstress lured to London with the promise of a waitressing job and tricked into prostitution once she arrived. An early correspondent wondered: did the premium on having a substantial income before marriage keep too many men single for too long, thus creating a demand for prostitutes? For weeks after that, under the rubric "Marriage or Celibacy?" dozens of readers debated the question. The letters came, according to John M. Robson's study of them, "from a broad range of readers, taking up common points in expository, argumentative, hortative, and interrogative modes, with dashes of humor and lashings of self-interest." The sometimes pseudonymous contributors—including "Benedick," "A Simple Country Girl" and "One Who Looks Before He Leaps"—ended up debating emigration, a potential solution to the bachelor's economic difficulty and its attendant social ill.

To the modern eye, this public discussion appears like a slow-motion computer chat room, with less salacity and better spelling. Today, most letters to the editor arrive electronically and run just a day after the material to which they are responding—or minutes later, if you're posting online. Their watchdog function endures, and for certain scolding, didactic personalities they are the genre of choice. Some years back a *New York Times* reporter visited one of the paper's most prolific, if unpaid, contributors. Mr. Louis Jay Herman had succeeded in getting 123 letters, out of the 859 he'd sent, published in the paper. Among his arguments: one "against the need to floss daily."

Graham Greene was made for the form. Relentlessly corrective, and just as frequently wrong, he wrote letters to the London *Times* and *Spectator* and *Telegraph* for nearly fifty years. Many of them were published not long before his death in a volume titled *Yours Etc.* That peculiar, time-honored sign-off, in which the abbreviation of courtesies seems almost a calculated rudeness, was exactly the note on which to end these communications.

Greene most enjoys setting straight any errors concerning himself: incorrectly reported sales figures, falsely alleged encounters—whatever might proceed from the "wild imagination" of some reporter or profile writer. He has much to say, over the years in bits and pieces, about all that authors put up with. He writes against how the Bank of England treats their earnings; in defiance of obscenity prosecutions and television censorship; in favor of the author's right to suppress his own early work.

When he protests the supposed ban on productions of *Pygmalion* that Bernard Shaw's literary executors had countenanced in order to boost the play's musical adaptation, one feels sure that what's really exercising Greene is *My Fair Lady*'s being an *American* success, one more loud triumph for a detestable country at its bloated peak of influence. The opportunities that the United States and its enemies provide him! There is the McCarran Act to be derided; Charlie Chaplin to be welcomed home to England; the jet that Britain should be selling to the dictator he likes to call "Dr." Castro. As late as 1979, he writes that the Soviet Union should grant more exit visas, since it "is highly unlikely that there would be a mass immigration of the proletariat—and that in itself would be a good propaganda point." A dozen years before, he had already announced that, if forced to live in either the United States or the USSR, he would "certainly choose the Soviet Union." And why not? He could pal around with friends like Kim Philby, who had already chosen it over Britain.

Letters to the newspaper allowed Greene certain antic indulgences, too. He began unserious feuds; solicited support for a nonexistent Anglo-Texas society; and entered a competition to produce the best parody of Graham Greene. But more often, when he remembered the *Times*'s address, he was in drunken high dudgeon.

Yours Etc. pieces together what Evelyn Waugh called Greene's "fatuous and impertinent" protest against the Catholic Church's refusal to have a priest offer public prayers at the funeral of Colette. Waugh explained (to Nancy Mitford) that the protest derived from Greene's being "tipsy when he wrote it at luncheon with some frogs," who got it translated and mailed. Greene himself would remember being "tipsy with rage," not liquor, but on other occasions he did acknowledge the alcoholic muse that got him to write some of these letters to the editor.

The Church, about which he was always so conflicted, becomes a godsend when it bumps up against other habitual irritants. Take the persecution of Catholics inside the USSR: "I would rather see my church honourably suppressed than corrupted within by such [American] war propagandists as Cardinal Spellman and Bishop Sheehan [*sic*]." But it doesn't take subjects this mighty to prod Greene toward snit and vendetta. A host of lesser devils will do: modern architecture; a cleanup of prostitutes in the West End; misprints in the *Times;* a change of typography in the *Spectator.* The essential requirement is an opportunity to appear bravely perverse. In 1976, he finds new grounds upon which to oppose a helmet law for motorcyclists: "Here motor-cycle helmets are more and more used in bank robberies, for they are less conspicuous than a stocking mask, especially the latest mode which provide a tinted shield against the sun. Not of course that one wants to make things difficult for bank robbers (we had eight in this region last month), for they may keep away tourists who are a pollution problem."

The postal service, which conveyed his cracked pots to the papers, was itself a preoccupation. On one occasion Greene proposed that *Spectator* readers clog the system with postage-due letters that recipients would then refuse, thereby bankrupting the whole service, "so that it may be taken over quite cheaply by some efficient business organization—say, Marks and Spencer." Decades earlier, according to the editor of *Yours Etc.*, Greene had suggested bringing down Neville Chamberlain's government by mailing packages of pornography that would appear to be coming from its cabinet members.

Here one may be arriving, to swipe a famous Greene title, at the heart of the matter: the slithering, insidious opportunities the mail provides—the way, for pennies, one can dispatch the most disturbing sentiments around the globe, and slip unbidden into a person's home. Much of Greene's life and character—all the secrets and seediness and despair that went into "Greeneland," the territory of his novels—suggests that his letters to the editor were a kind of self-assertion pretending to be the disinterested advice offered by those Victorians in the columns of the *Telegraph*. The conventions of letter-to-the-editor writing allowed him to hide all sorts of private rage in plain sight on a million breakfast tables.

UNLESS ONE SUBSCRIBES to the more extreme forms of expressionist criticism, hate mail is the only literary genre to be, fundamentally, a psychological symptom. The genre provides satisfaction not only to its practitioners but to many readers as well. These readers—not the original, individual recipients of the mail—derive a sort of pleasure that is also, no doubt, symptomatic: a safe displacement of their own aggressive impulses. They can satisfy themselves with a whole little shelf of anthologized epistolary spleen, which includes hate mail's more benign cousin, the prank letter. Published collections include: *Dear Sir, Drop Dead!* (1979); *Drop Us a Line . . . Sucker!* (1995); *Crank Letters* (1986); *Idiot Letters* (1995).

The true hate letter does not artfully crescendo. It flings itself, with sudden, unsubtle surprise, like a rancid cream pie. *Dear Sir, Drop Dead!* shows a number of targets getting it right in the face with the salutation: "Dear Heathen Communist Bitch" goes one greeting to the American atheist Madalyn Murray O'Hair, who inspired correspondents to work harder by her own manifest enjoyment of scorn, even the ad feminam sort: "All you are is nothing but a big old witch with a big ugly fat face and mouth on you."

Sarcasm ("My dog left home when he heard I had voted for you") depends, in both the writer and the reader, on an appreciation of distortion. Paranoia has no time for such contrivances. It is terribly urgent, under the gun and ready to assert itself in ALL CAPS, which even now pack an unsettling punch when they show up in the pixels of angry e-mail—though nothing can be more upsetting than the slithering hate fax, whose paper seems to come, somehow, from the sender himself and not the recipient's own machine.

Hate mail wants an answer—"I am speaking from experiance [*sic*]. I expect a reply from you"—and it will not be thwarted by a quickly executed "return to sender." Escalation may take the form of small packages—the dead animal; the soiled garment—or, most spectacularly, the letter bomb. As the Unabomber, Theodore Kaczynski became the most famous hate-mailer of our time, through both the explosive devices he posted and, toward the end of his slow-motion spree, the lengthy manifesto, a sort of giant letter to the editor that *The New York Times* and *The Washington Post* agreed to run in exchange for his pledge to stop the violence at three killed, twenty-three wounded.

Among the more seriously hurt was Yale professor David Gelernter, who lost part of a hand and part of his eyesight. In his book *Drawing Life: Surviving the Unabomber,* Gelernter reflects upon the irony of his having made Kaczynski's list: "He picked me out originally, my guess is, with no idea who I was aside from some guy who worked with computers." Only later, it seems, did Kaczynski discover, from Gelernter's book *Mirror Worlds,* that his target, a historian of technology, was actually "one of the very few persons in the field who doesn't *like* computers."

But Kaczynski, whom the media often treated as a serious if dangerous thinker, was hardly notable for consistency. As Gelernter points out, "He used a typewriter and rode a bus—go figure; but the machines he loved best are the ones that kill people." Gelernter diminishes his attacker by refusing to use his name; he instead employs the sort of mocking epithets one finds in the salutations of less lethal hate mail than the kind sent by Kaczynski. In Gelernter's coinages, Kaczynski becomes "Mr. Bucolic Cottage-in-the-Countryside," "Hut Man," and "Saint John of Montana."

Kaczynski's bomb came in "a book package with a plastic zip cord," which Gelernter found on a chair in his office beside a stack of mail that had piled up while he was away on vacation with his family. Since then, the pleasure of opening the mail, even what comes from whittling down a stack of business correspondence, is gone from Gelernter's life. After the attack, and the receipt of a "truckload of crackpot letters," he found that "all inbound communication channels are radioactive." He would "look at the strange message on curling fax paper in the shadows as if it, too, might start hissing and explode." By 1997, there were thousands of unopened messages in his e-mail queue. Having to type answers with one hand became too embittering a prospect; "the system has all the appeal of a flypaper that has trapped so many creatures it's disgusting."

Kaczynski's own fate was sealed, in part, with a kiss. He left DNA evidence against himself on an envelope and stamp that he had licked.

CHAPTER FIVE *Love*

I have something stupid and ridiculous to tell you. I am foolishly writing to you instead of having told you this, I do not know why, when returning from that walk. Tonight I shall be annoyed at having done so. You will laugh in my face, will take me for a maker of phrases in all my relations with you hitherto. You will show me the door and you will think I am lying. I am in love with you. I have been thus since the first day I called on you.

Alfred de Musset to George Sand, 1833

SEVERAL YEARS AGO, when Jennifer Hofer set herself up in Los Angeles as an *escritorio publico*, she did so as a kind of performance art. And yet, as she told Zachary Block, a writer from her Ivy League alumni magazine, the Latin American tradition of letter writing for hire "really does provide a service." Sitting behind a manual typewriter set up on one of the city's sidewalks, Hofer composes not only business correspondence for immigrants who can't write English, but also romantic missives for those not confident of their ability to put things with the proper ardor. Like a sympathetic but disinterested Cyrano, Hofer can fill in sentiments the sender can't fully dictate himself. According to the *Brown Alumni Magazine*, she charges "$3 for a love letter. Illicit love letters—she's written just two, including one for a woman with a crush on a married man—cost $5." Hallmark used to advertise its Valentines to those who "care enough to send the very best," but any printed greeting card is second best in the realm of authenticity. Hofer, part amanuensis and part author, offers something that by its one-of-a-kind nature comes closer to being the real thing.

Love letters can, in fact, seem so alive that, if one object of affection gets replaced by another, any letters that went to the first should be hunted down and gathered up, for sacrificial destruction or especially safekeeping. When H. L. Mencken got ready to marry Sara Haardt, he asked the silent-film actress Aileen Pringle if he could have back the letters he'd once sent her; he now encloses *her* letters to *him*. Miss Pringle was unhappy about this, but years later would come back into the critic's life by sending him a letter of condolence upon Sara Mencken's death.

Amorous e-mail can be deleted even faster than paper can be torn, although it tends to live on, like a potential stalker, somewhere in the hard drives of sender and recipient. In the realm of love, however, e-mail's most peculiar characteristic is the way it so often becomes not a means to romance but the entirety of any involvement. The e-ffairs into which so many postmodern people stumble are, like the chaste pen-palships of times past, relationships sufficient unto themselves, whereas epistolary romances traditionally sought their own extinction—the moment when physical separation ended, along with each party's need to write to the other.

More than a decade ago, at the dawn of cyber love, Meghan Daum mused upon her dates in the ether with the screen-named PFSlider: "Thanks to the computer, I was involved in a well-defined courtship, a neat little space in which he and I were both safe to express the panic and the fascination of our mutual affection. Our interaction was refreshingly orderly, noble in its vigor, dignified despite its shamelessness. It was far removed from the randomness of real-life relationships. We had an intimacy that seemed custom-made for our strange, lonely times." Operating inside the often wildly mendacious realm of cyberspace, Daum and PFSlider actually told the truth about themselves. But when they decided to meet for real, things soon enough went nowhere: in the older meaning of the term, they just didn't send each other.

In times past, the paper letter was nicely capable of the restraints and hesitations its computerized descendant later shook off; penmanship and typing could always don just the right amount of formality required to escort sender and recipient into, or out of, love. In May 1903, Roscoe Conkling Bruce, the son of Blanche K. Bruce, an ex-slave who represented Mississippi in the U.S. Senate during six years of Reconstruction, wrote to his young fiancée, Clara, from his administrative post at Tuskegee Institute: "Ask your woman doctor at Radcliffe for literature on the physical aspect of marriage; I have already written to Doctor Francis for similar information. You see, dearie, we *must* know all about certain things; we must not in a matter of deep concern be ignorant blunderers. I know you don't like me to write these things to you but we mustn't be prudish."

A quarter century later, using the same forthright primness, Harold Ross, editor of *The New Yorker*, who had realized he would rather be married to the magazine than to his wife, sent her a letter requesting a separation: "We have different tastes, different interests, different instincts, different ideas. We are distinctly two entities, two personalities. We differ in almost everything . . . Living with you on the basis that I have in the past is, I have concluded, impossible." He owned up to being "a monstrous person incapable of intimate association," but hoped that he and Jane could avoid "the emotional element, which is the last thing that ought to be brought in" to any of this. "If you could send me a note here outlining your viewpoint I would appreciate it."

THE WESTERN WORLD'S first famous pair of epistolary lovers began their catastrophic twelfth-century romance as teacher and student, when Peter Abelard—thirty-seven-year-old nominalist philosopher and the toast of intellectual Paris—managed, while living in the house of her uncle, Fulbert, to become tutor to the lovely teenaged Heloise. Abelard accomplished his conquest with the kind of pedagogical confidence that's done the job from the Athenian agora to the campus of Bennington: "I flattered myself already with the most bewitching hopes. My reputation had spread itself everywhere, and could a virtuous lady resist a man who had confounded all the learned of the age?"

All went well until Fulbert found out and banished Abelard. The lovers proceeded to run away, have a child and marry in secret—developments that, in time, might have brought Fulbert around, but in the event succeeded in driving him over the edge. He hired a gang to castrate Abelard, who entered monastic life and convinced Heloise to enter a nunnery. Abelard chronicled the story of his romance and mutilation in a long letter, the *Historia calamitatum*, which he addressed to a friend that centuries of editors have called Philintus.

According to Heloise, this dramatic narrative "happened . . . to fall into [her] hands," prompting her to write a letter of her own to her maimed lover. Hoping for a renewed exchange, she tells Abelard that the likeness of him she treasures in her room would hardly be able to compete with the thousands of words he might now send her: "If a picture, which is but a mute representation of an object, can give such pleasure, what cannot letters inspire? They have souls; they can speak; they have in them all that force which expresses the transports of the heart; they have all the fire of our passions, they can raise them as much as if the persons themselves were present." Their correspondence can be, she argues, a kind of substitute romance, a post-facto fantasy that can flourish no matter what real-life damage has already been done: "I shall read that you are my husband and you shall see me sign myself your wife. In spite of all our misfortunes you may be what you please in your letter."*

Her uncle, Heloise assures Abelard, made a psychological mis-

*In Ian McEwan's novel *Atonement*, letters perform something like the opposite task, sustaining Robbie's hopes of eventual romance with Cecilia after he goes to prison because of her sister's false accusation of sexual assault. The letters are wonderful consolation until Robbie's release, when they force an unforeseen consequence upon his and Cecilia's reunion. The two of them "sat down, looked at each other, smiled and looked away. Robbie and Cecilia had been making love for years—by post. In their coded exchanges they had drawn close, but how artificial that closeness seemed now as they embarked on their small talk, their helpless catechism of polite query and response."

take in ordering the castration: "he measured my virtue by the frailty of my sex, and thought it was the man and not the person I loved. But he has been guilty to no purpose. I love you more than ever; and so revenge myself on him." As it is, she tells Abelard, she preferred being his mistress ("it was more free") to being his legally bound wife, and she is angry that he pressed her to enter the convent ("You know it was neither zeal nor devotion that brought me here"). Even now she so lacks penitence that she can scare herself with her own cloistered blasphemy: "Among those who are wedded to God I am wedded to a man . . . What a monster am I!" She doubts that Abelard's own passion will long continue, but she will settle for a Saint Augustine–like cure—eventually but not too soon—when it comes to her own: "Till that moment of grace arrives, O think of me—do not forget me—remember my love and fidelity and constancy: love me as your mistress, cherish me as your child, your sister, your wife!"

In response, Abelard can tell her that the monastery hasn't worked either: "I betray and contradict myself. I hate you! I love you! . . . You see the confusion I am in, how I blame myself and how I suffer." Their love has become "an evil we dote on," and they need God to put an end to it. In the meantime, however uselessly, he takes cold showers of philosophy: "I comment upon Saint Paul; I contend with Aristotle; in short, I do all I used to do before I loved you, but all in vain . . ."

The whole *historia calamitatum* started with her looks, and she has no right to be asking for an epistolary revival of his love: "Oh! do not add to my miseries by your constancy." He can still speak to her in the imperatives of a schoolmaster, assigning the task of renunciation as if it were homework: "Nay, withdraw yourself and contribute to my salvation." He would have Heloise remain in the nunnery, even though he now drops a bombshell about his original urging that she go there:

> I will do you justice, you were very easily persuaded. My jealousy secretly rejoiced in your innocent compliance; and yet, triumphant as I was, I yielded you up to God with an unwilling

heart. I still kept my gift as much as was possible, and only parted with it in order to keep it out of the power of other men. I did not persuade you to religion out of any regard to your happiness, but condemned you to it like an enemy who destroys what he cannot carry off.

In time, both of them get her Augustinian wish. Letters keep the relationship alive, but its passions dwindle into a business-like exchange of clerical concerns between a devoted priest and conscientious nun. Editions of their correspondence are sometimes divided into "The Personal Letters" and the later "Letters of Direction," in which Heloise will ask Abelard for advice on, say, the Rule of Saint Benedict and how its clear application to monasteries might be adapted to convents: "How can women be concerned with what is written there about cowls, drawers or scapulars? Or indeed, with tunics or woollen garments worn next to the skin, when the monthly purging of their superfluous humours must avoid such things?" Abelard will respond with such suggestions as the need for Heloise and her sisters to "subdue the tongue by perpetual silence, at least in these places or times: at prayer, in the cloister, the dormitory, refectory, and during all eating and cooking . . ."

Today, the lovers keep their own eternal silence, entombed together in Paris's Père Lachaise cemetery, an arrangement Abelard proposed long before either had gotten over the other. In his first letter to Heloise in the convent, he reassured her about their everlasting proximity: "Your cold ashes need then fear nothing, and my tomb shall be the more rich and renowned."

TWO SEPARATE CLOISTERS allowed Heloise and Abelard to retreat from their folie à deux. But a half millennium later, in another (and perhaps just legendary) case of lopsided epistolary love, a nunnery acted as the hothouse for sinning in haste and recriminating at leisure.

Sometime in the first half of 1666, in the midst of Portugal's twenty-eight-year-long war of independence, a nun named Mariana

Alcoforado may have looked out from the Our Lady of Concieção convent in Beja and spied the attractive form of Noël Bouton de Chamilly, a chevalier serving with the French forces who'd come to help liberate her country from the Spanish. His fellow officers were soon being entertained in the convent parlor, and he seems to have ventured a bit further, into Mariana Alcoforado's room and heart. A year or so later, after prudence and obligation had recalled him to France, he would remain in her imagination as the object of wild longing and anger. And he would take up even more permanent residence in the five long, anguished love letters that she is believed (by some) to have sent him.

For the moment, let's assume of these letters what Mariana assumed of Chamilly: that they're not too good to be true. Certainly, if anguish could prove authorship, we would embrace Mariana as their authentic creator. Let's also concede Mariana a few moments of brisk good sense, as when she addresses herself instead of the absent Chamilly: "Cease, cease, unfortunate Mariana, to be consumed in vain, and to look for a lover you will never see." But what Mariana raises most is the eternally baffled cry of the abandoned and unrequited: why did you let me—no, why did you *make* me—love you? "I die of shame," she wails. Chamilly has abandoned her even though the king of France didn't really need him to come home, and the other obligations he claimed were just as flimsy: "Your family had written; do you not know all the persecutions inflicted by my own? Your honour begged you to forsake me; did I have any care of mine?"

Chamilly seems to have had a talent for moderation: "you once told me I was somewhat beautiful," Mariana recalls. The soldier claimed to possess "a great passion" for her, but she now understands how unequal that was to her own self-consuming desire. Near the beginning of 1668, Mariana says that she really doesn't want him to be punished, but six months later, in what will be her last letter, she declares: "Should chance bring you back to this country I tell you I would deliver you up to my parent's vengeance."

Men, it would seem, are all alike. "The officer who will bring you this letter reminds me for the fourth time that he must leave. How he is pressing. He is abandoning no doubt some other unfortunate woman in this country." The chance to scatter animadversions like this is an incidental pleasure available in the midst of misery. Mariana admits to a certain enjoyment of romantic martyrdom ("I find myself rather attached to the unhappiness caused by you alone"), enough to exhibit the seventeenth century's delight in paradox: "love me always and make me suffer even greater woes." She rather likes the idea of other women loving Chamilly, at least under certain circumstances: "I think I would not be angry if affections found in others could, in some way, justify my own, and I would like that all the women of France found you charming, that none be charmed, and that none please you." She'll go a step further, in fact: she can sometimes even imagine herself serving "the one you love." Chamilly once told her that, pre-Portugal, there had been someone else. Has that woman, she wonders, come back into the picture? Getting news like that might have a healthful shock-effect: "send me her portrait with a few of her letters, and write me all that she tells you."

But Mariana doesn't really want to be jolted out of her suffering. Indeed, in contrast to it, she pities Chamilly's "indifference"; she's glad that he "seduced" her, because she "could not live without the joy I am discovering of loving you amidst a thousand sorrows." The worst fate, she decides, would be to forget him.

Her health deteriorates inside the walls of "this miserable cloister," which she tells him has been a prison to her since she was a girl. Even the most severe nuns "have pity on my state" and are "touched by my love." But they also believe she's mad. For them, in return, she feels only scorn. Chamilly is her vocation now ("I am resolved to worship you all my life"), and she might as well keep practicing it.

Mariana does not compose her letters within any writerly structure—how could she, when her mood must swing from rage to rapture and back in the course of a paragraph? Piercing the pages with interjections ("Ah!" "Ho!" "Forgive me!"), she worries that Chamilly will be put off by the length of what she sends. She faints as she finishes one letter, and wishes, as she completes another, that she could fall into Chamilly's arms the way the letter will.

Inevitably, she will scold: "why have you not written to me!" In fact, Chamilly does write, but for the most part unsatisfactorily, "only icy letters, full of repetitions—half the paper is empty, and I can see that you are dying to have them finished." We don't have his side of the correspondence, but one feels safe in saying that its reception depended less on its matter than on Mariana's mood. A month or two before her just-quoted complaint about his half-heartedness, some of his words drove their recipient toward an ecstatic convulsion:

> Your last letter reduced [my heart] to a peculiar state: its pounding was so extreme it made, so it seemed, efforts to leave my body and go find you; I was so overcome by all these violent emotions that I remained abandoned by my senses for more than three hours; I stopped myself from returning to a life I must lose since I cannot keep it for you; at last, despite myself, I saw light.

But more often Chamilly's letters, with their "ridiculous civilities," are poor, wet kindling for a mighty emotional machine that begs to be stoked. In June 1668, Mariana decides that she will keep only two of them; she will return the rest and stop writing any more herself. With new backbone and clarity, she puts to Chamilly a declarative question: "Am I obliged to provide you with an exact account of all my varied emotions?" The greatest argument against the letters' authenticity may be that this letter she says will be her last turns out to be just that; silence is not, after all, the sort of pledge that obsessive lovers are generally able to keep.

But even if she's henceforth able to hold her tongue, what about the words she's already committed to paper? "Would you not be very cruel," she asks Chamilly, "to use my despair so as to render yourself more engaging, and to have it known that you aroused the greatest passion in the world?" What if he shows the letters to others, or even publishes them?

According to a recent book by Miriam Cyr, most believers in Mariana's authorship have decided that the letters began to circulate in Paris when, home in France once more, the lionized Chamilly was invited to the salon of the marquise de Sablé: "guilty of a momentary lapse in moral rectitude, [he] flaunted the letters in an effort to shine." Cyr is unable to bear the thought of even this much caddishness, and she constructs an alternative, exculpatory explanation for the surfacing of the correspondence—a theory, alas, as implausible as it is intricate.

Most scholars believe that Mariana may have existed but that her letters were actually the creation of Gabriel Joseph de La Vergne, the comte de Guilleragues, who would have known enough about Chamilly's Portuguese escapade to fabricate the letters, which he published early in 1669, while Chamilly was away on a different, this time ill-fated, military campaign, against the Turks. That little book, "small enough to be concealed by a fan," writes Cyr, made a spectacular debut, and its contents have never quite stopped speaking since. The letters intrigued Rousseau (who thought their genuine understanding of passion argued for a male author), moved Gladstone and may even have influenced the titular disguise that Elizabeth Barrett Browning gave to her *Sonnets from the Portuguese*. (*Sonnets from the Bosnian*, an earlier choice, was discarded.)

Publication of the letters led to an investigation of the convent in Beja and ultimately much stricter rules governing visits. Mariana would continue to live there—losing two elections to become the abbess—until her death at the age of eighty-three. Chamilly took for his wife a clever but ugly woman who nursed the wounds he suffered against the Dutch in 1676. He lived to be seventy-nine and, according to Cyr, whatever may be said of him from the letters, "never denied his affair with Mariana."

AFTER SOME LONG-LOST CORRESPONDENCE between William Wordsworth and his wife was sold at Sotheby's in 1977, the letters' designated editor, Beth Darlington, even while arguing the case for their publication, could not resist quoting Oscar Wilde's sonnet "On the Sale by Auction of Keats' Love Letters":

> These are the letters which Endymion wrote
> To one he loved in secret and apart,

And now the brawlers of the auction-mart
Bargain and bid for each tear-blotted note,
Aye! for each separate pulse of passion quote
The merchant's price! I think they love not art
Who break the crystal of a poet's heart,
That small and sickly eyes may glare or gloat.

The appeal of letters as real property—tactile couriers of a lover's very DNA—can scarcely be denied, and certainly not to a third party with a platinum Visa.

But William and Mary Wordsworth did not, in their letters or lives, love "secret and apart," and the highest bidder on their exchange was buying a record of marital devotion, not illicit passion. Wordsworth's famous involvement with his French mistress, Annette Vallon, who bore his daughter, was really just a premarital interruption to the attachment he and Mary Hutchinson had begun as children. As husband and wife, their letters were occasioned by separations that came when Wordsworth traveled on personal and literary business. Lengthy and news-filled, the correspondence chronicles the doings of two people accustomed to sharing all dailiness, but it also allows the future poet laureate to be a player in an epistolary genre more associated with other more reckless Romantics: "Fail not to write to me with out reserve," he implores Mary on July 22, 1810; "never have I been able to receive such a Letter from you, let me not then be disappointed, but give me your heart that I may kiss the words a thousand times!" While writing this, he is staying at his sister-in-law's and is expected to share the contents of Mary's letters; but as he reminds his wife, "I need only read parts to the rest of the family."

Startled by her husband's request—"it was so unexpected—so new a thing to see the breathing of thy inmost heart upon paper that I was quite overpowered"—Mary tries rising to the amorous occasion but doesn't quite make it, producing instead a sort of domestic diary, full of tidings about the new curate, her small son's love of string, the children's health and her own.

Even so, happy to know that she was moved by his plea for a love letter, Wordsworth enlarges in his next dispatch upon the emotional vista he sees before them: "a deep affection is not uncommon in married life, yet I am confident that a lively, gushing, thought-employing, spirit-stirring, passion of love is very rare." There's no reason their letters can't have it all. And yet, however heated up he may now be, he gives Mary his news before his feelings, because he has only an hour in which to write, and fears that his emotions, if put before the "facts," will devour the entire time. It is only before rushing to catch the post that he manages some excited vocative ("O Mary I love you with a passion of love which grows till I tremble to think of its strength") and a line that recalls one of his most famous verses: "thus did I feed on the thought of bliss that might have been." He also reports a recurring fantasy of sexual frustration: since they parted he has "ten thousand times" thought of the mouth pain she had been experiencing, and has "fancied that I was caressing thee, and thou couldst not meet me with kindred delight and rapture from the interruption of this distressing pain."

Three days later, Mary, still occupied with the responsibilities of home, writes of her annoyance with the servants and about her attempts to cure their daughter of left-handedness. She also makes fun of her own domesticated appearance: "I believe the fine folks at the church style fancy as I pass with the Baby in my Arms that I am a shabby Nurse Maid at the great house." The discomfort that letter writing causes her, its disruption of her domestic routine, is different and more easily alleviated than the trouble endured by stock epistolary lovers, whose plaintively passionate letters tend to inflame the condition they are seeking to quench.

Wordsworth's later paean to marital affection—"What rapture is . . . a kiss from a lip of the wife & mother, even if time have somewhat impaired the freshness of her virgin beauties"—is, as presents go, more on the order of a flannel nightgown than black lingerie, but its comfort to a wife unused to her husband's absence was probably considerable. By the time Mary reaches middle age, conscious of her missing teeth and graying hair, she assures her husband that one of his letters has even occasioned an improvement in her looks and apologizes for what she sends in return: "pray do not measure my love by my letters," she asks; they would be longer but for the demands of her noisy children.

From London in 1812, Wordsworth's unfavorable comments on the manners of Lady Davy—"All this has originated in affectation, but she now does without knowing what she is doing"—remind a reader, as much as anything, of the poet's own future pomposity. But for the moment, still in his early forties, he can yet send Mary spontaneous accounts of life in the capital, whose bustle forces him to rise early if he's going to get his letters written. We hear of such diverse matters as the prime minister's assassination; a young Lord Byron "who is now the rage"; and the Lambs: "Charles seems to think the dawn of [his sister's] recovery is at hand." (Lamb, by the way, saves his friend money through the time-honored means of abusing the office mail: he can receive letters for Wordsworth at the East India House without having to pay postage due.)

From the time of his and Mary's first separation, Wordsworth makes plans to put their letters "side by side as a bequest for the survivor of us," and while he understands the maternal pressures that keep Mary from writing at the length and pitch he would like, he proposes a scheme by which she might do better: "Surely by taking a little pocket book You may have a Letter going forward and may finish it by snatches, at those intervals when you are resting. I was half hurt when you said that you would '*write if you can.*' Can there be a doubt that you may."

What Mary's letters do convey is the extent to which our so-called distractions are really the warp and woof of life. "I am sitting in thy study," she writes to her husband on a Saturday night in August of 1810. The "rain beats against the window—the fire is flapping & the Baby in the Cradle upon the Sofa, nestling about warning me that he will presently awake, but all these quiet sounds are disturbed by a restless, noisy, chirping, dying (I am afraid) chick that is within the Fender & which the children left to *my* care therefore I have not the heart to dismiss it." We are most essentially ourselves when frantic and fidgety; we worry more about whether and how soon our letters will arrive than about what they have to say: "your former letter was written on a Saturday & it came by Wednesday's post this by Friday's," Mary writes her husband, trying with unintentionally comic complexity to sort things out. "Yet I cannot but think that *this* was written on Saturday likewise, because you say this day 3 weeks in the one, & this day fortnight in the other—without mentioning that you have departed from your intention—Yet I do not positively expect you so soon as tomorrow week, anxious as I am to have you here, therefore I shall send off this letter to Hindwell—had I been *confident* I should have directed to Mr. Crump's." The misnamed poste restante, always one step behind or ahead of where it should be, is perhaps the most perfect literary projection of ourselves.

HER FAMOUS FICTIONAL INCARNATION strides into *Orlando* "slicing at the head of a Moor." In her actual sex and century, Vita Sackville-West swept over the land like some fifth season, harvesting sensations as soon as the earth could thrust them up. On May 29, 1926, her letter to "darling Virginia" has her shingling her hair, felling an oak, delivering puppies, and reading a lover's book, "propped open by a fork," at the dinner table. To Virginia Woolf, Vita was "all fire and legs and beautiful plunging ways like a young horse." They met in 1922, became lovers a few years after that and then counted themselves among those lucky people who see eros burn itself into devotion instead of recrimination.

Each of their marriages is by now a legend of accommodation. Leonard Woolf put his talent at the service of his wife's genius, and Vita's husband, Harold Nicolson, finally saw no reason why his own homosexuality or his wife's should preclude their having the satisfactions of marriage and family. The frequent separations brought on by his diplomatic career were described by Vita as genuine "matrimonial miseries"—even if the night prior to lamenting these separations to Virginia she had been enjoying a German revue in which "two ravishing young women sing a frankly Lesbian song."

What do *these* two women, Vita and Virginia, want from each other?

For Vita there is the excitement of talking to her imaginative superior: "I don't know whether to be dejected or encouraged when I read the works of Virginia Woolf. Dejected because I shall never be able to write like that, or encouraged because somebody else can?" Vita can flatter her "gentle genius" back to the physical health and creative confidence that Virginia Woolf is always losing. *Mrs. Dalloway*, she declares, makes it "unnecessary ever to go to London again, for the whole of London in June *is* in your first score of pages." Where Woolf's books are experimental, diaphanous, endlessly flinging metaphors, Vita's poems and novels are sturdy productions of regular metrics and reliable narration that make a good deal of money for the Woolfs' Hogarth Press. As an artist, she was never in the race with Virginia Woolf. That she never tried to be is only one of the indicators of healthy self-awareness found in her letters.

To Virginia, Vita is the "scandalous ruffian" who can scold and soothe her childlike anxieties, who can bring her reports from realms that she might imagine but which Vita, with her aristocratic birthright and natural gumption, will actually maraud. Who else can tell her of embassy parties in Teheran and Berlin ("gold plate in rivers down the table"); or about pouring bowls of the shah's crown jewels through her fingers ("We came away shaking the pearls out of our shoes")? A train crossing the Russian steppes is stuffy: "So," Vita writes, "I have smashed the window with a corkscrew, and a thin shrill pencil of frozen air rushes in reviving us." Vita treats inanimate objects as if they are the lower orders, and to a correspondent for whom shopping for a dress was social torture, these reports must have been dazzling. Vita remains Virginia's standard of "real-womanliness," whether she's stealing men's wives, sending sons to Eton, or supervising a Boy Scout jamboree at the family estate. She brings adventures home like Othello, and they are incomplete until Virginia can hear the news: "Oh Christ, how much I always want to see you when life becomes exciting." For her part, Virginia seizes what she calls "eunuch" pleasures: "Here in my cave I see lots of things you blazing beauties make invisible by the light of your own glory."

All love survives and imperils itself by manipulation. We try to regulate our lovers' psychologies, reposition their caresses. We even prescribe their epistolary styles. In 1929, Vita cries in mock exasperation: "You said I was to write an intimate letter, and this is the result!" But she can give her own stylistic orders: "Put 'honey' when you write." In fact, it is the voice of power, loving and authoritative, that is her best note. On January 11, 1926, she writes to an ailing Virginia: "I don't care a damn, not a little row of pins, whether I catch it [influenza] or not; I'd travel all the way to Egypt with the fever heavy upon me sooner than not see you." Among the greatest pleasures provided by their two decades' worth of letters is the chance to recall every love affair's keenest intoxication—the thrill of hearing the thing you want insisting that you take it.

Virginia and Vita ought to remind us of Oscar Wilde and Lord Alfred Douglas—genius pursuing aristocratic beauty; minor talent feeding off greater gifts—but they don't. How much less sad, how utterly unsordid, is these women's story. Early in the relationship, Vita writes to Harold: "I love Mrs. Woolf with a sick passion." But that wasn't really the case on either side. Love was never allowed to overwhelm work, marriage or self-protection. Vita kept her distance from the alien territory of Bloomsbury, and Virginia did what she could to minimize the inevitable rejection: "But you dont see, donkey West, that you'll be tired of me one of these days (I'm so much older) and so I have to take my little precautions."

During one crisis of jealousy, over Vita's relationship with Mary Campbell, Virginia chooses to invent rather than rant. She writes *Orlando*, that protean fantasy whose muse and center is Vita. Reading it charms Vita into renewed reverence: "I feel like one of those wax figures in a shop window, on which you have hung a robe stitched with jewels."

The relationship survived. In the wartime months before her death in 1941, Virginia would be writing Vita thank-you notes for gifts of butter and wool. Sense always triumphed over sensibility, so much so that there is a kind of erotic rationality to their correspondence. Not the least sexy thing about these lovers is that they never ran away with one another.

AMERICAN READERS long familiar with Chekhov's letters only through the 1955 selection edited by Lillian Hellman (a dramatist he couldn't have been less like) more recently have gotten a chance to view the last portion of his life as a concentrated, two-character play. *Dear Writer, Dear Actress*, published about a decade ago, begins in 1899, nine months after the thirty-eight-year-old Chekhov has met Olga Knipper; it goes on to present five years during which the tubercular playwright spends most of his time convalescing at Yalta, while Knipper and Stanislavski's Moscow Art Theatre perform's his repertory and premiere both *The Three Sisters* and *The Cherry Orchard*.

The beginnings of the correspondence are tentative and courtly ("I take your hand in mine, if you will allow me," writes Chekhov), but the volume's main divisions follow Knipper's progress from "Friend" to "Lover" to "Wife" and then "Widow." So important was letter writing to their relationship that she continued to write Chekhov after he died.

Eight years his junior, Knipper is all chatter and charm. She requires constant, almost comical, reiteration of both Chekhov's affections and his acceptance of her absence: "You're not angry with me and haven't stopped loving me? Anton, you haven't changed? You still have your nose, teeth, hair, eyes, beard?" She is a champion seeker of left-handed compliments, a virtuoso of the passive-aggressive: "You're sick of writing to me, you don't feel anything when you write to me, isn't that right?" She will sometimes retract yesterday's letter (once its obsolete sentiments are already in the mail), and can be just as unhappy when Chekhov is well as when he's ill: "I couldn't help feeling stirrings of jealousy, why are you doing so well without me?" She is, classically, the one who wants to Talk About the Relationship, while he goes on deflecting her real-life complaints: "Dear heart, you are getting worked up over nothing." However gentle and self-mocking, he can exasperate her, too, as when he signs himself "Father."

Knipper cannot fully grasp his invalid's frustration. "An endless stream of visitors, idle, provincial tongues chatter away and I am bored," Chekhov complains from Yalta. "I get furious and envy the rat that lives under the floor in your theatre." He promises to love her "wildly like an Arab" when they are at last together, but with his body not up to such a standard of exertion, the excitement he more realistically craves is backstage gossip. Time and again his letters rush through the personal to get to the professional: "Why don't you write anything about *Three Sisters*? How is the play going?"

Both their personalities can seem almost too Chekhovian to be true. Each counsels the other to stay out of the doldrums, but listlessness is often the emotional rule between them. When Chekhov sighs "If only we could arrange things so that we could live in Moscow!" the reader checks to make sure one of the Prozorov sisters hasn't made an unexpected entrance from the right margin.

The theatre, which is most of what the lovers have in common, is also what keeps them apart. Even as Chekhov's illness worsens, Knipper is, despite what she writes, not ready to drop everything and rush to his side. Her guilt may be genuine, but Chekhov never forces her to act on it: "You're a goose, sweetheart. Never, while I'm your husband, will I take you away from the theatre." His doting mother and sister may fault his absent wife, but he himself finds the marriage more civilized than peculiar. The letters, which in many respects have had to *be* the marriage, remain to him the chief thing. Instead of summoning her to his bedside, he orders her to buy better ink, since what she's now using makes the paper stick to the envelope.

The correspondence is one of its own principal subjects. Endless complaint is made about the other's not writing, even though the other has, of course, just written: neither of them, despite years of evidence, ever learns to ascribe the other's silence to the vagaries of the czarist mails. A reader will be glad that Chekhov made as little use as he seems to have of the telephone at Yalta (it's referred to as early as 1899), but the written cross talk lends a farcical aspect to the narrative. The volume's editor must also deal with another sort of awkwardness, always the strangest-seeming irony of any long-distance epistolary romance: whenever the lovers do manage to get together, the letters stop dead.

Chekhov's gentle forbearance toward Olga provides a pleasing contrast to the super-logical declamations in another famous correspondence between playwright and actress. "Is this dignified? Is it sensible?" shouts George Bernard Shaw, near the start of his infatuated letter-writing to Mrs. Patrick Campbell. "At my age—a driveller—a dotard! I will conquer this weakness, or trade in it and write plays about it." He, too, had only one style, onstage and off.

It was a strange *coup de foudre* that knocked Shaw to his bony knees. He had been acquainted with Beatrice Stella Campbell for more than a dozen years before the 1912 meeting during which he fell "head over ears" in love with her. He was a placidly married man of fifty-six, she a widow of forty-seven. Within two years, the popular "Mrs. Pat" would play Eliza, and *Pygmalion* would carry them to a joint peak of fame. For a quarter century after that, while Shaw's achievements piled up and Mrs. Campbell's star declined, the two of them would continue a chaste lovers' quarrel, as "Joey" and "Stella," in their letters.

Shaw asks for nothing except "to have [his] own way in everything," exercising control and good sense to the extent of writing on green paper (more soothing) when he has headaches. Though at first badly smitten with Stella, he maintains a mixture of authoritarian kindness and casual cruelty in almost every paragraph. From the beginning he decrees that this Platonic affair will be manageable: "we great people have no need for happiness," he assures Stella, adding (not quite accurately) that his wife Charlotte is amused and unthreatened by it all.

Insisting that it is "unprofessional to write under the influence of deep feeling," Shaw nonetheless admits that he "badly need[s] some sort of humanizing," or at least temporary relief from being "the supersane man" whose brains are forever "grinding like millstones." If friendship, according to Byron, is love without its wings, Shaw's feeling for Mrs. Campbell amounts to love with snow tires—feelings deliberately restrained by irony and ego. He suggests that, when he dies, they put a plaque on one of their rendezvous sites reading HERE A GREAT MAN FOUND HAPPINESS.

It took a great diva to stand all this, to tell him how ridiculous he could be: "Oh dear me—its too late to do anything but *accept* you and *love* you—but when you were quite a little boy somebody ought to have said 'hush' just once!" Stella's own thunderbolts are flung in a perfect mess of penmanship and usage. The correspondence's editor, Alan Dent, notes how the actress's "epistolary style . . . does not always translate easily to the printed page," not with some words underlined up to seven times, and a thousand punctuation marks missing in action.

Each of these two natural scolds dishes out, and requires, the other's contempt. Invective is their sweet nothing. During one early quarrel, not long before Stella has the nerve to remarry, Shaw pronounces her an "Infamous, vile, heartless, frivolous, wicked woman! Liar! lying lips, lying eyes, lying hands, promise breaker, cheat, confidence-trickster!" His Majesty's mails being faster than the czar's, it takes her but a day to respond: "You vagabond you—you blind man. You weaver of words, you—and black and purple winged hider of cherubs—you poor thing unable to understand a mere woman." And then, to twist the knife, she calls him "my dear friend all the same."

She thinks of them as two "Lustless lions at play." The possibility of a final break never occurs to either beast, no matter how much flesh it's verbally clawed from the other. "No you dont wound me," Stella declares in 1914. "I saw into your heart a long time ago." But where else can she get such loving abuse? "You must be frightfully lonely in New York," Shaw writes when she's playing *Pygmalion* there. "I believe you would give your soul for five minutes even with me, the cast-off. Or are you wallowing in infinite adulation?"

Once the first years of their carefully unconsummated passion are spent, substantial gaps begin to interrupt the correspondence. Shaw settles into eminence while Stella ages out of her best roles, spending most of her time abroad, lucklessly in Hollywood and then, more and more impecuniously, in New York and Paris hotels. (She vows never to return to England if it means subjecting her Pekingese "Moonbeam" to a six-month quarantine.) As time passes, neither lover can any longer get the same rise out of the other. Now and then Stella requests the old abrasion ("come and call me a fool soon"), while at other times she claims to lack the strength for it: "Don't be angry with me any more. Life has taken some skins off me and I can't battle with your jibes and jests."

Joey and Stella eventually fight over their own early letters as if the words are children: publication rights are contested like custody or visitation. Whatever she may have said in 1913 about detesting "letters written for an audience—in hopes of publication after death," Stella comes to realize the financial rescue that publication can offer. The battle she and Shaw conduct over her attempts to print his private words goes on for years, a tedious postcript to the self-controlled romantic fireworks they once shot each other's way.

Stella cannot grasp the distinction between physical property (she owns the actual letters—that is, the stationery) and copyright, which remains with Shaw. She argues that publishing the letters will make Charlotte seem admirably forbearing; Shaw, changing the tune he whistled in 1912, disagrees. Stella fires back that he's being suburban, but he insists that their communications be revealed only when "we are both dead. Then we can be added to Heloise and Abelard and all the rest of them." It doesn't matter, she tells him; she needs the money now.

Mr. Dent, dealing posthumously with the letters, reminds us that it was Alexander Woollcott who described Mrs. Patrick Campbell as "a sinking ship that fired upon those who tried to rescue it." Her resistance to Shaw's resistance is never quite so furious as that—she usually sends love with her obstinacy—but money certainly killed the peculiar romance they'd composed for years. "Dear Joey," she writes on June 30, 1931, "My letters are worth 2d.—yours 50 quid—so don't bother to answer."

"IT IS A DIFFERENT THING working here at this desk now that you preside over it." A prophetic element hides within this letter of Woodrow Wilson's, written at seven o'clock in the morning on June 3, 1915, to the woman who would become his second wife and, eventually, after his disabling stroke, a secret surrogate president.

Mrs. Edith Bolling Galt was, in 1915, the forty-two-year-old widow of Washington jeweler Norman Galt, whose store did business in the capital for two hundred years. Wilson's cousin Helen

Bones and his physician, Dr. Cary Grayson, hoped the lively, plump Mrs. Galt would bring the president out of the "grief and dismay" that he himself called his "terrible companions in the still night." A year and a half into his presidency, the same week in August 1914 that war began overseas, Wilson had watched his first wife, Ellen, die of Bright's disease. In the months following, the depleted president had struggled both to mediate and steer clear of the Europeans' fighting; Edith Galt's appearance proved a sudden, wild tonic, beyond any doctor or family member's expectation.

Edith knew that she was "playing with fire," but she let her imagination be captured by Wilson's muffled charm, as well as by "the picture Helen gave . . . of a lonely man, detached from old friends and associations." Within weeks of their first meeting in March 1915, the president declared that his "*private* life had been recreated," and the two of them embarked on a months-long letter-writing romance that led to a Christmastime wedding.

On paper, Edith professes anxiety about the coldness of written words, but the love letter had always been Wilson's favorite mode of communication. His missives to his first wife had continued beyond their courtship through nearly thirty years of marriage; he "was never away from home more than a day without writing to her," says Ray Stannard Baker, an early biographer, "and not mere letters full of dusty cares." When Edith came into his life, one letter a day was often not enough, and he took to heading what he wrote with the hour as well as the date.

Our image of Wilson as a skinny pillar of rectitude, remapping the world into an abstract rationality, undergoes a comic transformation in his letters to Edith; he inflates like a cartoon genie. Eager to be goofy instead of brilliant, the author of *Congressional Government* and "The Modern Democratic State" seizes the opportunity to talk baby talk: "you are a bad girl to sit up so late!" Beyond anything, this fast worker (he first proposes in May) is eager to be helpless: "I *need* you. I need you as a boy needs his sweetheart and a strong man his helpmate and heart's comrade." He is "a longing man, in the midst of a world's affairs," "Your devoted friend, and your dependent friend."

The tendency toward self-plagiarism is greater in the love letter than almost any other genre. Compulsive utterance comes up against a finite number of terms of endearment; limited supply recycles itself to meet demand. Suitors will also find the opportunity to court one lover with words they've written earlier to another; Laurence Sterne, for example, the sort of classic English author Wilson enjoyed, romanced his mistress with lines he'd once sent his wife. In the president's case, the overlapping occurred in the enclosures: early on he sent Mrs. Galt a travel book by Philip Gilbert Hamerton, the same author he'd made an engagement present of, back in 1883, to Ellen.

It was through Ellen that Wilson had become acquainted with much of English literature (in fact, she introduced him to Sterne), which he developed into a frame of personal reference. After hearing her talk about *Middlemarch*, he went out and read the novel, finding "a very distinct parallel between Lydgate's aspirations and my own." Like George Eliot's young doctor, Wilson craved both intellectual and emotional companionship in a wife. "No man who isn't *merely* a student, simply a thinking machine," he wrote Ellen, "could wish to marry a woman such as John Stuart Mill married and doted on."

Edith Galt was a less cerebral companion than Ellen had been. In one décolleté portrait, this juicy, corporeal presence looks like Madame X as seen through the eyes of Botero, and it's not hard to imagine how Wilson, who once said he was "carrying a volcano" inside, felt ready to blow: "If ever again I have to be with you for an hour and a half," he writes her on June 5, "with only two stolen glances to express my all but irresistible desire to take you in my arms and smother you with kisses, I am sure I shall crack an artery!" Two weeks later, while Edith has tea at the White House with Helen Bones, Wilson hides behind some lace curtains in the Green Room, writing afterward that he "feasted [his] eyes on the loveliest person in the world,—with, oh, such a longing to go to her and take her in my arms and cover her with kisses." He more than once talks about his competing personalities ("the boy that is in me and who has found a perfect playmate, the lover in me who has found love like his own . . . the man of affairs"), and in a summer of war fevers, he turns Edith's love for him into her patriotic duty: "I am absolutely dependent on intimate love for the right and free and most effective use of my powers . . . what it costs my *work* to do without it."

Not everyone was so sure. Wilson was so occupied with gushing out letters to Edith's "own dear, wonderful, delightful, adorable self, the noblest, most satisfying, most lovable woman in the world" that he didn't notice the displeasure some of those around him, like the White House usher, Ike Hoover (still there from Theodore Roosevelt's time), were themselves feeling or confiding to their diaries. Hoover thought that the president was forgetting his job, whereas Wilson was merely charmed by the usher's performance as love's messenger: "The faithful Hoover," he writes Edith one night when she is out of town, "went down to the Post Office after all the deliveries had been made, but there was nothing there. He is going down again, bless him, and will report again about 10 o'clock tonight whether the 9:30 mail from New York has brought me what my heart waits for." The president suffered writer's cramp from all he was putting down on paper; aboard a jostling train, he would type his effusions on a Hammond portable.

He knows that the world, already at war, has "gone mad," and that it is depending "in part on *me* to steady it and bring it back to sanity and peace." But one disagreement with Edith makes him scrub a day's worth of appointments, including a Cabinet meeting, just to sulk. Even after coming to his senses—by resolving, in the common lovers' breakthrough, no longer "to *discuss* our love, but live upon it"—he can still declare that "there is nothing worthwhile but love," a scary enough sentiment in a president.

Wilson is sure that Edith improves whatever he writes, including drafts of his protest against the Germans' sinking of the *Lusitania:* "I have brought it nearer to the standard my precious Sweetheart, out of her great love, exacts of me." He even appreciates her influence over what his recent biographer August Heckscher calls "one of the major errors of his career," the speech in which he said there "is such a thing as a man being too proud to fight," a remark that would require some backtracking after Roosevelt and others snarled in disgust. "If I said what was worth saying to that great audience in Philadelphia last night," he writes Edith on May 11, "it must have been because love had complete possession of me."

With Edith making visits to the White House, and Wilson's orchid deliveries following her home, even people well outside his circle soon knew something was afoot. Continuing the letters was a substitute for going out in public together, and Wilson, who in drafts of some official correspondence used a shorthand comprehensible only to himself and his White House stenographer, must have enjoyed the subterfuge. As with Chekhov and Olga Knipper, the correspondence is one of its own main themes. In prose as purple as her writing case, Edith asks the president if he can feel her letter "throb and beat" as he holds it. She tells him to "let it nestle" close to his heart, leaving "no room between for loneliness or sadness." One night in August she lets him know that the pencilled letter she'll be sending from Geneva, New York, is being written in bed. Realizing it's "absurd," Wilson sends a letter that may be traveling to her on the same train he'll be taking himself.

From the beginning, he wants Edith's opinions. His troubles with his secretary of state become an early bond between them, and her tough line ("Hurrah! Old Bryan is out!") brings to the contemporary reader's mind that other presidential second wife, Nancy Reagan. "You are so sweet in your judgments of people and I am so radical," Edith will say after calling Roosevelt a "villain." Wilson must remind her how much he relies on his chief secretary, Joseph P. Tumulty, even though Tumulty isn't her idea of a gentleman.

After a couple of months, Wilson begins sending state papers along with his letters ("By the way, do not trouble to return any of the documents I send, Sweetheart, unless I specifically indicate that I should like to have them back"). He annotates them with explanations, for which Edith professes gratitude ("You are a dear person to take the time to write little sentences on each of the papers you send me"). Neither one knew that this would be training for the year and a half she would serve, in the estimation of some, as the nation's first woman president. Back in 1915, she merely loved holding one of Wilson's hands "while with the other [he turned] the pages of history."

Midway through one letter written to Edith on a Saturday night in August, Wilson provides an unforgettable glimpse of his presidential self: "I got back to the house before the band concert on the South Lawn was over and heard, I fancy, the greater part of the program as I sat writing at my desk. At the end, when they played 'The Star-Spangled Banner,' I stood up all alone here by my table at attention and had unutterable thoughts about my custody of the traditions and the present honor of that banner. I could hardly hold the tears back! And *then*, the loneliness!" He had always been a victim of the high achiever's fraud complex, writing his first wife, thirty years before, that "Complete success, such as I have had at [Johns] Hopkins, has the odd effect . . . of humiliating rather than exalting me." Later he saw himself as only "the (temporarily) beloved President of 100 million people."

In October of 1915, with his dependence on Edith so evident, and the gossip so embarrassing (one Washington paper, excitedly dropping a syllable, reported that the president had spent an evening "entering" Mrs. Galt at the theatre), the official announcement of their engagement must have come as a relief to anyone in the know. At that point a direct phone line was run between the White House and Edith's Twentieth Street home, where they were married on December 18. As was not the case with Wilson's first marriage, the letters now ceased, Edith's physical proximity more than compensating for whatever pleasures the two of them might have kept supplying each other on paper.

After five years in the White House (together, in 1918, they dedicated the first air-mail service), they moved to their own state-of-the-art house on S Street, which Edith had adapted to the president's infirmities. It is now open to the public as a relic of the Wilsons' brief life there together, and of Edith's subsequent forty years alone. The ermine cape she wore to John F. Kennedy's inauguration is upstairs, and on the piano in the second-floor library, one can find sheet music for the song that Colonel Starling of the

Secret Service overheard Woodrow Wilson, in top hat and pince-nez, singing to himself on his wedding day: "Oh, you beautiful doll! You great big beautiful doll!"

FOR A NUMBER OF DECADES the duchess of Windsor had the distinction of being simultaneously the world's most prominent socialite and its most notable outcast. Reviled by a royal family that owed its throne to her, she put her best face-lift forward at a thousand parties during her exile with the little man who'd given up his crown for her. A volume of their letters, published as she wished after her death in 1986, turned out to be something of an apologia. In particular, she wanted it known that, far from having tried to grab a crown for herself, "the twice-divorced Mrs. Simpson" (as she was always called) did everything she could to make Edward VIII renounce her instead of the throne in December 1936.

Although called *Wallis and Edward*, the volume contains not only letters between the duke and duchess but also ones from Wallis to her aunt Bessie Merryman of Baltimore. This proves a blessing. For one thing, it is through these postings to Aunt Bessie that we get to hear how everything happened. For another, those letters from the duke to the duchess that are included contain such treacly nonsense (well beyond the usual infantilism of billets-doux) that a reader couldn't stomach many more of them.

"Was Wallis socially ambitious?" wonders Michael Bloch, editor of the correspondence. One might as well ask if the present queen likes horses and corgis. But was Mrs. Simpson's specific ambition, from the get-go, to land the Prince of Wales? Bloch says that their first meeting came about "through accident rather than design," though shortly after it occurred, in 1931, Wallis did write to Aunt Bessie that "it was quite an experience and as I've had my mind made up to meet him ever since I've been here [in London] I feel relieved."

It seems clear that she didn't entertain the idea of actually marrying him. She continued to see the good sense in her comfortable, passionless marriage to businessman Ernest Simpson, even long after the prince had come to depend on her for constant attention ("this man is exhausting," she informs Bessie) as well as marching orders. She juggled things; and Ernest didn't slam the door until early 1935.

However shallow, Wallis Simpson was no fool; that was always clear, and her letters make it more so. Cautioned by memories of the "flat where mother had the café and was forever working herself to death to give me things," she shows no desire to pursue an affair that will end in her own penniless notoriety. She thinks of her liaison with the prince as temporary grandeur; she savors his notice and hoards her press clippings.

It is he who won't take no for an answer. At the time of the abdication crisis, with her mail full of insults and death threats, the prince insists she go through with her divorce from Simpson and marry him instead. The abdication leaves him somewhat bewildered, but eleven days after it's done, he writes Wallis that he is "really happy for the very first time in [his] life."

A reader of their letters has no reason to doubt it. The prince can only be described as besotted. Never a deep thinker (he liked jigsaw puzzles and needlepoint and standing on his head), he writes Wallis notes that have him reveling in his own dependence. He refers to the two of them as WE (Wallis and Edward) and seems to find this coinage the acronym of the age, using it constantly, along with their private word "eanum" (meaning puny or pathetic). A typical example of his epistolary prose: "Your lovely New Year message helped a boy a lot in his lonely drowsy and he was feeling sad. Give Mary [Wallis's maid] an eanum note for me to keep until WE can be alone together again."

The prince (and for eleven months king) comes off in these letters as His Royal Ickiness, unable during his brief reign and after to perceive how Wallis really needs to give him a dose of Lady Macbeth. After true humiliations have been heaped upon his exiled head, it is she who urges him to fight back against Prime Minister Stanley Baldwin ("You cannot allow that man to finish you") as well as the new king and queen: "I blame it all on the wife [the eventual Queen Mum]—who hates us both." But in the months following the abdication, moved by the full realization of what he has given up for her, Wallis lets her affectionate mothering bloom into something that looks like real love.

From the start, her letters are a huge contrast to his. True, she is preoccupied with money, clothes and parties, and on occasion shows Bessie a hint of Marie Antoinette: "The Hunger Marchers arrive in London tomorrow," she writes in February 1934, "so we are going to the country in time for dinner." But she is acute and amusing, too. Early in the affair, she tells her aunt: "The English would prefer that he marry a Duke's daughter to one of the mangy foreign princesses left."

The collection ends with the duke and duchess's wedding on June 3, 1937—a good place to call a halt. For years they remained more or less devoted to each other but to little else of consequence. In January 1937, the duchess writes that "whatever happens we will make something of our lives," but it's hard to see what, if anything, that turned out to be. In the end, one has to agree with those who have said that her chief public service was to take her husband out of the line of succession. Being king of England is a pretty eanum job these days, but his own letters make a good case for thinking that Mr. David Windsor wouldn't have been up to it.

THE SUPPOSED BLINDNESS of love has always been a measure of its irrational intensity and even nobility. In its purest form, love fails to notice physical appearance, social obstacles, or anything but love itself. To fit it with lenses would be to cure and thereby kill it. By contrast, except for the "deaf ears" upon which the pleas of an unsuccessful suitor may fall, deafness rarely provides metaphors for romance. And yet it is within the surrounding silence of actual deafness that Eva Weintrobe and Morris Davis, an English seamstress and a tailor, conducted a flinty and spirited epistolary courtship during the late 1930s.

Thirteen years older than Eva, Morris, at thirty-eight, has just returned to England from a decade in New York when he meets her at the Warrington Deaf Club in Liverpool in the summer of

1936. The son who will eventually publish their letters explains that Morris "had seen a photograph of Eva while he was in London and went to Liverpool with the express purpose of meeting her." As fast a worker as Woodrow Wilson, he will be suggesting marriage after about a dozen letters and a third as many meetings.

In fact, the lovestruck tailor is pressing two suits at once: he wants Eva not only to marry him but to settle in America as well. But she is skeptical of any future there: "How can you make money in one year as you say if you have been in the States twelve years & made nothing," she asks in April of '37. What's more, she does not like emigration being made into the test of her devotion. And anyway, why can't he just "act like other boys & give in to the girl."

Only Eva's side of the early correspondence survives, so Morris's arguments must be heard in her rebuttals: "You said I should not doubt your love for me as you were the first to declare & also the first to propose marriage, well this is the proper thing to do, did you expect me to propose first." The way Eva sees it, there are things that women just don't do, and as for Morris's idea that he might go back to America by himself for a while, after they've married—well, who does he imagine he is? "It is allright [*sic*] for cricketers & film stars, Jewish people never do things like this."

Morris does go back alone, and still single. Soon afterward, Eva says she's "honured [*sic*]" to have his first letter from the States, and in August of '37 she thanks him for the five dollars he's sent as a birthday present. Even so, ever cautious and charmingly stubborn, she reveals seven months later that she's yet to spend it: "I do not know why but I have not wanted to change it to English money, but if all is well between us I will buy something for my trousseau with it."

As they keep arriving, Morris's letters do convince her that she will be "safe in America," and Eva finally agrees to cross the ocean, saying she is "happy & excited at the prospect of seeing you again." Her exuberance is new, but still not high enough for her to put an exclamation point to it. As it is, what's been most crucial in making up her mind to emigrate is Morris's news that he's been able to get back his old American job.

Red tape and a consular official's discomfort with her deafness ("he was afraid you would not marry me & then I would be destitute & be dependent on the city") delay Eva's departure for a full year, during which a reader sees the conscientiousness and worry that she carries to her job every day. She can't write the "more sentimental & intimate letters" that Morris would like from her; after all, she's not a poet and she doesn't have the *time.* She reminds him that she couldn't get off from work even to say good-bye when he sailed from Southampton, but when the seamstresses are given an hour and a half's leave to greet the new king and queen during their visit to Liverpool, Eva does use the time to write to Morris.

The two of them quarrel and apologize and then justify themselves a little further, before agreeing to drop whatever the current bone of contention may be. In the meantime, they've hurt each other. During their biggest misunderstanding, Eva complains: "You also write that you will be fair to me & will marry me, although you do not love me as much as before. Morris you would be doing me a great wrong if you do, only if you love me will I marry you . . ." Replying from Brooklyn, Morris imparts evidence that his love remains deep: "Perhaps you will wonder differently if I tell you how much I suffered for almost ten weeks and how I lost 9 lbs. in weight within a few weeks, although I neglected my training in my [track and field] club."

Morris and Eva are proud, vulnerable people, full of wariness. An absence of gush makes their courtship letters a truer preview of married life than most beribboned clutches of old love letters would be. Eva assures him, "You have no need to worry, I will be a good wife to you, & will do everything for you as long as you are good to me." Morris needs to remember that she is "going to give up a lot for you leaving all my family & friends, so this ought to prove something to you." Eva relaxes only the least little bit in the direction of playfulness when he tells her about the kind of apartment they might soon have. She responds: "I am very glad & happy Morris & I do love you very much. I am waiting for the day when you will be telling me that there is too much pepper & not enough salt."

Each of them—even the more demonstrative Morris—is muffled in a cloak of reserve and formality; their manner of expression seems the opposite of our own era's compulsive, therapeutic directness. Both strain to sound correct and self-assured: "I received your parcel this morning & thank you for same," Eva writes to Morris. Prior to her departure for America, he declaims: "I hope you will enjoy yourself very much during your trip on the high seas, and please take good care of yourself and enjoy yourself in the company of your fellow passengers." Eva employs the phrase "your welcome letter," that archaic courtesy letting the earlier sender know that his envelope has been ushered into the house. The effect of such language is less pretentious than touching; the letters are whisk-broomed with the same kind of aspirant self-respect that can be seen in the couple's snapshots, where Morris and Eva and their friends are beautifully spiffed up and turned out.

This regard for convention extends to the letters' closings, where Eva finds subtle opportunities for variation. Her sign-offs are a barometric reading of the state of her feelings for Morris: her "best love & kisses" can be replaced with "kindest regards," and when she's truly angry she will dispatch a letter "From" Eva, or with nothing but a signature. Her emotional precision is such that the first time she calls Morris "Darling," he seizes the word like a victory: "I sure like it, and you can see now how easy it is for you to express your feeling in your letters, whenever you feel like doing so."

How much more reflectively some of our personal dramas played out before electronic mail, let alone text-messaging, which has now made e-mail seem almost sealing-waxed. Morris tells Eva that he will "always write the names of the fastest liners on the envelopes of the letters I send you so that the letters may catch these boats just in time before they sail." Once, just after mailing a letter in which he confides to Eva his worry that a case of mumps may have rendered him sterile, he decides that he's been foolish to alarm her and put their engagement at risk. So the amateur track star races to the post office in Manhattan and manages, in his peculiar-sounding voice, to convince a clerk to let him retrieve the letter. Today, multitasking at her sewing machine, Eva would already have clicked open the fateful e-mail. "If the letter had gone through," wonders the son who decades later edited their correspondence, "perhaps I would have never been born."*

To the question of whether his parents' long married life in America was a success, Lennard J. Davis gives "a qualified 'yes,'" the answer one would expect for two such "stoical people." Davis—who recalls from his early childhood a lot of arguments conducted via "emphatic signing, with its audible hand-slapping, and [his parents'] involuntary verbal expostulations"—grew up to be an English professor "who specialized in eighteenth-century novels" and "read many epistolary romances."

AFTER MEETING IN 1924, Russell Cheney and Francis Otto Matthiessen would spend twenty years together—a period almost equal to the difference in their ages—and just enough time apart to prompt the exchange of three thousand letters.

Cheney was forty-three and Matthiessen only twenty-two when the two began what might have been no more than a shipboard romance: the older man, an increasingly established artist, was on his way from New York to Italy to paint; the younger one would disembark first, in order to take up the second year of a Rhodes scholarship at Oxford, where he planned to write a thesis on Oliver Goldsmith.

In the year following the ocean voyage, except for brief reunions on the Continent, the two of them work out, in near-daily letters, the nature of the permanent relationship they are determined to form. "That there have been other unions like ours is obvious," writes Matthiessen, "but we are unable to draw on their experience. We must create everything for ourselves." Coltish, literary and idealistic, he declares that he and Cheney will have "a marriage that demands nothing and gives everything," even if they won't use that heterosexual term for the union. "Feller, my own dear feller, we have found the key to life, haven't we?"

*Davis's most recent book, *Go Ask Your Father* (2009), recounts his DNA-based quest to determine whether Morris was indeed his biological father.

Matthiessen tells Cheney that he is trying to make himself "worthy of your love," a process that includes struggling to keep sex a pure thing between just the two of them. Courting temptation in order to resist it, he takes a late-afternoon stroll by Marble Arch ("The place in London most flagrant") and reports the results: "Of course I could have stopped in that gesturing crowd. I could have drunk in a lot of luscious slime through my eyes. But who would want to when he can throw back his shoulders, and walk into the sunset, and be at peace with his soul and you?" Cheney, also prone to lust (and to renunciations even more sweeping and unsustainable), gently urges the younger man "to live and stop watching yourself live."

Eager for Cheney's protection and tutelage in the ways of the world and the heart, Matthiessen already has his own serious vocation for teaching, a calling that, coupled with the books he would produce about classic American writers, will make him a star professor at Harvard. His view of literature is forthrightly Arnoldian; what's inside a novel or poem remains without value "unless it can enrich a man's life." The young critic's political engagement follows logically from this, and it proves serious: we see him voting for the New Deal (until something more plausibly radical can come along) and rallying support for a Cambridge bookseller who's been threatened with the workhouse after selling *Lady Chatterley's Lover*.

But the life of action can take place only during hurried breaks from the academic assembly line of lectures and papers and conferences and committees to which Matthiessen is lashed: "This morning I was sent a senior who is working in the eighteenth century and wants to write his dissertation on Beattie (My God! I couldn't even remember who Beattie was . . .)." Even before he becomes the head tutor in one of Harvard's undergraduate houses, Matthiessen wonders to Cheney if he isn't letting himself "be spread as thin as shellac." Repeated term after term, his routine is "nerve-wracking, alternately very interesting and exhaustingly futile." For all Matthiessen's desire to enliven academic writing and enlarge the audience for it, he can never quite shake his sense that scholarship may be smothering the life of the very literature it's supposed to clarify: "with such sand slowly piling up how long is it going to be before the house is entirely covered?"

Though far more disciplined than Cheney, whom he scolds for squandering time away from painting, Matthiessen still knows that the older man he loves is the one engaged not in the business of mere explication but in actually creating something. Within months of their first meeting, Cheney had reflected that, thanks to Matthiessen's enlivening presence, "[t]he black hateful veil between myself and my work is torn." Six years later, finishing the portrait of a gas-station owner in Santa Fe, he speaks of another breakthrough, one that erases any remaining separation between himself and his work: "the painting of that picture was as sudden as a flashlight explosion. No consideration, no careful preparation, and God damn it, it lives and breathes and this studio is a different place because it is here." In fact, he tells Matthiessen, he has "crossed the border line into being *me*."

The very nature of criticism keeps the younger man from ever experiencing such transport. His books can admirably illuminate the works of others, but they cannot glow from within, and the yearning for it to be otherwise seems visible in the style of his letters. Compared to Cheney, he is the more self-conscious performer, wishing to appear clever ("[my] trick little mind") and inclined to self-reference in the third person.

Like literary criticism, love letters are a form of writing that can never quite compete with the real thing—the flesh-and-blood presence of the beloved. But even so, in their long correspondence Cheney and Matthiessen succeed in making themselves remarkably available to each other. Early in the relationship, Matthiessen claims to "keep going entirely on the anticipation of [Cheney's] letters"; all he has to do is "tear the envelope and Oxford and the world fall away." A letter from Cheney converts the older man's "evening alone with Beethoven" into a still-living hour into which Matthiessen can now step. The letters, Matthiessen marvels, "let me live your whole life with you," a phenomenon that Cheney, thousands of miles away, assures him is mutual: "I live with you all the time."

When in 1929, Matthiessen holds Cheney's letter to his cheek, "letting the full sense of you flood over me," he probably doesn't realize that he is making a gesture learned from Cheney himself, who five years before had written of the exquisite frustration involved in receiving one of Matthiessen's letters

> just as my friend Henry Poor came to take me out for all day. I couldn't read it till I stole the time to do so down in the Museum. Couldn't read the letter, but there it was in my pocket, and I'd slip my hand in and hold it, and a couple of times I'd hold it against my cheek, the sense of being with you strong.

Even during the Second World War, when Matthiessen is in Massachusetts and Cheney away in the Southwest, they will connect themselves by listening to the same live radio concert: "Mahler has just finished—very rich and full, wasn't it?" writes Cheney on a Sunday in November 1944.

What they are up against, socially and psychologically, is never far from the page. At the start of their partnership in 1924, the very young Matthiessen pronounces the two of them "beyond society. We've said thank you very much, and stepped outside and closed the door." But he can never long stop worrying about what might be getting said back in that room he's vacated. Six years later, in the thick of his Harvard success and responsibilities, he writes: "My sex bothers me, feller, sometimes when it makes me aware of the falseness of my position in the world. And consciousness of that falseness seems to sap my confidence of power. Have I any right in a community that would so utterly disapprove of me if it knew the facts?" When the university's professor of public speaking comments on his "blurred and soft" enunciation, Matthiessen wonders: "Am I just like any fairy?"

Cheney absorbs similar hurts even in the bohemia of Santa Fe. "I hate like poison to write it to you," he tells Matthiessen around Christmas 1929: "A telegram to [Phelps Putnam] was on the table when I got up containing the words: 'our best to Cheney and his little boys' signed Hester and Larry . . . I wrote 'inexcusable' across it and am sending it back to Larry. At least I leave it here on the table [for] Put to mail if he thinks best. It plain broke me—such indecency."

In the long run, alcoholism did the worst damage to Cheney and his relationship with Matthiessen, who observed the affliction with a mixture of perplexity and anger. In April 1942, when Cheney is in a sanatorium, the younger man writes: "I don't think that I goad you into drinking but once you're started I'm sure that my intensity doesn't help matters any. I wish that I could learn not to be so torn to pieces by your deceptions, which, though ugly, are only symptoms of your by then desperate state." For his part, Cheney is contrite, resolute and naïvely optimistic about the possibility of change. But he never conquers his condition, and less than a year before his death in 1945 is writing in a manner that seems already posthumous: "don't worry about me. [Dr.] Mera will fix me OK in about four days. I will look out. Weedsie, you have the most beautiful loyalty the world has known. You are a very lovely character, and you have had the entire love of another feller."

Matthiessen may have been mystified by Cheney's binges, but he was no stranger to his own kind of blackness, a severe recurring depression. His occasional sense of life's pointlessness ("God how I want to put my head in your lap," he writes Cheney) could sometimes be alleviated by working even harder than usual, but he was still left to wonder whether his own "bright scrutiny, the self-knowledge which I have believed to be my sureness in making my life an integrated one" hasn't "left nine-tenths of the iceberg hidden."

In late 1938, having become suicidal, he receives treatment in Massachusetts at McLean Hospital, the site of so much Brahmin literary misery. Determined to "find my way back to the light," he receives a guilty letter that Cheney writes from their house in Maine: "I fight my own devil who whispers I have drained too much life from you by my constant demand lately for help and backing." The reference is to a terrible bender Cheney went on after the great hurricane of that year, an episode that left him wanting to die and left Matthiessen confronting the possibility that he would. In a long journal-letter written at McLean, Matthiessen reflects: "Having built my life so simply and wholly with Russell's, having had my eyes opened by him to so much beauty, my heart filled by such richness, my pulse beating steadily in time with his in intimate daily companionship, I am shocked at the thought of life without him. How would it be possible? How go on from day to day?" He has become, he realizes, his own hostage to fortune: "When you give yourself entirely to love, you cannot demand that it last forever. For then fear intrudes and there I am."

During this breakdown, Matthiessen's "death wish" assumes the form of "agonizingly vivid images of jumping out of a window"—the fate he would actually inflict upon himself, from the twelfth floor of Boston's Manger Hotel, in 1950, five years after Cheney's death. However terrible this end, readers of the love letters Matthiessen wrote and received may be drawn to see it as the high price life demanded for fulfilling the hope he had expressed, as a shining certainty, to his new love a quarter century before: "You'll give me balance, a touch with life. And instead of being an energetic accurate little machine, why I may be a personality."

CHAPTER SIX *Spirit*

Jesus has a very special love for you. As for me, the silence and the emptiness is so great that I look and do not see, listen and do not hear.

Mother Teresa, letter to
Rev. Michael Van Der Peet, 1979

THE WRITER OF A BOOK such as this finds himself grasping at synonyms for the main subject—whatever will let him avoid the sentence-after-sentence repetition of "letters." What's available, alas, seems pretty musty and artificial-sounding. One might get away with "missive" a couple of times in the chapter on love letters, but the word looks awfully silly anywhere else. "Epistle" is another creaky, thesaurus choice—except perhaps here, at the start of a chapter about the letters of priests and philosophers and other seekers after life's essential spirit.

"Epistle" remains the agreed-upon term for the open letters—apostolic spreadings of good news and chastisement and doctrinal elaboration—addressed to the early Christian church's far-flung potential converts. Saint Paul is the New Testament's most prolific letter writer, and his Epistle to the Romans perhaps the central explanation of his new faith's demands. This momentous communication really had two initial audiences, as Thomas Bokenkotter explains in his *Concise History of the Catholic Church;* it was "intended for Jerusalem as much as for Rome," in the hope that it would "clear up any remaining doubts the Jewish Christians still entertained" about the Gospel's new precedence over all previous Law.

The epistle begins, more or less, as a thank-you letter, expressing gratitude to the Romans for their remarkable ongoing conversion. But it doesn't take many short chapters for Paul to hit his stern or-else stride. The choice for waverers, he makes plain, is between joy and death: "Behold therefore the goodness and severity of God: on them which fell, severity; but toward thee, goodness, if thou continue in his goodness: otherwise thou also shalt be cut off" (11:22). The apostle's favorite technique is to harrow his new flock with rhetorical questions—"What shall we say then? Shall we continue in sin, that grace may abound?"(6:1)—and to say "God forbid" when the temptation for his audience may be to answer yes.

But the weak in spirit can take comfort from the autobiographical shout that splits the epistle in two: "O wretched man that I am! who shall deliver me from the body of this death?" (7:24) cries Paul—a daunting admission of need from someone who's been vouchsafed visions on a road to Damascus that the recipients of his epistle will never get to travel themselves.

Thirteen centuries later, Ibn Abbad of Ronda would be trying, through his *Letters on the Sufi Path*, not to get a spiritual movement off the ground so much as to keep the factions of an existing one united in the celestial air. The advice he writes to his followers is marked by, more than anything else, a calm, soothing empathy: "In short, you are a man with faults," he tells one correspondent. Well, so is Ibn Abbad. It is actually a gift to be disgusted with one's spiritual condition and sins, he argues; what else provides the opportunity to repent?

The high decibels of Pauline epistle are largely absent from Ibn Abbad's letters. (In fact, after laying out one complicated piece of theology, he charmingly confesses, "I am not swayed by my own line of argument.") But the two proselytizers have in common a strong belief that while the spirit gives life, the letter—i.e., the law—killeth. The importance of mystic truth over formal learning is perhaps Ibn Abbad's principal message. He himself may move from topic to topic, but he urges his listeners not to wear themselves out with spiritual searching: "If, therefore, what you seek is already found and present to you, why do you look beyond Him and why do you search for mediation from other than Him?" Ibn

Abbad is happy for his letters of individual counsel to be seen and debated by others, no matter if they earn the scorn of "Zayd or 'Amr"—individuals his translator identifies as the Arabic equivalents of "every Tom, Dick, and Harry."

Even for this comforting Moroccan mystic, urging the seeker to look for what's already in sight, the *journey*, the needy man's self-chosen setting out on foot, remains, as it does perhaps in all the creeds of the world, the central metaphor for spiritual growth. The religious epistle probably has its closest genre-cousin in the travel letter; on occasion, even today, the two will combine into one. The director of the Western Buddhist Order, the former Dennis Lingwood, who became the monk Sangharakshita following his World War II service with the British army in India, has for years stayed in touch with his disciples ("Dear Dharmacharis and Dharmacharinis") through open letters, keeping them posted (as we still say) about his activities and whereabouts, sometimes in rather numbing travel-diary detail: "we had a late meal at Hockneys, followed by a quiet browse in the Centre bookshop." As the leader of an established sect—neither the upstart Church of Paul nor the troubled movement of the Sufis—Sangharakshita can often make his trip reports sound like filings by a UN secretary-general ("In the course of the last three-and-a-half months we have visited eight FWBO centres in four countries"), but even if the author seems more occupied by the bureaucratic than the beatific, there are still the occasional self-examinations that get made and then offered as strength for others' journeys: "Was thought indeed dependent on physical energy, and if so to what extent?" These speculations, ready for mass spiritual mailing, can be prompted by simple personal discoveries, such as Sangharakshita's late-in-life one that, Buddhist contemplative though he may be, he is suffering from high blood pressure—perhaps exacerbated by stress.

IN NOVEMBER 1833, a year after resigning as a pastor of the Second Church of Boston, thirty-year-old Ralph Waldo Emerson first mounted a public lecture platform, secular wooden space that he would come to regard as the "new pulpit" of New England. Emerson spent most of his life preoccupied with what he called, in a letter to his aunt Mary Moody Emerson, the "stone walls of incommunicability [that] exist between mind & mind," but in shifting back and forth from the public hall to the private letter, he occasionally had trouble adjusting the tenor and amplification of his own utterance: "I really did not mean when you asked me for a letter to write a homily," he apologizes to Harrison Gray Otis Blake, one of the Harvard students who asked him to give the Divinity School address, in August of 1839.

Letter writing appears often enough as a subject in Emerson's letters to give the reader a strong feeling of their moment of composition, whether it occurs on the high seas ("Forgive these ricketty faltering lines of mine; they do not come of infirm faith or love, but of the quivering ship"), or in a parlor, when Emerson finds himself distracted by others' chatter: "forgive me this gossiping letter—I had company in the room so you must fill out its elliptical logic."

His mother had urged her young sons to write one another "improving" letters, filled with what they'd gleaned from their reading, but as he matured Emerson saw far richer opportunity in the genre than the creation of yet another commonplace book. He would tell his own daughter to think of a letter as "a kind of picture of a voice," and would complain to Margaret Fuller about how the production of our most pleasurable correspondence tends to be postponed for those letters "that, like duns, do threaten & chide to be answered." One can sense him prolonging epistolary delight when he carries around, instead of mailing, an Italian travel letter he's been writing for his Aunt Mary: "I began this letter at Rome, I am finishing it at Florence close by the tombs of Galileo, of Michel Angelo, of Machiavel & the empty urn of Dante. My letter sheet has got sadly soiled & so I give the history of its places."

Despite his mother's premium on seriousness, the young Emerson's letters to his brothers could be quite playful and entertaining. And in later years, albeit with a certain effort, he could still put an amusing show onto the page. He probably never wrote a funnier paragraph than the one he sent to Charles Anderson Dana in 1843 about the Transcendentalists' short-lived magazine, *The Dial:*

> It has coaxed & wheedled all men & women for contributions: it has sucked & pumped their brains, pilfered their portfolios, peeked into their journals, published their letters, and what it got, it has mutilated, interpolated, & misprinted, and never so much as said, Thank you, or Pardon me; on the contrary, a favourite method has been to extract by importunity a month's labor from its victim, & when it was done, send it back or suppress it as not fit for our purpose.

These lines have a calculated charm, but Emerson's egotism (charged against him by many, including his second wife) usually keeps him from spreading charm's more basic mischief. When in 1840, he decides against joining Brook Farm, he writes to its founder George Ripley that "the Community is not good for me," and that he must not burden it with "the task of my emancipation"—as if that had been the utopian commune's raison d'être.

The all-for-one-and-one-for-one attitude that's detectable between the lines of his long and polite letter to Ripley surfaces elsewhere, sometimes with a great self-loving clang. What, finally, are we to make of a shipboard communication to his brother William in which Emerson claims to wonder how people

> have borne with me so long—, and the oddity & ridicule of it all, is,—given me a literary reputation too, which I make dangerous drafts upon, every day I live. The will o' the wisp, the light invisible except in certain angles, & in all but impossible circumstances, seems to me how often the type & symbol of us all. We cannot overestimate or underestimate these strange goodfor-nothing immortal men that we are.

Does all this self-deprecating, oxymoronic, philosophical flummery really *mean* much? It's certainly less revealing than a peculiar train of thought that Emerson sends toward Margaret Fuller in a letter written during the summer of 1841:

> Friends are luxuries, are they not? things that honest poor people can do without but indispensable as serenades & ice to all fanciful persons. Thus the other night I found myself wishing to die because I had friends,—which sounds very like nonsense but was a veritable reverie very pleasant to entertain.

Does he wish to die from guilt over having the friends an honest, *un*fanciful person doesn't require? But if that's the case, why would such a reverie be "very pleasant to entertain"? One can't help but believe that the reverie's real pleasure is the chance it gives Emerson to imagine his own funeral, at which he can be serenaded by the eulogies of those delightful friends.

He writes with great force and feeling after the deaths of his first wife and son ("fled out of my arms like a dream"). But in less extreme circumstances he is, by his own admission, "negligent of professing love." When Margaret Fuller and the poet Caroline Sturgis accuse him of too much coldness and caution, he overcompensates with ardent pledges of friendship and a promise that he "shall never go quite back to my old arctic habits." Two months later, however, he confesses the likelihood of relapse: "tell me that I am cold or unkind, and in my most flowing state I become a cake of ice."

Emerson's admiration of Carlyle surpasses what he feels for all others, and yet the buoyant letters he sends from Concord to London float along on a certain obliviousness as well as intellectual ardor. Emerson brags about his own independent income two paragraphs before complimenting Carlyle's honorable poverty. (One thing he never transcends is the bottom line: Emerson keeps after his brother William about repaying a loan, and says he would rather have his lectures abused than transcribed, since the latter fate would cut down the size of his next audience.) Well-enough traveled himself, he tends to mock others when they take to the road; and yet when he's the one abroad, he can be quite blind to the sights en route. Passing the coast of Ireland in October 1847, he sees only "a country as well cultivated & plentiful as Brookline & Brighton"—this a week before deciding that Carlyle and his unhappy wife Jane "live on beautiful terms."

He ages with surprising grace, inspiring a reader, when he's nearly seventy, with the stock-taking he does after a bad house fire: "this late calamity, however rude and devastating, soon began to look more wonderful in its salvages than in its ruins." Age shortens his letters, but only to make keener their depiction of age's depredations: it has "tied my tongue & hid my memory."

One admires him for not sinking into the "velvet life" he believes Goethe to have indulged in. And yet, having inveighed against writing "luxuriously" as well as living that way, he's unable to feel the wacky plush in some of his own spiritual sentences through which he moves "God-ward, striving to keep so true a sphericity as to receive the due ray from every point of the concave heaven." By famously pronouncing a foolish consistency to be the hobgoblin of little minds, he fashioned for himself the biggest loophole any philosopher ever created, one that could lasso the whole earth. Is ours a "little coloured world," he wonders in his correspondence, or a "sickening planet"?

He declares this place we live to be merely "the apparent the partial," but it's hard to see Emerson transcending Nature when he's so busy running it: "what is [Nature] but the circumference of which I am the centre, the outside of my inside, object whereof I am subject?" He is using these last two terms in their grammatical, not monarchical, senses: the subject governs the object.

"My creed is very simple," he writes in 1841; "that Goodness is the only Reality." Are sentiments such as this the reason why, like Melville, we resist him? Or do we resist because, just after calling Reason "the highest faculty of the soul—what we mean often by the soul itself," Emerson will go on to say, without telling us what the pronoun "it" even stands for, that "it never *reasons*, never proves, it simply perceives; it is vision." From such a formulation we want nothing so much as the chance to reason our way back toward the hard and plain and clear. And yet, Emerson's most provocative idea about God has to do with the Supreme Being's own possible inarticulacy: "Does the Power labour, as men do, with the impossibility of perfect explication, that always the hurt is of one kind & the compensation of another?"

In carrying out what he called the "gravest acts" of his life, Emerson always preferred to write instead of speak, certain that what a man puts to paper gives a more authentic idea of him than his conversation can. His own letters, as he feared, do turn into homilies, and for succumbing to that occupational hazard of the preacher and sage he's easily enough forgiven. But still, after too many pages of yearning and abstraction and sky-high-mindedness, what relief a reader takes from the concrete glimpse that Emerson gives to Thoreau, in June 1843, of some ordinary road-builders: "The town is full of Irish & the woods of engineers with theodolite & red flag singing out their feet & inches to each other from station to station"—men making the hard human journey not in one oversoul'd leap, but step by halting step.

"MAIL IS VERY EVENTFUL TO ME," Flannery O'Connor wrote a college friend in 1951. The novelist answered letters "at once and at length," but a collection of her correspondence, published in 1979, fifteen years after her death at thirty-nine, reminds one of the slowness with which a writer's editorial life was conducted before the fax and e-mail—or even, in O'Connor's case until 1956, the telephone. More important, though, it proves to a reader how natural letter writing—with its opportunities to question, affirm and exhort—is to any spiritual journey, even one conducted along a much more straight-and-narrow path than Emerson's.

Literary figures come and go in O'Connor's letters, but mostly it's just "Me & Maw"—O'Connor and her widowed mother, Regina—on the farm in Milledgeville, Georgia, where Flannery, throughout her thirties, raises peacocks and writes her books while fighting off lupus and the deterioration of her bones. The local farmworkers provide the sort of daily dramas and epistolary material that servants do in the letters of Virginia Woolf: "Louise recently stuck an icepick in Shot," O'Connor reports in 1961, "but otherwise we go on our peaceful way around here." The sightseeing opportunities for her visiting French translator include "the local monuments, the reformatory, and the insane asylum," along with, over in Eatonton, the home of Uncle Remus. O'Connor's own room is such a security-inducing clutter of books that any enforced tidying by her mother makes her feel that she is "being sawed in two without ether." Her sincere belief that "Routine is a condition of survival" was surely a blessing to her life as an invalid; her single visit to Europe includes a trip to Lourdes, a place so crowded and dirty the real miracle "is that the place don't bring on epidemics."

She views her illness with a detached bravery that the reader of her letters comes to understand as a manifestation of grace. She explains her ACTH injections to the playwright Maryat Lee in 1958: "I owe my existence and cheerful countenance to the pituitary glands of thousands of pigs butchered daily in Chicago Illinois at the Armour packing plant. If pigs wore garments I wouldn't be worthy to kiss the hems of them." The crutches she requires are her "flying buttresses," and since crossing the room on her "own four legs" requires "a major decision" every time it's done, she ends up living as painstakingly as she writes. After seven years' work on her novel *The Violent Bear It Away*, she has "to begin thinking of the next one—one damn book after another."

A reader expecting self-pity is upended, in letter after letter, by two varieties of humor—the cornpone lingo and persona she puts on for correspondents like Maryat Lee and Sally Fitzgerald (eventually the letters' editor) and, sometimes in the same paragraph, examples of her own forbearing sophistication in front of Maw and the neighbors:

> Regina is getting very literary. "Who is this Kafka?" she says. "People ask me." A German Jew, I says, I think. He wrote a book about a man that turns into a roach. "Well, I can't tell people *that*," she says.

O'Connor's crustiness ("I divide people into two classes: the Irksome and the Non-Irksome") is only a comic amplification of her clear-mindedness and integrity. Letter writing allows her to be herself, only more so. "In person I lack command," she declares; but she can manage it "through the mail."

Her grotesque fictions invite wild misapprehension and a "lunatic fringe" of reader correspondence, some of which she cherishes. (In 1955, *A Good Man Is Hard to Find* provokes much mail "from gentlemen who have got no farther than the title.") But her work also attracts an awed response from serious young writers; *The Habit of Being*, as Sally Fitzgerald titled the volume of letters, contains O'Connor's thoughtful, lengthy replies to novelists and poets like John Hawkes and Alfred Corn. If her spelling is sometimes doubtful, her paragraphing demonstrates a mind as organized as it is definite. Typing strikes her as more personal than handwriting since one uses "ten fingers to work a typewriter and only three to push a pen"; what emerges from her machine is the most vital collection of letters produced by any American writer during the mid-twentieth century.

Her gift—or grace—is for making an imaginative virtue of necessity. Having spent a few years up North in the "delusion" that her "writing depended on [her] staying away," she returned South to the certainty that it "is great to be at home in a region, even this one." If, as she says, "Experience is the greatest deterrent to fiction," there are worse fates than not being able to get out much.

Her inventions run to the gaudy and distorted because that "is the only way to make people see," but critics usually fail to notice the deadly forest of faithlessness for all its blasted trees: "when I see these stories described as horror stories I am always amused because the reviewer always has hold of the wrong horror." And yet she seems inclined toward the twisted as much from personal taste as for its potential revelations: "Did you see the picture of Roy Rogers's horse attending a church service in Pasadena?" she asks Sally and Robert Fitzgerald in 1952. "I forgot whether his name was Tex or Trigger but he was dressed fit to kill and looked like he was having a good time."

Professors who turn her books into schematic exercises in symbol and message are her special cross, and she bears it unwillingly. When she doesn't know the teacher who's written her for an answer key, her response will be harsh. When she does, it will be merely exasperated: "My Lord, Billy," she writes William Sessions in September 1960, "recover your simplicity. You ain't in Manhattan. Don't inflict that stuff on the poor students there; they deserve better." A writer who takes so long to produce her books cannot afford to be anything but practical, sometimes even in her choice of reading: "I keep clear of Faulkner so my own little boat won't get swamped." She confines her worry over the death of the novel to the question of "whether the one I'm working on is dead." Opposed to progressive education, to "learning for life" and to the pursuit of happiness (quite different from salvation), she pronounces literary "Theories" to be "worse than the Furies"—and dies a merciful decade before their still-current mutations devoured the academic study of English.

Catholic doctrines are another matter. These are necessities of faith, not delusions of the intellect. They humble the mind into its proper place: once inside the Church, a person's intellect "will cease to be tyrannical." Dogma, she insists, *increases* her vision and freedom to create. To the young writer Shirley Abbott, in 1956:

> It is popular to believe that in order to see clearly one must believe nothing. This may work well enough if you are observing cells under a microscope. It will not work if you are writing fiction. For the fiction writer, to believe nothing is to see nothing. I don't write to bring anybody a message, as you know yourself that this is not the purpose of the novelist; but the message I find in the life I see is a moral message.

She does not want religious mysteries explained and cannot see man being truly free unless Hell continues to exist. O'Connor and John Hawkes conduct an ongoing epistolary argument about their two very different devils. "My Devil," she explains,

> has a name, a history and a definite plan. His name is Lucifer, he's a fallen angel, his sin is pride, and his aim is the destruction of the Divine plan. Now I judge that your Devil is co-equal to God, not his creature; that pride is his virtue, not his sin; and that his aim is not to destroy the Divine plan because there isn't any Divine plan to destroy. My Devil is objective and yours is subjective.

She calls herself a "hillbilly Thomist" and, as early as 1955, has an exact sense of how her faith must drive her work: "I write the way I do because (not though) I am a Catholic. This is a fact and nothing covers it like the bald statement. However, I am a Catholic peculiarly possessed of the modern consciousness, that thing Jung describes as unhistorical, solitary, and guilty. To possess this *within* the Church is to bear a burden." She shows palpable agitation when Robert Lowell and Betty Hester, her most frequent correspondent, leave the Church: "The loss of [faith] is basically a failure of appetite, assisted by sterile intellect." She loves to hate the *Atlanta Journal-Constitution*'s positive-thinking columnist, Dr. Frank Crane, and in 1963, finds John F. Kennedy's somber funeral "a salutary tonic for this back-slapping gum-chewing hiya-kid nation."

Beset with "a stomach full of liberal religion," O'Connor takes every opportunity she has to set straight interested correspondents on the subject of divine intervention. God does not engage in any "continuous miraculous meddling . . . in human affairs." His grace is not sprinkled like fairy dust but obtained through "faith and the sacraments" and over our own great capacities for resistance. O'Connor's literal belief in Purgatory is a personal necessity to someone whose "virtues are as timid as [her] vices." Faith is not meant to be "emotionally satisfying," and self-knowledge is a waste of time unless it leads to salvation.

Her theology is finally as practical as her literary criticism. "Do you know the Hopkins-Bridges correspondence?" she writes William Sessions, the same man she urges to "recover [his] simplicity" in aesthetic matters. "Bridges wrote Hopkins at one point and asked him how he could possibly learn to believe, expecting, I suppose, a metaphysical answer. Hopkins only said, 'Give alms.'" She had doubts about the efficacy of this advice, but she repeated it to others and tried to use her own letters in an ad hoc missionary way. Toward the end, as her death approached, they became occasions for asking instead of answering. "[T]oday in bed I did a day's work," she informs Janet McKane in late June 1964. "This must be the result of my friends' prayers"—spiritual favors she has taken to requesting through the mail.

LET'S TAKE A LOOK AT Hopkins's letters to Robert Bridges, which must have had a special appeal for O'Connor, coming as they did from another writer living in spiritual fervor and literary isolation.

In 1866, John Henry Newman, making sure that the twenty-two-year-old Gerard Manley Hopkins was "acting deliberately," reminded him that he "must come to the church to accept and believe," which is just what Hopkins proceeded to do with disciplined intensity. (He gave his parents the news of his conversion in a letter.) Submitting to the Church and entering its priesthood, Hopkins would eventually choose a very different law and canon to rebel against: the rules and pantheon of English poetry. Having burned his own youthful work and denied himself all verse writing for the half dozen or so years of his novitiate, Hopkins later burst into renewed composition, upending English metrics with an almost Luciferian clatter.

He required a correspondent who was, like himself, vocationally split, and he found one in Dr. Robert Bridges, a young writer pulling a long double shift of medicine and poetry. Their twenty-three-year-long epistolary exchange may be free from the more familiar competitiveness of full-time men of letters, but it is hardly without its strains. Hopkins can never quite get over trying to be Bridges's confessor as well as his critic. Thirteen years into their letter writing, the Jesuit proselytizes his correspondent: "You understand of course that I desire to see you a Catholic or, if not that, a Christian or, if not that, at least a believer in the true God." But Bridges is a tough sell. He upsets Hopkins by implying that the priest's own zeal is somehow temporary and unserious; disgusts him by taking pleasure in another priest's abandonment of his vows; and generally exasperates him with earthbound thinking. "You do not mean by mystery what a Catholic does," Hopkins scolds. "You mean an interesting uncertainty . . . But a Catholic by mystery means an incomprehensible certainty . . . the interest a Catholic feels is, if I may say so, of a far finer kind than yours. Yours turns out to be a curiosity only."

In 1879, lest there be an epistolary breach, Hopkins proposes not compromise but compartments: "Morals and scansion not being in one keeping, we will treat them in separate letters." Unsurprisingly, this separation of church and verse fails: two years later Hopkins is trying to make Bridges a believer by means of Bridges's own poetry: "This poem as well as that sonnet express your belief that the mind is immortal . . . You cannot wisely neglect this world of being to which you imply that you will come. In it or above it is the sovereign spirit of God, to whom you should now at once make your approach with the humblest and most earnest prayers."

When he does confine the subject to versification, there is still nothing gentle about Hopkins's ministry. He is compulsively corrective of Bridges's work—its technical shortcomings, figurative flaws, unconscious imitations. As he giveth ("The *Early Autumn* very beautiful and tender"), so must he taketh away ("but in the octet at all events not perfectly achieved"). He can, very occasionally, contrive wonderful compliments ("If I were not your friend I shd. wish to be the friend of the man that wrote your poems"), but the dominant message is that very little of Bridges ever measures up. Even someone else's positive notice of the poet falls short: "The review in the *St. James's* is pleasing and appreciative, though it might have been stronger."

When speaking of his own work, Hopkins may worry about the cloistered routines that have left him with "so little varied experience" compared to other poets, and he may pick homely metaphors for his own creative process (he has "two sonnets soaking" and another "hot on the anvil"), but none of this really conveys his confidence—perhaps even sinful pride—in the excellence and rightness of his enterprise. By the summer of 1877, when revising "The Wreck of the Deutschland," he has "fixed [his] principles" and wed himself to the sprung rhythm of irregular stresses that will give his poems their unique, torrential sound. As he urges it upon Bridges ("I hope to convert you"), he can make the technique sound more like a political platform or production quota than an aesthetic ("I have consistently carried out my rhyming system"), and he rebuts Bridges's objections in the manner of a commissar: "your criticism is of no use, being only a protest memorialising me against my whole policy and proceedings." What he's doing is not *meant* to be completely clear, he insists; Bridges should "take breath and read it with the ears."

Bridges's breath must sometimes have been taken away by the pugnacity of this unpublished cleric, who finds portions of Tennyson "commonplace and wanting in nobility," and judges the Brownings to be "very fine . . . in their ghastly way." But Hopkins gradually loses hope of seeing his own eccentric poems in print. As the years pass, teaching, clerical duties and poor health confine him to a "coffin of weakness and dejection"; he approaches the end of his short life with more plans than finished productions ("all my world is scaffolding"), worn out, the modern reader of his letters feels, by a grinding vocation that stole him from his real one.

"You are my public," he wrote Bridges in 1877. The substitution of a single man for a whole readership in some ways equals the letters' replacement of any face-to-face relationship between the two correspondents. Throughout the long exchange, especially in its early days, Hopkins declines opportunities for the two men to rendezvous in person ("I daresay we may not meet again for years"), even though limits can be put on the number of letters he may receive or send and his superiors have the power to censor incoming and outgoing mail.

Hopkins's unwillingness to address Bridges by his Christian name ("for first it wd. not feel natural to me and secondly it wd. be unnecessary, for your surname is the prettier")—even while he enjoys Bridges's use of *his* first name—gives the reader a sense of the odd, magnetic field of reserve and intimacy over which this correspondence travels. One finds a teasing element on Hopkins's side of it, a flexing of emotional strength that one associates with a lover who's in control: "As for this letter," he explains, "it is to soothe you and stop your mouth; I will write more elsewhen." On December 18, 1881, however, it's Hopkins who pouts: "Bridges, my dear heart, why have you not written?" Perhaps because less than two months before, Hopkins had pronounced a letter he was sending a piece of "charity to wile away your time, for I ought to be at other things than letterwriting: it certainly has wiled away mine." After Bridges takes a bride, a certain awkwardness, bordering on the creepy, encloses itself with one or two of Hopkins's letters. The priest confesses to "a kind of spooniness and delight over married people," and closes with a "goodnight to Mrs. Bridges or (what is more beautiful) to your wife."

Hopkins sometimes lets us see the correspondence's real importance to him through nervous, mock-heroic flourishes. On April 6, 1877, he sends a postcard, like a small herald, to announce the dispatch of a full-length letter "laden to her gunwales with judicious remarks"; four years later he acts surprised to find that his "magic nib has . . . minuetted and gavotted into the syllables of [Bridges's] name," as he writes a letter whose "first movement shall be something of a stately saraband." Even so, one finds him, at least once, ending with "No more now"—that age-old envoi as strange as it is commonplace, by which a letter writer acts as if what he's composing is a dalliance to be resisted, or a bedtime story whose prolongation would be good for neither teller nor listener.

In Hopkins's case, it is only when there is truly to be no more—six weeks before his death, in his last letter to Bridges—that he finally signs off with his Christian name. "Gerard" is the final word he mails his correspondent, who goes on to outlive him by forty years and who, in 1918, publishes Hopkins's poems. The priest's one-man "public"—the doctor he couldn't bring to God—at last secured Hopkins a real audience, and a second kind of afterlife.

IT IS DIFFICULT to imagine an aspiring poet *more* in the literary thick of things than Keats. If creative isolation was Hopkins's condition, the letters of his Romantic predecessor show a crush of collegiality: "Shelley was there"; "Haydon is in Town"; "I have seen a good deal of Wordsworth. Hazlitt is lecturing on Poetry at the Surrey institution—I shall be there next Tuesday"; "I met Mr. Green . . . in conversation with Coleridge—I joined them, after enquiring by a look whether it would be agreeable." Yes, it would be—to us, too. Letters from this scrappy, five-foot-tall versifier still burst out of their envelopes with every sort of vigor and longing, from the careerist to the ethereal.

Keats's professional ambitions never tire a reader, because his pursuit of them usually resembles that of the young man trying to get the girl. In fact, poetry *is* the girl. On a Saturday in March 1819, he declares: "I know not why Poetry and I have been so distant lately—I must make some advances soon or she will cut me entirely."

More often, he's all over her. This aspirant youth, in such a hurry that he nicknames himself "Junkets" (say "John Keats" very fast), will "read and write about eight hours a day" and think about Poetry even longer than that—"so long together that I could not get to sleep at night." At twenty-one, he's swinging for the fences of posterity, banishing doubts as fast as they can arise:

> I have asked myself so often why I should be a Poet more than other Men,—seeing how great a thing it is,—how great things are to be gained by it, what a thing to be in the Mouth of Fame,—that at last the Idea has grown so monstrously beyond my seeming Power of attainment that the other day I nearly consented with myself to drop into a Phaeton. Yet 'tis a disgrace to fail even in a huge attempt, and at this moment I drive the thought from me . . . I intend to whistle all these cogitations into the Sea . . .

Despite critics' attacks on his ornate, upstart productions, he has a brazen confidence that he "shall be among the English Poets after [his] death." His letters seem full of foreknowledge, for himself and for us; all through them one hears signals of the poems that are yet to come: "I never can feel certain of any truth but from a clear perception of its Beauty," Keats writes to his brother and sister-in-law in December 1818, five months before writing "Ode on a Grecian Urn."

Still, the road up Parnassus is an obstacle course. Along with reviewers determined to block passage by a Cockney interloper, there are editors bent on taking too much credit for Keats's own efforts. Add to this the landlady's children, who make too much noise for any poet's concentration, and top it all off with the torment of going to the bank—"to me worse than any thing in Dante." His friends and acquaintances are always quarrelling, and there is never a time when everyone's healthy at once. More often it's nearly the opposite: "Every body is ill." His brother Tom spits blood like a motif, reminding a reader of the tuberculosis that will soon kill two of the three Keats boys, including Junkets, who even so never loses faith that there is "something real" in life, or that he has "that in me which will bear the buffets of the world."

"Real" is a favorite word, one he puts, for example, into a note thanking Benjamin Bailey for an epistolary kindness: "Your tearing, my dear friend, a spiritless and gloomy Letter up to rewrite to me is what I shall never forget—it was to me a real thing." And yet, we would not want the same favor from Keats himself, because his troubles never lie on the page as mere complaints. They're superior grist for his spiritual business here on Earth: "Do you not see how necessary a World of Pain and troubles is to school an Intelligence and make it a Soul?" he writes in 1819, at the age of twenty-three. We live "where the heart must feel and suffer in a thousand diverse ways. Not merely is the Heart a Hornbook . . . it is the text from which the Mind or intelligence sucks its identity."

Keats didn't have to dare himself to eat a peach; he was prepared to bite into life's whole bushel of fruit, rotten apples included. Among the Romantics, the term "gusto" may belong to Hazlitt, but it's Keats who's the quality's real practitioner. He'll get so hungry that "fowls are like Larks"; will rhapsodize on claret for lying in one's stomach "as quiet as it did in the grape"; and resolve to be ever more efficient in feasting on female beauty: "I never intend hereafter to spend any time with Ladies unless they are handsome—you lose time to no purpose." What's wanted is always more; and then more still. It's the same with matters of the spirit. The letter about soul-making describes a process that builds and builds, ever onward and ever upward: "what are circumstances but touchstones of his heart? and what are touchstones but provings of his heart? and what are provings of his heart but fortifiers or alterers of his nature? and what is his altered nature but his Soul?"

Hiking in the Lake District, this thoroughgoing Londoner discovers "an amazing partiality for mountains in the clouds." And yet, "human nature is finer," always, than scenery: "The Sward is richer for the tread of a real, nervous English foot." Ordinary human imperfection—not epic virtues and titanic flaws—constitutes Keats's true sublime. He famously discriminates between a street quarrel ("a thing to be hated") and the energy that goes into it (something "fine" and full of "grace") and makes the compensations of defeat more satisfying than success: "The first thing that strikes me on hearing a Misfortune having befallen another is this—'Well it cannot be helped: he will have the pleasure of trying the resources of his Spirit.'" Keats's own moments of discouragement often seem positively exuberant. No matter how hard circumstances press, the bedsprings of his self are available for falling back on: the harder his fall, the more cheerful their squeak.

However much he may have cried "for a Life of Sensations rather than of Thoughts!" his intellectual appetites were, if anything, more avid than his physical ones. Any of his letters, no matter the recipient, is likely to brave three different themes in the course of a paragraph. For a reader today, their greatest philosophical excitement lies in the writer's movement toward "Negative Capability," his most important aesthetic belief. He describes it in a letter to his brother as the creative condition in force "when a man is capable of being in uncertainties, mysteries, doubts, without any irritable reaching after fact and reason"—a susceptibility to Beauty above all other considerations. The "intensity" man seeks in art is best achieved by a paradoxical passivity, an extreme receptiveness.

Men of real genius, Keats has decided, "have not any individuality, any determined character." His own empathies are both simple and extreme: "if a Sparrow come before my Window I take part in its existence and pick about the Gravel." At any gathering to which he brings his vital personality, "the identity of every one in the room begins to press . . . so that I am in a very little time annihilated—not only among Men; it would be the same in a Nursery of children." This young man so bent on fame achieves his true identity by giving up the one he has.

Keats's ideas about religion are, by his own admission, nothing special. The afterlife he imagines is just one more variety of earthly more-more-more: "we shall enjoy ourselves hereafter by having what we called happiness on Earth repeated in a finer tone." But when he talks of each man being able, mentally, to spin "his own airy Citadel," as a spider spins its web, he speaks powerfully to the spiritualists of a later age. "Minds would leave each other in contrary directions, traverse each other in numberless points, and at last greet each other at the journey's end." Late in 1818, he proposes a telepathic experiment to his brother and sister-in-law in America: "I shall read a passage of Shakespeare every Sunday at ten o'clock—you read one at the same time and we shall be as near each other as blind bodies can be in the same room." He induces them, with a kind of virtual reality, into taking the same walk he likes to take himself: "Then I pass across St. Cross meadows till you come to the most beautifully clear river—now this is only one mile . . . I will spare you the other two till after supper when they would do you more good. You must avoid going the first mile just after dinner."

Almost all of Keats's letters are conscious entertainments, full of humor—which he preferred to wit. He sends up the lyrical conventions of travel writing; turns mock-heroic over the unpaid bills piling up; and passes on the story of "the fattest woman in all Invernesshire who got up this Mountain some few years ago—true she had her servants—but then she had herself." Eager not to try the patience of his audience, he'll apologize for a letter that's too heavy (the recipient being responsible for paying the postage); admit that his epistolary style suffers when he waits too long to reply; and concede the difficulties he causes his correspondents with his changeable, nothing-by-halves personality: "I carry all matters to an extreme," he writes Benjamin Bailey in July of 1818,

> so that when I have any little vexation it grows in five Minutes into a theme for Sophocles—then and in that temper if I write to any friend I have so little self-possession that I give him matter for grieving at the very time perhaps when I am laughing at a Pun. Your last letter made me blush for the pain I had given you—

Keats's own greatest pain comes from Fanny Brawne, described to his brother and sister-in-law, after he first meets her, as "graceful, silly, fashionable and strange." Only eighteen, "she is ignorant—monstrous in her behaviour, flying out in all directions"—which is to say, the sort of mercurial creature guaranteed, when placed against Keats's own quicksilver nature, to produce a romance of wild fluctuations. "Miss Brawne and I have every now and then a chat and a tiff," he tells his brother and sister-in-law two months later. Writing to Fanny herself, this great epistolary philosopher will settle for the dull boilerplate of ecstatic love ("I know not how to express my devotion to so fair a form").

A year into knowing her, Keats attempts withdrawal from Fanny's undependable affections, but five months later he is still riding the whipsaw: "the extasies in which I have pass'd some days and the miseries in their turn, I wonder the more at the Beauty which has kept up the spell so fervently." In May of 1820, still not twenty-five but with his health and money and time running out, he continues to beg for Fanny's "whole heart." The following winter, in Rome, he will be buried, as he instructs a friend, with one of her unopened letters.

WITH ITS LOVE OF fashioning opposites, nature seems to have set down Keats's a century later in a provincial Polish town, in the shy, dark shape of Bruno Schulz. To Keats, melancholy was merely what comes from recognizing the finite, temporary nature of things fabulous ("Ay, in the very temple of Delight / Veil'd Melancholy has her sovran shrine"). To Schulz, melancholy is an omnipotent scourge, not pleasure's price but its absolute denier. If Keats's imagination was sponsored by the world, Schulz's only darts through life's alleys and cracks, forever expecting to be snuffed. And yet, the letters of this discouraged, menaced artist have a poignant Chaplinesque charm. We never tire of Schulz amid his troubles.

Stuck teaching drawing in a local gymnasium, the already middle-aged writer finds himself unable in the mid-1930s to capitalize on his recent literary debut, the critically praised prose fantasies—

a sort of Polish magical realism—of his book *Cinnamon Shops.* "I don't know if I can stand this drudgery much longer," he writes to one editor. In truth, it's worse than that; Schulz's inability to control his students is both comic and nightmarish:

> the violent and desperate measures of intimidation I must resort to in order to keep them in check fill me with disgust. Every day I leave that scene brutalized and soiled inside, filled with distaste for myself and so violently drained of energy that several hours are not enough to restore it.

The schoolmaster-artist hopes for a grant that will give him a respite. He's blissful when he's awarded one; crushed when the stipend runs out. Additionally burdened with family problems (a neurotic sister) and poor health (kidney stones), Schulz also despairs of his on-again, off-again engagement to a troubled and usually absent fiancée, Józefina Szelińska. Still, whatever their difficulties, she "represents my participation in life," he tells one correspondent; "only by her mediation am I a human being and not just a lemur or gnome." And yet, it's in these delighful, miniature incarnations that Schulz, wearing his mournful cap and bells, seems to look up and resize the world for our imaginations.

"I am a reactive creature," he writes to Romana Halpern, one of several artistic women who offer appreciation and aid. His self-diagnosis may shift all the time, but he pinpoints one afflicting constant when he tells "Roma," in August 1937: "What I lack is not so much faith in my own gifts but something more pervasive: trust in life, confident acquiescence in a personal destiny, faith in the ultimate benevolence of existence." Through all his premonitions of doom ("I've left springtime behind for good," he declares in 1934), he goes on writing and sketching, marvelously, knowing that his depression—which, among other symptoms, keeps him from answering letters—has ironic roots in a preoccupation with contentment, one that makes him spend "every other minute testing the balance of satisfaction in exploring the art of happiness. Every other minute I ask myself the question: Do I have the right to be satisfied, is the undertaking 'Schulz' worth carrying on, does it justify further investment?"

In fact, he steadily tries to grow that frail, fabulous enterprise. We find Schulz looking up from letter after letter with those bright lemur-like eyes, making himself ingratiating, clever, winsome—doing what needs to be done to keep his writing career alive: proposing translations of his own work; securing letters of introduction; complaining about the favoritism and fixes involved in literary prize-giving; even soliciting blurbs for the incomprehensible verse of a rich man whose favor he needs. Schulz eventually becomes embarrassed over the abundance of good turns done him by Romana Halpern, and on February 21, 1938, must tell her: "How sweet of you to remember my affairs even while you are in the hospital, to escape from medical care to run an errand I hadn't even asked you to do."

But he keeps her on the job, and it is to Roma that Schulz admits suffering from "the misconception that literary creation can begin only when all difficulties have been cleared away over the entire range of one's life." His own writing life disproves this idea utterly, but he still can't let go of it, or allow Roma the opposite misconception, "that suffering is necessary for creative work. This is a worn old cliché." Schulz tells her she's making a mistake to "overrate" him; her "emotional binge" of artist-worship may provide him flattery that he finds "very pleasant," but he fears "the 'morning after.'"

And yet Schulz himself, in letter after letter, exalts the creative life over the one he's forced to lead each day in Drohobycz: "One must . . . fence off one's inner life, not permit the vermin of ordinary cares to infest it." As with Keats, the goal of his writing seems ultimately less aesthetic than spiritual: "I long for some outside affirmation of the inner world whose existence I postulate. To cling to it by sheer faith alone, to lug it along with me in spite of everything, is a toil and torment of Atlas."

Whether writing to Roma or, as in the sentences just above, to the novelist Tadeusz Breza, Schulz betrays no embarrassment over his abject wants. He believes in something like the opposite of ripeness, positing "immaturity" as the life force, and art as a kind of "regression" into genius. "My ideal goal is to 'mature' into childhood. That would be genuine maturity for you." A reader realizes, from such declarations, that the weird near-gaiety to be sensed in Schulz's letters is not conscious whistling in the dark of circumstance but the laughter of a childhood self that remains alive behind a single, but thickening, wall.

In 1936, during an exchange of open letters with Schulz, the writer Witold Gombrowicz conjures up the figure of a doctor's wife who, he says, has pronounced Schulz "either a sick pervert or a poseur." Like Virginia Woolf's Mrs. Brown or J. D. Salinger's Fat Lady, this bourgeois matron becomes the avatar of a mighty challenge. Gombrowicz dares Schulz to abandon his more rarefied imaginings and "Get back down here on earth!" to grapple with this real and unpleasant woman.

But Schulz won't take the fleshy bait: "Oh no, dear Witold, I have liberated myself from this sort of thing." He is bent on transcending sexuality (however hard he finds it "to resist the charm of [the woman's] legs"), as well as everything "cynical and amoral, irrational and mocking." With this doctor's wife, he adds, Gombrowicz may be pretending to "defend vitality and biology, against abstraction, against our detachment from life," but as a fellow artist, whether he knows it or not, Gombrowicz is really, like Schulz, chasing something newer and better: "The avant-garde of biology is thought, experiment, creative discovery. We, in fact, are this belligerent biology, this conquering biology; we are the truly vital."

Schulz's reply, published in the journal *Studio*, was probably no more self-consciously composed than many of his private letters, which he was known to put through outlines and drafts. Indeed, *Cinnamon Shops*, his masterpiece, grew directly out of his well-wrought letters to Debora Vogel, a writer friend and philosopher. As Jerzy Ficowski, Schulz's posthumous editor, explains: "piece by piece, the brilliant stories which would become the stuff of Schulz's first book [were] couched in extensive postscripts which gradually took over the whole substance of the letters." Publication saved both the *Cinnamon Shops* stories and the exchange with Gombrowicz; most of the rest of Schulz's large correspondence was destroyed during the Holocaust. He himself was killed—shot in the head by an SS officer—in 1942.

Four years earlier, he had composed for Romana Halpern one of the most vivid assessments ever made of the imaginative challenge posed by letter writing:

> Spatial remoteness causes the written word to seem too weak, ineffective, powerless to hit its target. And the target itself, the person who gets our words at the end of that road through space, seems only half-real, of uncertain existence, like a character in a novel. . . . One probably shouldn't say such things but fight instead that weakness of imagination which refuses to believe in the reality of remote objects.

Any reader who finishes Schulz's surviving correspondence—a slender single volume—ends up applying this kind of imaginative effort to the rest of it, all the letters that were set ablaze, somewhere beyond the pale.

WITHIN A FEW YEARS of Schulz's murder, Poland had found a new, different gruesomeness in Communist subjugation. The poet and diplomat Czeslaw Milosz took flight from it in 1951, two years before publishing *The Captive Mind*, a book that would find an enthusiastic reader in the American Trappist monk and author Thomas Merton. In 1958, Merton began a ten-year-long correspondence with the Polish exile by sending him a sort of spiritual fan letter: "It is an important book," he wrote of *The Captive Mind*, "which makes most other books on the present state of man look abjectly foolish."

The letters that Merton continues sending to the self-exiled Milosz, first in France and later in California, often make it hard for a reader to remember that their writer is in his forties and early fifties and has already been settled for two decades at the Abbey of Gethsemani in Kentucky. Merton may be established as a literary figure (he offers Milosz help securing an agent), but it is Milosz who sets the moral and intellectual pace of their exchange, into which the monk seems gratefully to relax, a needy and agreeable postulant.

Merton admits to naïveté about Communism and sees what some members of a later generation would sarcastically call "moral equivalence" between the Cold War's superpowers. Looking for "a third position," he predicts to Milosz that "One day we are going to wake up and find America and Russia in bed together (forgive the unmonastic image) and realize that they were happily married all along." Milosz has to warn the priest about "placing both camps on the same level," let alone in a connubial embrace. Milosz himself is squeezed inside the bipolar world: "For *The Captive Mind* I have been denounced to the police: 'not enough' anti-communist and probably an agent; while [giving off a] hideous smell in Paris literary circles: a bourgeois, he writes against what is sacrosanct." Even so, he can remind Merton that "of the two [camps] not the West is pushing and probing for new ways of expansion." He can also warn him against peace movements that create only an "*exasperation* which pushes many people to the right."

A chastened Merton tends, almost always, to concede the point, though if he thinks, even for a moment, that he hears Milosz moving into an early sixties groove, he fairly clamors his encouragement. When the Polish poet worries briefly over the complacency that leaves America "grazing like a cow," Merton cooks up an over-the-top metaphor of America as "this continual milkshake"—or, better yet—this "Calypso's Island where no one is ever tempted to think and where one just eats and exists and supports the supermarket and the drug store and General Motors and the TV." It's easy for a reader to see Milosz, only four years older than his correspondent, as a sort of elderly bishop, offering the overeager novice a sympathetic but cautionary pat on the head.

And yet, their minds do meet, often provocatively, on the treacherous ground of politics and religion. When Milosz explains the unexpected spiritual benefit of Poland's experience with Communism, which "made [the] inner life of human beings more intense" there, it's a paradox that can be appreciated by Merton, who recognizes sinners as "the ones who attract to themselves the infinite compassion of God." Milosz confides that the writings of Simone Weil helped him through the worst of the despair that produced *The Captive Mind*, and admits to a belief in the Resurrection, if not the soul's immortality. He settles for calling himself "crypto-religious," the pull of the Church being still strong enough that he has trouble finding the right sign-off for his letters to Merton: "there is this respect for the priest's robe," he explains, so "let me say with brotherly love . . ."

The two men's connection is made easier by Merton's own feeling that he is, even within the walls of the Church, a "complete lone wolf" as a Catholic. "I have *not* coped with the basic theological questions," he writes in 1961. "It only looks that way." The censors of his order give him trouble, and his religious searching will eventually send him, at the end of his abbreviated life (he died at fifty-three), toward Buddhism and the Far East.

But Milosz is the more reluctant customer when it comes to any sort of ontological comfort. He explains his own ill-suitedness to Merton's Trappist silence and solitude by saying: "I cannot afford too great interiorisation and have to keep myself on the level defined by *The Cloud of Unknowing* as contemplation of one's own wretchedness." He complains, too, that Merton does "not pay much attention to torture and suffering in Nature"—provoking a rare rebuttal from the monk: "Nature and I are very good friends," Merton writes, "and console one another for the stupidity and the infamy of the human race and its civilization . . . Spiders have always eaten flies and I can shut it out of my consciousness without guilt."

In fact, Milosz agrees with Merton about the ultimate separateness of nature and mankind but draws a very different—and finally more optimistic—conclusion from the split. He may "have always felt the burden of blind and cruel necessity, of mechanism, in Nature, in my body, in my psychology," and yet, "History, as a purely human domain, alien to Nature, meant liberation." What to Merton seems a friend is, to Milosz, a chrysalis—one that humans can transcend together, if not individually.

The Merton/Milosz letters are the kind of considered exchange to which e-mail is now doing such chatty, hurry-up violence. In the manner of Hopkins and Bridges, the men write each other for more than two years before using first names in their salutations. Both have a sense that the correspondence is sufficiently important to be conducted only at thoughtful intervals. Because each takes pains, in Milosz's phrase, to "avoid bavardage," their published letters (*Striving Towards Being*) take up fewer than two hundred pages. When Merton apologizes for "rambling," he's actually done nothing of the kind; the apology is just a tic of epistolary politeness, as old as Pliny the Younger, and forever peculiar, since people almost never apologize for the real rambling that they do in conversation.

A couple of years into the correspondence, each writer admits to the other that he would enjoy meeting face to face. That ends up happening just twice, once at the abbey and once in Berkeley, and it is one measure of the letters' richness that their production falls away to nearly nothing, as if by some literal disenchantment, after the word turns flesh. The sacred or at least rarefied nature of their correspondence becomes ever so slightly profane. Whereas in 1959, Milosz would pose the question "perhaps Prometheus was not an ancestor of modern revolutionaries, perhaps he was in revolt against a heavy, false God, but not against God the Father?"—Merton will eventually just ask, "What is new with you?"

History was slowly carrying Milosz, and Poland, to something better. But during 1968, what would be the last year of Merton's life, the monk seems increasingly sad, caught, a bit like Milosz in the early fifties, in a spiritual-political vise, in his case between "puerile optimism about the 'secular city'" and the displeasure of conservative local Catholics "burning my books because I am opposed to the Viet Nam war." Though by now a theological celebrity, one whose published writings, including volumes of letters, are ready to be consumed as good-news epistles by thousands of readers, Merton still feels the need for private, epistolary devotion to Milosz's obvious moral authority. He last writes him on November 21, 1968, from Darjeeling, amidst India's "monasteries, temples, lamas, paintings, jungles." He is weeks away from the accident that will kill him, unaware, as Paul wrote the Romans, that "The night is far spent, the day is at hand . . ."

CHAPTER SEVEN *Confession*

Sam's a thirsty lad and he won't let me stop killing until he gets his fill of blood.

David Berkowitz, "Son of Sam," letter to columnist Jimmy Breslin, 1977

IN A LETTER WRITTEN to her new spiritual advisor, Father John Hamilton Cowper Johnson, near the beginning of Lent in 1951, Rose Macaulay, the English novelist, worried about "the time I must cost you, and the trouble, and the stamps." By then nearing seventy, the author of *They Were Defeated* (1932) was still trying to recover from two blows she had been dealt a decade before: the death of her married lover, Gerald O'Donovan, and the destruction, during the Blitz, of all the possessions in her London flat: "I am bookless, homeless, sans everything but my eyes to weep with," she had written a younger friend in May 1941.

The particular loss of O'Donovan's letters stimulated Macaulay, not long after the bombing, to write a short story in which the only remaining token of the heroine's lover is a "charred corner of paper," less than one page of a single, quarrelsome letter quite uncharacteristic of the couple's long and peaceful, if illicit, devotion: "all that was legible of it was a line and a half of close small writing, the o's and the a's open at the top. It had been written twenty-one years ago, and it said, 'leave it at that. I know now that you don't care twopence; if you did you would' . . . The words, each time she looked at them, seemed to darken and obliterate a little more of the twenty years that had followed them . . ."

Gerald O'Donovan was an ex-priest and novelist whom Macaulay had met in London during the First World War, when both were employed by the government's Department of Propaganda. Having once broken his clerical vows, O'Donovan seemed determined to hold on to his marital ones, and Macaulay never pressed the point. Without the survival of their letters, it is difficult to know the exact nature of their relationship throughout the 1920s and 1930s, though biographers have tried to draw inferences from whatever other evidence—including her novels—the decidedly private Macaulay left behind. In her 1991 life of the writer, Jane Emery proceeded cautiously, but did feel able to conclude that the secret affair with O'Donovan resulted in "the continued suppression of emotion in [Macaulay's] work."

A measure of the romance's depth can be found in the letters Macaulay writes to Father Johnson during the early 1950s, while she is trying to find her way back to the Anglican church. Macaulay sends the priest—a distant relative and long-ago acquaintance now living in America—frequent and pain-filled communications by both air and sea, wondering if God has ordained this new correspondence in order to end her absence of almost thirty years from the sacraments.

She tells Father Johnson that her losses are helping to motivate the search for "another sphere of life." With abashed simplicity, she explains: "The people I love most have died. I wish they had not. But there is nothing to be done about it. Not only my parents—that was to be expected, of course—but my favourite sister, two brothers, and the man I loved." Though unnamed and otherwise undescribed, O'Donovan, placed at the end of Macaulay's sentence, seems to bring her grief to a crescendo. And yet, in the letters to Father Johnson, Macaulay appears bent on abandoning his memory as much as cherishing it, because O'Donovan is the heaviest of the sins she believes herself to be carrying through her exile from God's grace: "is the whole basis and structure of character sapped by the long years of low life? I see horribly clearly how low it was, and how low I am." After she has returned to confession and the Eucharist, she feels more conscious, not less, of her decades as a sinner: "I told you once that I couldn't really *regret* the past. But now I do regret it, very much. It's as if absolution and communion and prayer let us through into a place where we get a horribly clear view—a new view—so that we see all the waste, and the cost of it . . ."

The local priest who hears her confession and absolves her of her sins frustrates Macaulay by having little to say beyond what's mandated by sacramental procedure. The reader of her letters to the faraway Father Johnson realizes that the mailbox provides more relief than the confessional, but even so, Macaulay's agony remains. She may include her "beloved companion" in the prayers she's saying these days and may tell Father Johnson that he and the still-unnamed O'Donovan would have liked each other, but she is compelled to disavow the romance that once sustained her and to do it in a way that seems brutally self-punishing: "Not all the long years of happiness together, of love and friendship and almost perfect companionship (in spite of its background) was worth while, it cost too much, to us and to other people. I didn't know that before, but I do now. And he had no life after it to be different in, and I have lived the greater part of mine. If only I had refused, and gone on refusing."

Macaulay compliments Father Johnson on the "range, depth, breadth, humour, wisdom, interest, sympathy" and affectionateness of his own letters, qualities a reader cannot assess, since Macaulay asked that Johnson's part of the correspondence be destroyed after her death. She claims to understand the benefits to posterity in having the letters of such priests and saints as Fénelon and Françis de Sales, but tells Johnson she is queasy about the publication of an Anglican cleric's once-confidential counselings in *The Life and Letters of Father Andrew* (1948). She finds it "interesting trying to construct, from [Father Andrew's] answers, the kind of situations his correspondents had written to him of," but points out that "some of them seem too private, and, though veiled by anonymity, one would know that some of one's friends and relations would recognise things in them."

Father Johnson had no such scruples. After Macaulay's death in 1958, he provided "constant encouragement" to a third cousin of the novelist, Constance Babington-Smith, as she prepared Macaulay's side of the correspondence for publication.

One contemporary critic in the *Telegraph* recounts how "the conventionally pious" praised the letters' appearance and "the more bohemian writers' lobby" voiced reprehension. (Writers of course always have to fear the sort of letter-hungry "publishing scoundrel"—i.e., the literary biographer—first decried by Henry James's Juliana in *The Aspern Papers.*) The *Telegraph*'s critic goes on to note that Evelyn Waugh expressed himself at least twice on the subject of Macaulay's letters, once to Nancy Mitford ("I met [Macaulay] once and thought her sharp but ladylike. Not at all the kind of person to gush to a parson") and once to Graham Greene: "Do you think her adultery was an hallucination?" he asked.

Actually, any delusion seems doubtful. Of Greene himself Macaulay had once written: "What a mess his mind must be; nothing in it, scarcely, but religion and sex, and these all mixed up together." Her own scarifying refusal to let those two things coexist animates the authentic struggle she confessed to Father Johnson's encouraging and treacherous ears.

E. M. FORSTER ADDED his own long life to a line of long-livers. His great-aunt Marianne Thornton, whom he knew and whose biography he wrote, was born in 1797, and Forster himself died in 1970, the year the Beatles broke up. The most famous two words he ever wrote were also the most characteristic: "Only connect." This epigraph for *Howards End,* his novel about the hazards of attempting to bridge gaps in the English class system, might have done just as well for *A Passage to India,* in which he explored the thwarted efforts by some English and their subjects to become friends. Few novelists have written more perceptively of the forces that separate people or have been more aware of their own separation from passions they felt a duty to know.

Perhaps the most poignant thing a reader learns from Forster's letters is how long it took him to grow up. Raised by his mother amid the company of many aunts, he left home poorly armed for the traditional awfulness of English public schooling. Even when he reached Cambridge, a place so congenial he would end up spending much of his life there, he seems to have glimpsed most of what went on from a distance. It won't surprise readers of *A Room with a View* to find its author, in his letters, observing life instead of living it: "O such fun on Friday night! all the undergraduates ran up & down the streets yelling at the tops of their voices. Very foolish, but I much enjoyed it, for I saw it from my window beautifully."

A sense of incompleteness continues to frustrate Forster throughout his early success as a novelist. He travels in Italy with his mama; tutors for a wealthy family in Germany; makes a visit to India that excites but somehow fails to enlarge him. He experiences his first hangover at twenty-six and doesn't lose his virginity until thirty-seven. Exclusively homosexual in desire, he manages to write a novel about homosexuality (*Maurice*, unpublished until after his death) before he's ever had a complete homosexual experience. His initiation finally comes during World War I, while he's doing Red Cross work in Alexandria; like Walt Whitman with Peter Doyle, he falls in love with a tram conductor, Mohammed el Adl.

The letters Forster sends home are suddenly alive with joy and discovery. If his love is something he cannot confess to his mother, it is something he *must* confide to his friend Florence Barger: "I want it to be known if ever I should die . . . I was resting my head on him all the time . . . and his hands were stroking it." Realizing that he will not, after all, die only having guessed at the intimacy he's always sought, he exults in his luck: "I wish I could convey to you what I feel at this unique time . . . It isn't happiness; it's rather—offensive phrase—that I first feel a grown up man."

It's hard to think of another collection of letters that describes the finding of love more delicately or movingly. With correspondents other than Florence Barger, however, the younger Forster does not rise to great letter-writing heights. He lacks both spontaneity and contrivance, generally pitching things down the middle. In 1913, he tells the novelist Forrest Reid that "it bores [him] to write insincerely," but it's this lack of insincerity that may be his chief epistolary problem. A reader craves some sparkling artifice, not just sense and precision, from what he writes to relatives and friends.

The second volume of his letters opens in 1921, with Forster, now forty-two, serving as secretary to the Maharaja of Dewas: "The whole of this month has been wasted in cumbersome festivities; yesterday we had a funeral feast in commemoration of an aunt, before that 15 days on end to salute the arrival of a daughter." From this experience Forster gathers material for what will be his final novel, *A Passage to India*. After returning to England, he will spend the last decades of his career composing essays in the service of a culture running to barbarism. But as his fiction dies out, his letters gain liveliness. There are fewer dutiful communications to "Dearest Mummy" and more to such artists as Constantine Cavafy, Siegfried Sassoon, Christopher Isherwood, Benjamin Britten and Virginia Woolf. And yet, as the rest of his correspondence opens up, his letters to Florence Barger constrict: "My relation to her is queer," Forster writes his friend Jack Sprott in 1929. "I told her all about myself up to 1921—i.e. the year Mohammed died, and she has made something sacred and permanent for herself out of this, which fresh confidences would disturb." Without her having preserved Forster's letters from Egypt, one might have to depend on the cautious, retrospective characterization he made of that time when writing to the novelist Hugh Walpole: "not bad years on the whole: any how I learnt how to use the telephone and how to swim."

Forster offers various explanations for his long silence in fiction. Aware of his "creative impotence," he sometimes makes foolish excuses for it: "I never felt work was a duty—indeed, the less one adds to civilisation the longer perhaps it will take to topple over." He has wearied of the "conventionalities of fiction-form" but has no ardor for modernist experimentation in the manner of his friend Virginia Woolf ("I expect even Virginia will get bored finally, though she has scooted down a very exciting passage of which I can't predict the end"). He thinks for a while that his abandonment of the novel may have something to do with the fact that his "patience with ordinary people has given out," but by 1966, he can "only suggest that the fictional part of [himself] dried up."

Other possibilities present themselves in the letters. For many years his mother's longevity forbids the appearance of *Maurice*, and after her death the respectable position of his lover Bob Buckingham (a married policeman and probation officer) presents another obstacle. From time to time, Forster appears to consider taking the risk, only to end up feeling annoyed by his own lack of courage. He may finally have tired of fiction from a kind of resentment: if he is prohibited from writing about the emotions that have touched him most deeply, why should he write novels at all?

His despair over the world's prospects, particularly during the 1930s, pushes him onto the platforms of public life. He becomes a literary politician, working with the National Council for Civil Liberties and PEN, earnestly writing and broadcasting to his countrymen about the threat to "personal relationships and the arts" in "this age of break-up." He takes false steps—credulous participation in the Communist-dominated International Congress of Writers (Paris, 1935), a foolish declaration that he would rather betray his country than his friend—but he lives on the whole a civilized and civilizing life. His epistolary status rests, curiously, upon a stack of confessional letters he wrote not to the object of his love but to an encouraging third party—as if he at last wanted someone to see *him* through a window.

ASSIGNED TO OCCUPY the Trinity College rooms of George Gordon Byron during a year when their regular tenant would be away from Cambridge, Charles Skinner Matthews was given a warning by his tutor: "I recommend to your attention not to damage any of the moveables, for Lord Byron, Sir, is a young man of *tumultuous passions.*"

From birth, Byron seemed bent on becoming an adjective; he brawled toward his destiny inside a body that must have felt like a kettle at full boil. Prone to migraines ("*thunder* headaches"), fainting, "hysterical merriment," depression and more or less constant lust, he was inclined to loathe—and love—himself excessively, and to cast sharp scorn upon others. As he assured his poet friend Thomas Moore: "agitation or contest of any kind give a rebound to my spirits."

More than most poets', Byron's life may legitimately be sought within his works, those liberty-loving, score-settling productions of exile and priapism. "As to 'Don Juan,' confess, confess," he orders his friend and banker, Douglas Kinnaird: "It may be profligate but is it not *life*, is it not *the thing*? Could any man have written it who has not lived in the world?—and fooled in a post-chaise? in a hackney-coach? in a gondola? against a wall? in a court carriage? in a vis-à-vis? on a table? and under it?"

The only three women he truly detested turned out to be, alas, his mother, wife and mother-in-law. Instead of finding medical help for her child's clubfoot, Catherine Gordon Byron preferred to see it as an emblem of his inherent sinfulness, and from the time he was an adolescent, her son treated her in turn to bold, epistolary contempt. After being insulted by one of his masters at Harrow, Byron sends his mother an ultimatum: "If you do not take notice of this, I will leave the School myself"—not that it's home he'd care to come back to. "I dread the approach of the holidays," he explains to his half sister, Augusta, "more than most boys do their return from them."

After refusing his mother's written order to dismiss a particular servant, he writes Augusta from Trinity: "I sent back to [her] Epistle, which was couched in *elegant* terms, a severe answer." This response "so nettled her Ladyship, that after reading it, she returned it in a Cover without deigning a syllable in return." By November of 1808, he can proudly inform his sister that "Mrs. Byron I have shaken off for two years, and I shall not resume her yoke in future." His heart is not naturally bad, he insists, just "hard as a Highlander's heelpiece" from all the abuse it's been dealt.

Byron may have "no very high opinion" of the female sex, but he declares this position to a woman whose letters he values for their "traits of discernment, observation of character, knowledge of your *own sex* and sly concealment of your *knowledge* of the *foibles* of *ours*." Lady Melbourne, the correspondent in question, occupies in 1812 a pivotal position in Byron's life as both mother-in-law to Caroline Lamb—whose notorious affair with the poet will prompt her famous judgment that he is "mad, bad and dangerous to know"—and aunt to Byron's future wife, the misery-inducing Annabella Milbanke.

Byron dismisses Caroline's claim that she can make any man fall in love with her, by asking Lady Melbourne: "was there ever yet a woman, not absolutely disgusting, who could not say or do the same thing? Any woman can *make* a man in *love* with her; show me one who can *keep* him so!" But right now it's the niece, Annabella, who "requires time and all the cardinal virtues," none of which Byron has in large supply, since he's also romancing a married woman with olive skin, black eyes and too much of an appetite. "I only wish she did not swallow so much supper," he tells Lady Melbourne; "chicken wings, sweetbreads, custards, peaches and port wine."

Byron would be making a play for Lady Melbourne herself were it not for "the very awkward circumstances in which we are placed." Even so, amidst all the other women and girls, she is to remain uniquely his confidante and confessor: "you always must know everything concerning me. It is hard if I may not have one friend." If she ever suffers his neglect, there will be a simple explanation: "When I don't write to you, or see you for some time you may be very certain I am about no good."

The letters to Lady Melbourne are so filled with female reference that in order to keep things straight, Byron resorts to what rhetoricians call "transitional markers": "Now for Caroline," he'll begin one passage; "As to Annabella," he'll start another. Additional women are reducible to initials and aggregate numbers. Commenting in disgust on Caroline's need for calling his attention to all the men in pursuit of her, he asks: "Can't she take example from me? Do I embarrass myself about A? or the fifty B., C., D., E., F., G. H's., &c. &c., that have preceded her in cruelty, or kindness (the latter always the greater plague)?" It strikes him as being really too much that, during this same period, he's also got to deal with the amorous delusions of Lady Falkland. A girl named Charlotte Harvey might solve everything "if she could always be only eleven years old." As it is, he'll likely marry her "when she is old enough, and bad enough to be made into a modern wife."

His actual choice of a wife proves disastrous. "Miss Milbanke is the good-natured person who has undertaken me, and, of course, I am very much in love," he assures one female friend in a letter that fairly howls with protesting-too-much. Even readers innocent of literary history won't give the union with Annabella more than twenty pages from where it begins—not when Miss Milbanke can be found explaining it to one of her friends in a starchy, footnoted letter that makes the match seem more like a disease than a romance: "You have also, I trust, a sufficient confidence in my principles to believe that I would not marry any man whom I could not 'honour' as well as 'love.' It is no precipitate step. The attachment has been progressive for two years."

A month after his own statement about being very much in love, Byron is still writing to Lady Melbourne about his attempts to make headway with the bride-to-be: "I am studying her, but can't boast of my progress in getting at her disposition . . . However, the die is cast; neither party can recede." Once the wedding has occurred, he can address Lady Melbourne as "Dearest Aunt" and make a joke of the whole just-consummated horror: "I got a wife and a cold on the same day, but have got rid of the last pretty speedily." A postscript to this letter makes its most important point: "Lady Byron sends her love, but has not seen this epistle; recollect, *we* are to keep our secrets and correspondence as heretofore, mind that."

Thirteen months later, Byron and Annabella have separated; their infant daughter is said to be somewhere in the countryside with her mother. But it's another little girl, Elizabeth Medora Leigh, now nearly two years old, who is the focus of rumor and scandal and the Milbanke family's implacable hostility. Is Byron the girl's half uncle, or is he her father? Are the ardent verses he composes to Augusta a literary extravagance or evidence of an incestuous romance with his half sister? In April 1816, Byron concludes a letter to Augusta with the suspiciously overripe pledge that he is "ever and again, and for ever, thine." She is later asked "not [to] be afraid of the past; the world has its own affairs without thinking of *ours* and you may write safely."

Self-exiled to Venice, Byron will look back, cryptically, on "the nightmare of my own delinquencies" in a letter to Thomas Moore.

At the trouble's height, he confesses, he "should, many a good day, have blown my brains out, but for the recollection that it would have given pleasure to my mother-in-law." For the next few years the poet fills his letters with offhand expressions of hope that this same woman will, along with her daughter and her husband, drop dead. He requests that Douglas Kinnaird "ask Lady Noel not to live so very long" and composes an elegy not upon her death, but upon her recovery from illness.

When Augusta and Byron were adolescents and often apart, his sister had requested that he burn her letters; in reply, he declared: "If you burn any of mine, I shall be *monstrous angry.*" And so should we be. Byron's epistolary production is a constant thrill ride, brave and preposterous and enduringly *loud.* Exile—and for this we must thank the Milbanke family—increases the necessity and frequency of his letter writing. Once settled in Italy, he refuses entreaties to come home, and the longer he's away, the less he regrets it. He hates running into the English in Venice, unless they're sick, in which case he's helpful: "I return my card for theirs, but little more." His time on the Continent passes "viciously and agreeably." He finds Italian life quiet, except for the native tendency to murder friends and relatives.

Love remains a "hostile transaction," but business is brisk. Upper-class Italian women may be ugly, but Venetian women kiss especially well. Most convenient is the nature of Italian loyalty: "You hear a person's character, male or female, canvassed, not as depending on their conduct to their husbands or wives, but to their mistress or lover." Byron himself starts out with Madame Segati, "the wife of a 'Merchant of Venice,'" who has a charming panoply of qualities to recommend her: "she is very pretty and pleasing, and talks Venetian, which amuses me, and is naive, and I can besides see her, and make love with her at all or any hours, which is convenient with my temperament." Madame Segati is soon, however, replaced by the Countess Guiccioli, whose three years with the poet end with her husband's threat to put her into a convent, "for doing," as Byron puts it, "that with me which all the other countesses of Italy have done with everybody for these 1000 years." Before this unfortunate dénouement, Byron has fallen in love with the countess's friend Geltruda, "who is very young and seems very well disposed to be perfidious; but alas! *her* husband is jealous." He concludes a report of these latest entanglements on an optimistic note: "there are hopes that we may quarrel."

Long before leaving England, Byron had observed to Lady Melbourne that egotism "is said to be allowable in a letter, and only in a letter." Like exile, this quality, too, helps to fatten his correspondence. The greatest rhymer of English poetry chronicles his exploits and imprints his face, like a cameo, upon each linen sheet he sends home. Eight years after his famous swim across the Hellespont, Byron can inform his friend John Hobhouse that he has now swum "from Lido right to the end of the Grand Canal"—though in a modest P.S., he notes: "*The wind and tide were both with me.*" Shelley, by contrast, cannot swim at all, a fact that Byron imparts to the publisher John Murray on May 15, 1819. Three years later he will be posting news of Shelley's drowning and funeral to Thomas Moore, composing his famous description of the pyre ("All of Shelley was consumed, except his *heart*, which would not take the flame") only after he has described his own sunburn: "I have suffered much pain; not being able to lie on my back, or even side." The difference is simple: he is alive and Shelley is dead. He writes one letter to Moore at four a.m., while "dawn gleams over the Grand Canal, and unshadows the Rialto. I must to bed; up all night—but, as George Philpot says, 'it's life, though, damme it's life!'"

Having seen how wrong his fellow Romantics could be about a figure like Pope, Byron takes the long view of his own literary reputation and digs in his heels with friends and editors. No, he won't cut *Don Juan*, he swears in January 1819: "I will not give way to all the cant of Christendom. I have been cloyed with applause, and sickened with abuse; at present I care for little but the copyright." Nor will he entertain the suggestion that he write an epic, presumably religious in nature: "is *Childe Harold* nothing? You have so many '*divine*' poems, is it nothing to have written a *Human* one?"

Well before meeting his death in Greece—where he would try,

almost against his better judgment, to liberate its people from the Turks—Byron had wrestled with a sense that his time (he was nearing thirty) had already passed. By 1818, he is insisting he's seen too much to *feel* anything anymore; not even the death of Lady Melbourne that year can impact his emotions. Dying young will make him a more valuable literary property; if he lives long—and he'd prefer not to—one of his children, legitimate or otherwise, will have to support him. In the meantime, he's "'in for a penny, in for a pound,'" determined to do what he can "for the Ancients." So it's off to Missolonghi, and death from a fever, one that measured perhaps a tenth of a degree higher than the one that had burned in him all along.

"ONE ALWAYS FEELS a little guilty writing next to someone who is asleep," admits Colette in a letter from the summer of 1925 to her actress friend Marguerite Moreno. But not too guilty; not when the breezes of the Côte d'Azur are coming over the terrace and the person asleep beside you is an amiable younger lover having his afternoon nap.

Now in her fifties, with two stress-inducing husbands behind her—she cut the second one loose after the affair she had with his son—Colette is free to relax with the thirty-six-year-old man who will become her third spouse, though not for another ten years. There's never any hurry with Maurice Goudeket; it's one of the nicest things about him. "He savors the heat, the sea, and my patio court," she tells Moreno in 1928 from Saint-Tropez; he's "always the perfect companion, warm, full of tact, and born under the sign of Apropos." She will never have cause to regret the "wise improvidence in my behavior" that made her get hold of him.

Several years before Maurice even enters the picture, Colette can be heard in one letter giving Moreno the Wildean advice to "make do with passing temptations." After all, "What can one be sure of if not what one holds in one's arms at the time one is holding it? And we have so few chances to be proprietary." Few? A reader of Sidonie-Gabrielle Colette's letters sees her living her long lifetime as a kind of giant maw. She originally titled her book of sexual adventuring, *Le Pur et l'Impur*, even more inclusively, as *Ces Plaisirs*, a phrase capacious enough that one might consider it for her collected letters, covering as they do the romancing of all her five senses—by lovers male and female, by food, animals, flowers and the warmth of the sun. In July 1911, assuring the French caricaturist André Rouveyre that he has moved from being an acquaintance to a friend, she informs him: "you may write me and tell me everything you wish, without wounding or shocking me." Her own letters, to all those occupying Rouveyre's new category of *amitié*, are a decades-long confessional cascade of pleasures sighted and pleasures taken.

"The state of the weather has always had a large place in my life," Colette tells Renée Hamon, the writer and diarist, on February 25, 1938. The climate is an exasperating lover, blowing hot and cold, and while Colette will do most anything to escape its chillier moods, she keeps every pore open to its other whims and possibilities: "The weather has been Rozven weather, that is, never cold, often stormy, dead calm without rain, or scorching hot with a light wind—deliciously variable." It's only the cold, especially the bronchitis-bearing northeast wind, that she looks upon as a foe. She's even willing to summon the warmth, like a gigolo, with cash. Stuck in Paris during a terrible December, she makes her wishes known to the hotel that soon awaits her in Brittany: "tell Madame Angèle that, even on moderately cold days, I shall gladly pay for supplementary heat." The best and most beloved things are marked by elevated temperatures, real or imagined. "Now I'm going to bed, beneath the large warm rug of the moon," she writes Marguerite Moreno from Paris on the night of July 15, 1943.

Rarely has anyone so avid felt so lazy. Early in her career Colette admits to an appetite for work, but by middle age literary labor seems frankly "unwholesome," the thing that's "poisoning my life." When she has to finish a novel, she can still "grab it by the scruff of its neck" and get it done, but unlike George Sand, whose general gusto extended to her hasty, exuberant writing, Colette doesn't "know how to work with joy"; she can only go about her writing with "exasperated resignation." Indeed, the beauty-products business that she and Maurice begin when they're in need of money during the early 1930s may surpass novel writing when it comes to fulfilling the personal creed she imparts to the novelist Anna de Noailles: "I have very often deprived myself of the necessities of life, but I have never consented to give up a luxury."

Whatever she's working at, "an hour's pleasure undoes the rest of [her] day," loosens its strings as if it were a corset, leaving it good for only *more* pleasure. An inflamed right knee forces Colette to work in bed, but that's her "preferred manner" in any case. At the age of sixty, she tells Marguerite Moreno from Saint-Tropez: "All I want to do is go on with the unbridled life I lead here: barefoot, my faded bathing suit, an old jacket, lots of garlic, and swimming at all hours of the day."

Enough garlic, in fact, that she worries whether one letter she's writing to her friend Léon Hamel doesn't smell of it. (Posterity, alas, will never know: the editor of Colette's correspondence tells us that the "tender and tactful" Hamel "carried delicacy to the point of destroying the originals of all of Colette's letters, but only after copying their contents, with coded names, into the sort of schoolgirl's notebook Colette herself used.") A writer should never, by Colette's reasoning, "lose his fat the way a pierced cask loses wine," and everyone needs to remember that a full stomach is a defense against flu: one friend, Anne de Pène, would have survived the 1918 pandemic, Colette feels certain, had she not "skipped a meal to lose weight." Colette herself stays full and round: "I had just enough time to eat your strawberries, wipe my mouth, and leave for Saint-Malo," she tells Rouveyre. When it comes to food, overdoing it has its own pleasures: in the same letter where she reveals "a bet with myself to eat four hundred nuts between lunch and dinner," she extols the "pure—and purgative—joy of eating black cherries which the sun has ripened on the tree."

Colette is so elementally attached to the earth that at one point she even discovers a gift for dowsing. More inclined to think of herself as an animal than a mind, she can be found "pawing the ground with impatience" or delivering a new book that's "moist as a new-born cat." She tells Marguerite Moreno that a real feline, a tom six months old, "has just walked across my paper"—attracted perhaps by the smell of garlic. In the summer of 1940, having fled Paris with Maurice, she finds herself in an old Lyon hotel where "the mice flourish. There is one in particular who has been loyal to me for a month. She is very tiny, but I feed her well and she's grown so fat that she can no longer get through her mousehole. She uses the door, and while I have been writing, she has appeared twice, looking for bits of bread I leave for her on the marble mantelpiece." Years before, Colette had caught "a little 75-centimeter shark" with her own hands and marveled at its "skin like a moist leather slipper"—a sensual treat on the order of the "dewy mushroom noses" on a pair of lambs. One August, after writing a letter from Saint-Tropez that's filled with mentions of cats, butterflies, swallows, lizards, snakes and toads, she finally asks its recipient: "Have you had enough?"

For herself, no; never enough of anything. "Lord, how sweet it is to live physically," she writes, after cleaning the roof with "muscles one had forgotten." Colette even claims the ability, or curse, to hear the sound of the quickly passing days in her own ears. During travels in Italy, she declares less enthusiasm for Herculaneum ("I remained cold before so much marble") than the Grotto of the Sibyl, "which you visit on the shoulders of a half-naked guide, with the delicious odor of torches smoking in the darkness." Her everlasting preference is for the body over the mind, for living above work. Her letters are the place to ravish everything a second time, and to own up to having possessed it, for real, the first. When her mother dies in 1912, she confides only one grief to Léon Hamel: "I am tormented by the stupid notion that I shall no longer be able to write to her as I always have."

WHENEVER *HIS* WIDOWED MOTHER had to leave his side, Proust would sign letters to her with "A thousand loving kisses." He took pleasure in complaining to her along the "sort of wireless telegraphy" he imagined connecting them, until Madame Proust's death in

1905 allowed him to inflate real grief into a kind of infantilism he seemed to crave.

Being able to admit that one has never finished Proust is a sign of cultural security, even if the admission is usually followed by a declaration of intent to try again someday, perhaps by starting in the middle. Opening up the second volume of his letters, which runs from 1904 to 1909, may be a way of warming up for the task.

"I have just spent an entire year in bed," he writes on August 6, 1907. A reader quickly finds that Proust's asthma—as famous as Milton's blindness, and in its way perhaps as propelling—is monitored with astonishing detail in this second volume of correspondence. At its beginning in 1904, the writer is thirty-two years old and has just endured the death of his father. He has pulled back from much of the social life he pursued in his twenties, relegated by his ailments to a strange nocturnal timetable: activity comes easier late at night. In May 1905, he writes his fellow invalid, Madame Émile Straus: "If I find an oculist who is prepared to see me at 11 o'clock in the evening I shall consult him."

By the time he is thirty-five, he can at last think of himself as an orphan. He won't attend a lecture near the anniversary of his father's death, finds "unspeakable" a novelist pursuing an antifamily theme and extends the worship of his own ancestors to everybody else's. He calls the mother of his friend Georges de Lauris "a person I never knew but whom I mourned and still mourn as though I had always known her."

As George Painter's biography showed, Proust's homosexuality eventually became feverishly active, but in 1908, he is still so confused as to be able to indulge and repress it in the course of a single letter. A paragraph after telling de Lauris of the joy he would experience "reciting in your presence the litany of your ankles and the praises of your wrists," he says he'll refrain—"because of the misunderstandings and misinterpretations which would spring up in others' thoughts."

If there is a confessional aspect to these letters, it resides not in the admission of sexual exploits or emotional duplicity, but in the stealthily increasing revelation of an ambition, a mission that he will have little more than a decade to fulfill once he has fully embarked on it. All of his personal preoccupations, so mannered and exaggerated, are actually the feathers and fuss of procrastination.

Take, for example, the art of the compliment. However assiduously it may have been practiced in the Belle Époque, Proust's ornate courtesies remain positively exhausting to read. The characters in the short stories of Anatole France are, he tells their author, "freshly born of the miraculous foam of your genius," and he reassures Anna de Noailles (also Colette's friend) that some praise he's passing on to her is "the inevitable echo of your divine accents in any human ear capable of hearing them."

Like all gossips, he is touchy, though a little anger proves therapeutic: "when I have a grievance against people I like them to be guilty of wrongs against me which sound warlike fanfares in my heart." He enjoys his epistolary tiffs with such aristocratic friends as Antoine Bibesco and Robert de Montesquiou, who more than once imputes hypochondria to him. It is, however, Prince Léon Radziwill who receives Proust's testiest sign-off: "I was your truly sincere friend. Marcel Proust."

Proust is well informed of both literary and national politics—where people stand on the Dreyfus affair is a basis for his judgment of their characters—and he eventually becomes adept at following the progress of his portfolio, which includes New York City bonds. But it is another sort of portfolio that is really on his mind, gnawing at it with a demand to be taken seriously.

As this volume begins, he is still hesitant about his literary career, devoting most of what energies he has to critical essays and translating Ruskin. Worried that he might "die without ever having written anything *of my own*," he moves on to parodies ("pastiches") and finally to his novel—but only by way of criticism: an essay taking issue with the biographical critic Charles-Augustin Sainte-Beuve turns into an early draft of *Remembrance of Things Past.*

His "horrible anti-asthmatic medicaments" may leave him unable to "remember what happened the day before," but it is a remoter past he now goes after. By May 23, 1909, he is asking de Lauris if he knows whether the name Guermantes is "entirely extinct and available to an author." The last letter in this volume mentions "some alterations which are essential for my peace and quiet [being] done to my room in Paris." The famous cork lining is being applied to the walls of his bedroom. His imaginative galleon is being assembled, against all odds, like a ship in a bottle.

OUR FIRST EPISTOLARY ACQUAINTANCE, Charles Lamb, could match Colette's gusto for anything emerging from the oven ("God bless me, here are the birds, smoking hot!"), but he tended to ask politely, rather than grab, for the platter. Even when trying to borrow an algebra text for his hapless friend George Dyer, Lamb confessed to the item's owner that, in seeking the right delicate manner for the request, he has consulted the letters of Pliny, "who is noted to have had the best grace in begging of all the ancients."

The "begging letter," when written with enough sincere chagrin and charm, may end up seeming as much a present, a kind of prefacto thank-you note, as a request. Indeed, the "bread-and-butter letter," which appreciative houseguests are supposed to send to their hosts the day after arriving home, seems with its curious name to show the codependence of supplication and gratitude. But there are those begging letters that spring from calculated greed, ones that exchange the downcast eye of embarrassment for a cunning tug of the forelock in order to make an entirely false confession of need. This variety of the letter survives even today in the sudden appearance, usually from overseas, of e-mailed opportunities to relieve a person's medical desperation through the simple act of providing one's bank account number. But the genre's low-tech traditions go back centuries. Here, from *The New York Times* of March 29, 1901, is an explanation for the arrest of the entire Patrick McCann family of East Forty-sixth Street:

> The scheme of the letters was for the woman to represent herself as a former servant of some rich person, in dire distress through sickness and to appeal for a contribution of $5 or $10 to help through pressing emergencies. Such a study the woman made of the system . . . that she read all the society announcements in the

> various newspapers in order to secure the names of fresh victims. The plan then was . . . for the woman to seek Mrs. Francis, the janitress of her house, and have her write the appealing letter, telling of an old servant about to be dispossessed, and then have one of the children present it at the house of the person to be swindled.

The Dickensian feel of this reconstruction reminds us of how, throughout his fame as an author, Dickens himself, that champion of the imprisoned debtor, received bagfuls of letters requesting his help and his cash. In the mid-1840s, he went so far as to report one schemer named John Walker to the Mendicity Society, whose very name Dickens would seem to have invented. But it was the mendacity, not the mendicity, that troubled the novelist. In an article for *Household Words*, Dickens wrote of his exasperation with the way the writers of begging letters were "dirtying the stream of true benevolence, and muddling the brains of foolish justices, with inability to distinguish between the base coin of distress, and the true currency we have always among us."

The crook Dickens typically hears from has, at various times, "wanted a great coat, to go to India in; a pound, to set him up in life for ever; a pair of boots, to take him to the coast of China; a hat, to get him into a permanent situation under Government." Dickens sometimes detects the pseudo-desperate writer "fuming his letters with tobacco smoke"—perhaps garlic, too—while he's in the midst of threatening suicide and assuring the recipient that he has never written this sort of thing before. The letters usually come via a messenger, often a child, who will later graduate to practicing the profession himself.

The cheap chiseling drives Dickens to a rhetorical scorn that he normally reserves for industrial-scale malefactors like Mr. Bounderby. Indeed, it says something, as the critic Michael Slater reminds us, that the novelist picks begging-letter authorship as the epilogic fate of Pecksniff, one of his pettiest, nastiest and most memorable villains. The actual poor, Dickens insists, "never write these letters. Nothing could be more unlike their habits."

BY THE MID-1980S, William S. Burroughs (1914–1997) looked less like the "connoisseur of horror" he once called himself, than someone's terribly frail grandfather, so stooped and skinny one could almost see his ribs through the back of his sport coat. That he lived for another decade, long enough to see the publication of his letters, seems a sort of medical mystery to their reader, who gets to follow Burroughs through the fifteen years of struggle that preceded the success of *Naked Lunch*, a time of solitary wandering and gluttonous drug-taking.

"I have given up junk entirely and don't miss it at all." These famous last words, written in 1946, are among the volume's first: the thirty-two-year-old Burroughs is spending a court-ordered summer with his parents after a narcotics arrest. As the next dozen years go by and the family's black sheep moves from growing vegetables in Louisiana to getting high in Colombia and on to buying boys and drugs in Tangiers, the reader almost requires a Burroughs calculator, source of the family fortune, to count Bill's climbings onto and off the junk wagon.

Dope proves a distraction from his farming ("Putting out feelers in the local junk market"), and Burroughs ends up being one of the few men who can say their rehab was thwarted by dislocations to the agricultural economy: "I had hoped to go to a sanatorium for a 10 day cure on my carrot money. Now that hope is blasted." On New Year's Day 1950 he writes Jack Kerouac to praise a lack of Mexican effort at "curtailing self-medication. Needles and syringes can be bought anywhere." By March of '51, he's taken "the Chinese cure and [is] off the junk," but thirteen months later, with the departure of a lover, he's "got another habit. Start cutting down tomorrow."

It goes on like this, year after year, from codeine to Eukodol, Peru to Morocco, in and out of "the straitjacket of junk," crawling between resolute cleanness and "[d]egenerate spectacle: I just hit a vein (not easy these days. I don't got many veins left). So I kissed the vein, calling it 'my sweet little needle sucker,' and talked baby talk to it."

Even so, Burroughs slogs through the cycles of kicking and lapsing and kicking and lapsing with more plainspokenness than the average social drinker manages to summon. Whether he's writing about the Texas drug laws ("For some idiotic reason the bureaucrats are more opposed to tea than to stuff") or making fun of Allen Ginsberg's short-lived "normalization program," by which the younger writer hopes to turn heterosexual, Burroughs somehow keeps a perspicacious head above the ocean of dope. Even while he wallows in Tangier, a sort of peripheral vision permits him to see the city for what it is: "Things here are so typically Tangiers—'My dear, *anything* can happen in Tangiers'—that it is positively sick-making."

Between hallucinations he is more than ordinarily respectful of common reality, going so far, in 1948, as to pronounce a philosophy of "factualism": "All arguments, all nonsensical considerations as to what people 'should do,' are irrelevant. Ultimately there is only fact on all levels, and the more one argues, verbalizes, moralizes the less he will see and feel of fact. Needless to say, I will not write any formal statement on the subject. Talk is incompatible with factualism." He means for his early writings, such as *Junky*, to carry no message beyond mere descriptiveness ("You might say it was a travel book more than anything else"). He writes mostly to stave off misery, though he prefers contracts and royalties to neglect and persecution. A good deal of what's in his letters ends up, sometimes word for word, in the novels he eventually publishes, and amid all the paranoid phantasmagoria those books contain, one can still detect a nod and a wink, the sly self-awareness of "That Junky writin' boy Bill," as he signs himself to Ginsberg in 1952.

American conservatism is hardly a seamless garment, and the question of drug legalization has always strained its libertarian lining. But Burroughs, no single-issue deregulator, can be found wearing the cloak with surprising frequency. In 1949, when renting the back house on his Louisiana property, he tells Kerouac of a dismaying discovery that he cannot evict his tenants "without removing the premises from the rental market. I tell you we are bogged down in this octopus of bureaucratic socialism." All liberals, he writes a few months later, are "vindictive, mean and petty," and when he heads for Mexico City on the GI Bill he delivers a word of advice: "I always say keep your snout in the public trough." Burroughs is frequently one step ahead of the local police, but the totalitarianism he fears is of the looming nanny-state variety. "Why can't people mind their own fucking business?" is his motto. Ginsberg, his intellectual foil for some of these libertarian pronouncements, thinks Burroughs's "b.s. about Statism and Cops and welfare state is just a W. C. Fields act," but there is a bit more to it than that: "There are 2 bases for any ethical system," Burroughs declares to him in 1950. "(1) *Aristocratic code* (2) *Religion.*"

That he is prepared to embrace neither doesn't keep him from being a kind of ethicist to the Beats. He recognizes Neal Cassady as an "inveterate moocher" and offers Ginsberg this moral evaluation of the cross-country trip Kerouac would turn into *On the Road:* "I can not forgo a few comments on the respective and comparative behavior of the several individuals comprising the tour, a voyage which for sheer compulsive pointlessness compares favorably with the mass migrations of the Mayans." Ginsberg himself needs few lectures in behavior. The letters provide consistent evidence of the poet's loyalty, patience and simple niceness to Burroughs, whom he serves diligently, and for a time quite hopelessly, as a literary agent.

Burroughs often lets his own letters simmer "on the stove" for days on end; their composition betrays more shaping than haste. In them he stages some of the vaudeville vignettes that dapple his novels, and he indulges in that fifties specialty, the sick joke: "in this life we have to take things as we find them as the torso murderer said when he discovered his victim was a quadruple amputee." He can mix hipster riffs, camp and Papa Hemingway's Injun talk in a single letter, but he's at his best when playing it starkly straight. His high-speed photos of Peru have a terrible vividness: "Lima, a city of open spaces, shit strewn lots and huge parks, vultures wheeling in a violet sky and young kids spitting blood in the street."

Burroughs was of course a gun nut, thanks to that aggressive sense of personal liberty and who knows what dope-soaked collision between the sexual and death-seeking urges. He famously killed his common-law wife, Joan, in a drunken game of William Tell that the two of them enacted with a gun and a glass. His literary exploitation of the incident is less repellent than his effort, a few years later, to explain it to Ginsberg. "May yet attempt a story or some account of Joan's death. I suspect my reluctance is not all because I think it would be in bad taste to write about it. I think I am *afraid.* Not exactly to discover unconscious intent. It's more complex, more basic and more horrible, as if the brain *drew* the bullet toward it."

He knew that a passage like this might eventually be read by more eyes than Ginsberg's. "Better save my letters," he'd written him three years earlier. "[M]aybe we can get out a book of them later on when I have a rep." Eventually he had one, and his letters by and large confirm it. But it is a reputation for talent, not genius, and so the lines above must stand pretty loathsomely amid all the grubby levelheadedness surrounding them. Genius may have its license, but talent is too common to be the basis for forgiveness, at least on the scale he required it.

VIOLENCE—AGAINST EITHER the superfamous recipient or the desperately obscure sender—never seems far from the extreme fan letter, the kind that confesses not a burst of infatuation but grinding obsession. During the 1980s, two rock 'n' roll chroniclers named Fred and Judy Vermorel "read about 40,000 letters" written to British pop idols before offering a sample of them in an anthology called *Starlust: The Secret Life of Fans.* The ghost of John Lennon and the gun of Mark David Chapman hover over the whole production.

The lonely devotion of "Cosima" to David Bowie ("please don't think I am crazy") is such that "every time people say bad things about you I feel the duty to defend you and sometimes I become violent." Cosima begs Bowie to understand that he is her "central life" and "the only human being for who I would be capable to do sacrifice." Of whom it is not entirely clear. One fan of Nick Heyward tells him that "It deeply disturbs me knowing you will never belong to me," while another explains that she has considered falling into a coma in order to get his attention.

CIA interception of these letters is sometimes feared by those who write them, and another of Bowie's fans, "Heather," suspects that the rock star is tapping her family phone. And yet, amid the threats and paranoia, one occasionally finds, especially in the closings, a peculiar sweetness. "Melanie" is startled to realize that she may have begun to feel Bowie's loneliness along with her own: "I am your friend, David. Feel free to push unmanageable emotions in my direction."

With more typical anger, however, "Cheryl" warns Nick Heyward that she "never got on well writing a diary because I couldn't communicate with a blank piece of paper," and if he thinks he can get away without responding to her letters, he's "got another think coming—what a nerve." Even unanswered, these letters have a usefulness to their writers beyond anything the diary's blank brick wall can afford. They entail a physical transmission, a penetration of the beloved's space, if only just his outer office; they offer themselves to be ripped open or flung into the trash, a fate that Cheryl imagines and protests even as some masochistic part of her is relishing the negative attention.

The Who's Pete Townshend, in an introduction to the Vermorels' anthology, admitted to being a bit scared by some of the letters he himself had received over the years, but he concluded that the writing of them is part of an understandable, if displaced, search for God: "what matters is that I have made myself available as what Jung called a symbol of 'transformation.'"

WHICH BRINGS US TO the most famous mail ever to pass between Vienna and Zurich.

"We must never let our poor neurotics drive us crazy," writes Dr. Sigmund Freud to Dr. Carl Gustav Jung on New Year's Eve, 1911. The revelations, humbling but healing, that Freud and his acolyte are in the midst of bringing to the human psyche result, the men's letters make clear, only from long, daily, tricky labor. Misapprehension and overwork are prominent themes of the correspondence conducted by mentor and disciple between 1906 and 1914. Jung is "swamped" by his practice and Freud "enslaved" by his, enough so that the toil threatens the latter's "so-called health." But if the therapeutic truth is to spread beyond the consulting rooms of central Europe, there are journals to edit, conferences to convene, converts to make and dissenters to punish. The letters shuttle back and forth like some great clerical superego, keeping everything organized.

Even in the years of Jung's fealty toward Freud, cracks are visible in their professional alliance and personal devotion. Freud, after all, scorns those who suspect a physiological cause of mental illness ("they are still waiting for the discovery of the bacillus or protozoon of hysteria"), leaving the more curious Jung to apologize at one point for having resorted to "a wee bit of biology" in explaining the libido. Before fully embarking on the expeditions that will make him see the unconscious as more than sexual and even collective in its nature, Jung tends to report any deviation from Freud's still-new orthodoxies with a certain embarrassment: "I have been dabbling in spookery again," he writes on November 2, 1907. Freud pronounces the occult "a charming delusion," and the younger man promises to be "careful" in his exploration of its precincts. By 1911, when considering astrology and mythology, Jung still seems bent on convincing himself that he intends no more than a temporary detour from the Freudian fold. He begs Freud for a bit of time: "Please don't worry about my wanderings in these infinitudes. I shall return laden with rich booty for our knowledge of the human psyche."

Freud will, of course, make his own investigations of mythology but continue to believe that it "in all likelihood . . . centres on the same nuclear complex as the neuroses." Whereas Jung would like to see Christianity regain the mythic symbols and joy it once contained, the home office in Vienna regards religion as the immature manifestation of a helpless, psychosexual need. Freud calls his own view of the matter "very banal," but he doesn't retract it: "After infancy [man] cannot conceive of a world without parents and makes for himself a just God and a kindly nature, the two worst anthropomorphic falsifications he could have imagined."

In his association with Jung, Freud craves not a parent but a son, someone more intimately bound to him than a mere trained successor. As for God: Freud can fill that role himself. Jung, at the start, is conveniently subservient, prone in fact to slavish expressions of admiration and loyalty. Early in 1908, he asks Freud "to let me enjoy your friendship not as one between equals but as that of father and son." Freud admits that he likes being in the right and throughout the correspondence is always delighted by signs of submission: "I was overjoyed at your interest in *Leonardo* [Freud's essay on da Vinci] and at your saying that you were coming closer to my way of thinking." Jung owns up to a "father complex," which Freud tends to notice only when the condition is prompting resistance by the son. Jung stages small rebellions followed by wholesale surrenders. In April 1909, after some disagreement over his interest in poltergeists, the younger man fancies that the dispute has "freed me inwardly from the oppressive sense of your paternal authority," but a year later he's once again asking that Freud "forgive me all my misdemeanours."

After their first face-to-face meeting in 1907, Jung had written to Freud less like a colleague than a patient engaged in transference: "I have the feeling of having made considerable inner progress since I got to know you personally; it seems to me that one can never quite understand your science unless one knows you in the flesh." Freud's own imagery for the relationship during this early period is sexual and Eucharistic: "when you have injected your own personal leaven into the fermenting mass of my ideas in still more generous measure, there will be no further difference between your achievement and mine." He even realizes that Jung's birthday is the same as his wife's.

Jung confesses that his "veneration" of Freud has "something of the character of a 'religious' crush" with an "undeniable erotic undertone. This abominable feeling comes from the fact that as a boy I was the victim of a sexual assault by a man I once worshipped." However startling this revelation, it occupies a less crucial position in the letters than an exchange concerning Jung's first patient, a "hysteric" Russian émigré named Sabina Spielrein, with whom Jung came to have a sexual relationship. By 1909, Spielrein is making trouble, causing Jung to write this half-candid, and quite put-upon, confession to Freud:

> a woman patient, whom years ago I pulled out of a very sticky neurosis with greatest devotion, has violated my confidence and my friendship in the most mortifying way imaginable. She has kicked up a vile scandal solely because I denied myself the pleasure of giving her a child. I have always acted the gentleman towards her, but before the bar of my rather too sensitive conscience I nevertheless don't feel clean, and that is what hurts the most because my intentions were always honourable. But you know how it is—the devil can use even the best of things for the fabrication of filth.

Jung, one should note, does not deny a sexual relation; he admits only his refusal to father a child. But Freud, who has heard about the woman's complaints from another source, refuses even to believe that Spielrein was Jung's mistress. He assumes that his son and heir is being "slandered and scorched" by "the neurotic gratitude of the spurned," and he tries to soothe Jung's feelings by explaining that the incident represents an occupational hazard for the psychoanalyst: "it will never be possible to avoid little laboratory explosions."

Jung is "relieved and comforted" by Freud's assurances, but he can't hide his telltale guilt or a seeming awareness that his confession has put him in a permanently vulnerable position with his mentor: "my father-complex kept on insinuating that you would not take it as you did but would give me a dressing down"—one more or less disguised as brotherly love. Nine days later, he adds: "Although not succumbing to helpless remorse, I nevertheless deplore the sins I have committed, for I am largely to blame for the high-flying hopes of my former patient." He goes on "very reluctantly [to] confess to you as my father" that he unprofessionally (and untruthfully) wrote a letter to Spielrein's mother saying that he "was not the gratifier of her daughter's sexual desires, but merely her doctor."

Two years earlier Jung had disclosed to Freud his view that "sexual repression is a very important and indispensable civilizing factor, even if pathogenic for many inferior people." But in the wake of his difficulties with Sabina Spielrein—who will go on to become a more orthodox Freudian analyst than Jung himself—he ponders the possibilities of "sexual freedom" and infidelity: "The prerequisite for a good marriage, it seems to me, is the licence to be unfaithful."

The real adultery that Jung requires is intellectual, a long-postponed apostasy that's no doubt been inhibited by all the invective he's accustomed to hearing—and speaking—against foes of the Freudian movement. Early on, Freud tells Jung of his own "inclination . . . to treat those colleagues who offer resistance exactly as we treat patients in the same situation." The "enemy camp" produces "emotional drivel." Dissidents are not merely sick; they are malicious and sometimes satanic. The psychiatrist Adolf Albrecht Friedländer, an opponent of analysis, is a horned "Beelzebub," according to Freud, who tells him off in person and then confesses to Jung that he had "a fiendishly good time" doing it; "I couldn't get enough." Jung quivers vicariously over the report: "I hope you roasted, flayed, and impaled the fellow."

Jung can be even more vivid than Freud in expressing disgust and fantasizing revenge. The opposition makes him "feel the urgent need of a bath," he says, and it's a "pity there are never enough good men around to applaud loudly whenever these weaklings, mixtures of muck and lukewarm water, have to eat humble pie."

Freud admits to a certain childishness in his own makeup but doesn't recognize the megalomania that from time to time has him sounding like Ayn Rand: "when a man stands firm as a rock, all the tottering, wavering souls end by clinging to him for support." He may advise Jung to treat the battle "with humour as I do except on days when weakness gets the better of me"—but that would be most days. Freud insists that his colleague not "regard me as the founder of a religion," but a certain cultishness seems distinctly permissible. As late as 1910, Jung himself suggests to the master that psychoanalysis "thrives only in a very tight enclave of like minds," and even a year after that he's asking: "May we know the names of the dissidents soon? In my view this purge is a blessing."

In one of his first letters, Freud speaks of "the torments that can afflict an 'innovator,'" and after his friendship with Jung has flowered makes a telling joke about his intellectual suffering: "sometimes it annoys me that no one abuses you—after all you too have some responsibility in the matter." But even when Jung at last rises to full-throated rebellion, Freud himself will not abuse the younger man, at least not forthrightly. His own letters remain a model of passive aggression—as they have been from the beginning, when he told Jung: "I should be very sorry if you imagined for one moment that I really doubted you in any way." Whether straightening him out on the subject of paranoia or playing him off against another disciple ("Apart from that, you have every advantage over him"), it has been Freud himself cranking the spin cycle that Jung speaks of being caught in: "The feeling of inferiority that often overcomes me when I measure myself against you has always to be compensated by increased emulation."

When Emma Jung grows concerned about the increasing tension between her husband and his mentor, she begins her own correspondence with Freud and pinpoints the nature of Freud's selfishness: "Doesn't one often give much because one wants to keep much?" She asks that he not discuss their exchanges with Jung ("he was astonished to see one of your letters addressed to me; but I have revealed only a little of their content") and admits to her own difficulties with her husband: "I find I have no friends, all the people who associate with us really only want to see Carl."

As the spring of 1912 approaches, Jung is quoting Nietzsche to Freud, on the need for the student to rebel against the teacher. He has begun tugging noisily at his chain, explaining to the possessive and suspicious older man, "I have not kept up a lively correspondence during these last weeks because I wanted if possible to write *no letters at all*, simply in order to gain time for my work and not in order to give *you* a demonstration of ostentatious neglect. Or can it be that you mistrust me?" Freud responds with tender manipulation: "The indestructible foundation of our personal relationship is our involvement in ΨA [psychoanalysis]; but on this foundation it seemed tempting to build something finer though more labile, a reciprocal intimate friendship. Shouldn't we go on building?"

In fact, a new dispute over the libido is ready to blow the house to smithereens. Jung has concluded that incest is "primarily . . . a fantasy problem," a desire that didn't even exist until it was forbidden. He stands his ground against Freud's more primal view of the matter and is soon delivering a series of lectures in New York that put his heresies on public display. He expresses a hope that things can remain friendly between them but also asserts that professional matters must now trump all else. His correspondent gets the message: for years Freud has saluted the younger man as "Dear friend," but the next letter from Vienna opens with a stiff new "Dear Dr Jung."

A move toward reconciliation proves futile, and Jung responds to Freud's attempt at an elegiac tone ("for me our relationship will always retain an echo of our past intimacy") with belligerence and sarcasm: "It is only occasionally that I am afflicted with the purely human desire to be understood *intellectually* and not to be measured by the yardstick of neurosis." Finally, after a letter in which Freud points out a Freudian slip that Jung has made, the younger man has had enough: "You go around sniffing out all the symptomatic actions in your vicinity, thus reducing everyone to the level of sons and daughters who blushingly admit the existence of their faults. Meanwhile you remain on top as the father, sitting pretty. For sheer obsequiousness nobody dares to pluck the prophet by the beard. . . ." Freud replies with a bland assertion that Jung is mentally ill; the only proposal he can now make is "that we abandon our personal relations entirely."

Amid all of Freud's bilious anger and comical formality and jargon (he at one point declares that an Italian vacation "has supplied several wish-fulfilments that my inner economy has long been in need of"), a reader of these letters may forget how much fright and pain Freud swept away from so many mental attics—let alone the bravery it took for him to accomplish that. Auden's famous elegy to the doctor concedes that "often he was wrong and, at times, absurd," but holds that when he died, "Only Hate was happy." One playful image from Freud's letters to Jung—"the ego is like the clown in the circus, who is always putting in his oar to make the audience think that whatever happens is his doing"—feels pleasantly similar to the homely, approachable ones in Auden's tribute. Alas, this clown simile arose in the course of Freud's denouncing one more heresy committed by one more errant psychoanalyst.

LIKE THE EPISTOLARY NOVEL, the suicide note caught on in the eighteenth century. In his introduction to an anthology called . . . *Or Not to Be*, Marc Etkind shows how newspapers catering to the "newly literate" of that era began to print suicide notes that would soon change society's view of their authors: "Once suicides were considered satanic, now the notes showed them to be human, suffering from such common problems as poverty, infidelity, and plain bad luck."

Such notes continue to range from the pointedly accusing ("May you always remember I loved you once but died hating you") to the wanly philosophic: "If we can enter eternal sleep," wrote the Japanese novelist Ryunosuke Akutagawa in 1927, before swallowing sleeping pills, "we may at least have peace, even if we may not enjoy happiness." Suicide notes are written not only to different audiences—sometimes even pets, Etkind points out—but also in an ever-expanding range of media. The minister who not long ago hanged himself and wrote "God forgive me" on the package containing the rope could today use one of the Internet bulletin boards available to both the sincerely desperate and the perversely joking.

How often an expression of apology enters these notes! Dying from Nembutal as he writes, Dr. Stephen Ward, the London doctor caught up in the Profumo scandal of 1963, manages to say: "I do hope I have not let people down too much." Virginia Woolf, before drowning herself during the Second World War, addresses her husband, Leonard, in the kind of simple declarative sentences she'd practically banished from the English novel:

> I feel certain I am going mad again. I feel we can't go through another of those terrible times. And I shan't recover this time . . . I don't think two people could have been happier till this terrible disease came. I can't fight any longer. I know that I am spoiling your life, that without me you could work. And I know you will. You see I can't even write this properly.

In the early days of Bill Clinton's administration, the president's depressed aide Vincent Foster, beset with an unexpected host of political enemies, devoted most of his suicide note to rebutting them, but he began by saying, "I made mistakes from ignorance, inexperience and overwork." And in the end, before shooting himself, Foster ripped his own note into twenty-seven pieces, which he then threw into his briefcase. As Etkind points out, such destruction is common, "since many who feel they are unworthy to live also feel their final thoughts aren't worth sharing."

CHAPTER EIGHT *War*

The sun is just rising and how beautiful! It makes one feel sad to think this beautiful spring day must be spent just slaughtering human beings.

Henry Morrison, Fourth Virginia Volunteer Infantry,
May 5, 1864

WHEN IT APPEARED time to fly "to war and arms" on behalf of his beleaguered king, the Cavalier poet Richard Lovelace first had to take leave of "Lucasta," in a hasty lyric that might as well be a letter. Lovelace's *Casablanca*-style apologia explains that the problems of two seventeenth-century aristocrats don't amount to a hill of beans in a world with Cromwell on the horizon; and so, however faithless it might seem:

> . . . a new mistress now I chase,
> The first foe in the field,
> And with a stronger faith embrace
> A sword, a horse, a shield.

Once he's gone, Lucasta will understand and be proud:
this inconstancy is such
As you too shall adore;
I could not love thee, dear, so much,
Loved I not honour more.

The history of letter writing demonstrates the human inability to make war without making love. Wartime encourages hasty romances, sunders existing ones (the "Dear John" letter is war's own epistolary innovation) and with its fiery tests of separation and danger solders the strongest marriage into something even stronger. As the World War II generation takes its long farewell, what once seemed a mundane tendency to do its duty has begun to look not just heroic but romantic. The veterans' aging children are making bestselling anthologies out of the micro-sized V-Mail their fathers sent home to sweethearts and young wives.

The generally plainspoken GIs tend to move us with their matter-of-factness, but an earlier century's emotional flourishes have not lost their affecting power, either. The great epistolary moment of Ken Burns's Civil War documentary came with a letter composed by Sullivan Ballou of the Second Rhode Island Volunteers a week before his death in the First Battle of Bull Run. Writing from Camp Clark, Washington, on July 14, 1861, Major Ballou assures his wife Sarah that

> my love for you is deathless; it seems to bind me with mighty cables that nothing but Omnipotence could break; and yet my love of Country comes over me like a strong wind and bears me unresistibly on with all these chains to the battlefield.
>
> The memories of the blissful moments I have spent with you come creeping over me, and I feel most gratified to God and to you that I have enjoyed them so long. And hard it is for me to give them up and burn to ashes the hopes of future years, when, God willing, we might still have lived and loved together, and seen our sons grown up to honorable manhood, around us.

However less jauntily, Ballou makes the same case Lovelace does about the competing claims of love and honor. Something "whispers" that he "shall return to my loved ones unharmed," but his letter is more alert to the possibility that war will have its own say about both honor and love. Should he die, Ballou offers his wife a ghostly substitute attendance until the two of them can meet once more in eternity:

> But, O Sarah! if the dead can come back to this earth and flit unseen around those they loved, I shall always be near you; in the gladdest days and in the darkest nights . . . *always, always,* and if there be a soft breeze upon your cheeks, it shall be my breath, as the cool air fans your throbbing temple, it shall be my spirit passing by.

Over and over, from Peloponnesus to the Persian Gulf, war acts as love's destroyer and enabler. The soldier, in his letters, follows the orders of both.

NOT ALL OF Ballou's comrades in arms could use the language so elegantly as he. But refinement and eloquence are not the same thing, and many ordinary Civil War soldiers do rise to the latter in the kind of straight, simple utterance now being rediscovered in their descendants' V-Mail. Private James Binford of the Twenty-first Virginia Volunteer Infantry begins one letter home, after the Battle of Cedar Mountain, with a sort of record-setting concision: "Dear Carrie and Annie: Thanks to merciful providence, I breathe and have all my limbs." On the Union side, Private Chester Tuttle of the Eighty-first New York tells of how his company tended its wounded inside a rebel's house after the Battle of the Wilderness. A spinet piano "was used to cut off legs and arms on. Ben Ballard . . . said that the blood run down in on to the strings."

If the Civil War had one letter writer able to use starkness and economy to astonishing effect, it was Private Tuttle's commander-in-chief, Abraham Lincoln. On his second-floor desk in the Executive Mansion, the president kept a small stack of cards, suitable for fast responses to pleading widows and office seekers, but the lawyer in him was generally averse "to getting on paper, and furnishing new grounds for misunderstanding." If Jefferson's letters can be a sort of Louisiana Purchase, lighting out for more territory than they require, Abraham Lincoln's are a struggle for union, battles for exactitude and strict coherence, limited-objective campaigns fought on short rhetorical rations. The mere three or four hundred letters Lincoln himself probably composed as president—similar to Jefferson's only in their neat, undemonstrative handwriting—have become, by their scarceness and brevity, as familiar to us as his speeches. They are the literal circumscriptions of a man hemmed in by catastrophe. In his White House correspondence, this great storyteller has no time for telling stories.

Lincoln passed many of his presidency's most important hours in the telegraph office at the War Department, receiving and responding to news from the battlefield. Samuel F. B. Morse, who grew considerably richer off the military's use of his invention, spent the war agitating for peace with the rebels, but he had provided the president he so disliked with a formidable instrument, one that made the most of Lincoln's natural powers of brevity and sarcasm. The telegram was practically designed for letting remarks hang in the air, for doubling the impact of the dead-bolt closings Lincoln had already mastered in his letters. "If the head of Lee's army is at Martinsburg," he cables General Hooker, "and the tail of it on the Plank road between Fredericksburg & Chancellorsville, the animal must be very slim somewhere. Could you not break him?" The president responds to a serving of McClellan's usual molasses—this time a dispatch about tired horses—with a wire that ends: "Will you pardon me for asking what the horses of your army have done since the battle of Antietam that fatigue anything?" McClellan had failed to heed two earlier sign-offs, the magnificently casual one just before Antietam ("Destroy the rebel army, if possible"), and the urgent underlining ("*But you must act*") in a letter five months prior to that.

Some of Lincoln's telegrams to the battlefield have a remarkable similarity to present-day, conversational e-mail. "Colonel Haupt," he wires during the second Bull Run campaign. "What became of our forces which held the bridge twenty minutes ago, as you say?" The speed and spareness of the dispatches kept the recipient to the point, and one wonders if the feeling of control they offered wasn't what inspired Lincoln to compose the most audacious gamble of his presidency not at his desk in the Executive Mansion but over at the War Department with one of the barrel-pens used by the cipher-operators. David Homer Bates, manager of the telegraph office, recalled in 1907 how Lincoln drafted the Emancipation Proclamation "a line or two" at a time, stopping when "a fresh despatch [*sic*] from the front was handed to him."

"If [Lee] stays where he is," Lincoln telegraphs Hooker three weeks before Gettysburg, "fret him, and fret him." These are the words of a man who thought that "nothing equals Macbeth" but who clearly knew *Othello*, too ("Put out the light, and then put out the light"). We know something of Lincoln's Shakespeare-reading from a private letter he sent the actor James H. Hackett, who let the president's "small attempt at criticism" find its way into the newspapers. When Hackett apologized for causing the snickers that ensued, Lincoln told him not to worry: "Those comments constitute a fair specimen of what has occurred to me through life. I have endured a great deal of ridicule without much malice; and have received a great deal of kindness, not quite free from ridicule. I am used to it." But not indifferent. Lincoln would die with some favorable press clippings in his wallet.

From the start of his presidency, Lincoln's letters are assertions of authority, instruments to control and stabilize a state of affairs that, like his own depressive temperament, requires a sly, firm hand. A month after taking office, he lets William H. Seward know that the president, not the secretary of state, will be running the administration. "When a general line of policy is adopted, I apprehend there is no danger of its being changed without good reason, or continuing to be a subject of unnecessary debate; still, upon points arising in its progress I wish, and suppose I am entitled to have, the advice of all the cabinet." Seward, who would come to understand Lincoln perhaps better than anyone, no doubt felt the sting of that "suppose I am entitled" in this letter's final sentence. One wonders if McClellan, forever preening in place, realized the insult, the deliberate subordination, in one envoi that he received: "The success of your army and the cause of the country are the same; and of course I only desire the good of the cause."

Lincoln shows none of Jefferson's contempt for the position he holds. His "heavy, and perplexing responsibilities here" provoke the reverent doubts of the postulant: "I could not take the office without taking the oath," he writes the Kentucky newspaper editor Albert G. Hodges. "Nor was it my view that I might take an oath to get power, and break the oath in using the power." Means and ends, the single end of preserving the Union, will not be confused. One letter he writes to Horace Greeley, that famously muddled mind, is a split-rail fence, notched and slotted with a precision designed to reinforce Lincoln's own conviction as much as to entrance the *Tribune*'s editor: "If I could save the Union without freeing *any* slave I would do it; and if I could save it by freeing *all* the slaves, I would do it; and if I could save it by freeing some and leaving others alone I would also do that."

No other president's image is so clouded with the stagy dry-ice vapors of Destiny; no other's words have been more often heard by posterity against actual musical soundtracks. The letters offer today's citizen as much chance as he gets with any of Lincoln's writings to turn off the special effects and attend to the sentences that so often seem addressed to their author, written for the moment instead of the ages, put together for personal clarity and their powers of reassurance. The control they exert more than any other is self-control.

The most famous rebuke Lincoln ever composed, to General Meade ten days after Gettysburg ("I do not believe you appreciate the magnitude of the misfortune involved in Lee's escape . . . Your golden opportunity is gone, and I am distressed immeasurably because of it") survives only as a draft, an expulsion of steam that never left the president's office. A week later General Meade once more had Lincoln's "confidence as a brave and skillful officer, and a true man"—even if that confidence was expressed in a letter to General Howard instead of to Meade himself. (The telegram about McClellan's supposedly fatigued horses could not be retrieved, only softened with another one three days later, in which Lincoln apologized for the hopelessness that "may have forced something of impatience" into his earlier wire.)

When he is free from doubt, when the letter Lincoln writes is meant only to command its recipient, parallels and antitheses make way for a buckshot spray of rhetorical questions that harry his correspondent into a corner. A year after issuing the Emancipation Proclamation on the basis of its military usefulness, Lincoln refuses the suggestion of his treasury secretary, Salmon P. Chase, that the order now be applied to portions of Virginia and Louisiana that had been exempted: "Would I not thus give up all footing upon constitution or law? Would I not thus be in the boundless field of absolutism? Could this pass unnoticed, or unresisted?"

Limiting himself to the tenable, Lincoln takes care not to turn up the flame of his displeasure any higher than necessary. He makes sure John C. Frémont knows he is being given "caution," not "censure," and that General Halleck understands how disagreement doesn't equal a lack of confidence. When telling his generals, as he always must, to speed it up, Lincoln will shamble on about his own "poor mite" of military judgment, his being "not competent to criticise" the views of D. C. Buell or even U. S. Grant. But the message will come anyway, at the end of the page, the bottom of the deductive, lawyerly funnel. "Now dear General," he writes, in denying Nathaniel Banks's request for some supplies that will only slow him down further, "do not think this is an ill-natured letter—it is the very reverse. The simple publication of this requisition would ruin you."

Forgiveness was a natural disposition and strategic necessity, required for dealings with underage deserters, his wife, and the wayward inhabitants of the Confederacy. "On principle," he wrote Secretary of War Stanton on February 5, 1864, "I dislike an oath which requires a man to swear he *has* not done wrong. It rejects the Christian principle of forgiveness on terms of repentance. I think it is enough if the man does no wrong *hereafter.*" Having narrowed his war aims to a single mystic tenet, he would also narrow down the prerogatives of peace. "I shall do nothing in malice," he writes Louisiana's Cuthbert Bullitt. "What I deal with is too vast for malicious dealing." Indeed, when he steps away from this vastness, leaves off preserving the Union to write to Mary, the lines can come out hasty and dull, the closing ("But enough") a mere banality beside the last words of his military communications.

If he requires, as he writes to Carl Schurz, "success more

than . . . sympathy," it is the latter he is called upon to give, over and over again—at the necropolis of Gettysburg (where his Address was itself a sort of telegram) and in individual expressions of condolence. John R. Sellers, a Lincoln expert at the Library of Congress, once described himself as being "constantly plagued by people finding the Bixby letter," that is, the missing original of what went out in the fall of 1864 to a woman who had lost five sons in the Union's service. (Or so Lincoln thought. Three of the five sons survived, and one of those was a deserter.) The Bixby letter's enduring popularity is sustained by even Lincoln's admirably unhagiographical biographer, David Herbert Donald, who finds it a "beautiful" production full of "sincerity" and "eloquence." But by Gettysburg standards, the eloquence is more like Edward Everett's than Lincoln's. The letter is an overblown affair ("to have laid so costly a sacrifice upon the altar of Freedom"), its tropes tumbling out with the modern auto-empathy of Bill Clinton. One feels inclined to let John Hay, Lincoln's principal secretary, take credit for the production—as does Lincoln scholar Michael Burlingame.

A more provable Lincoln resides in an earlier letter, to Colonel William McCullough's daughter, Fanny. Here one finds the president limiting his objectives of consolation, making statements into questions, addressing his own high-maintenance moods: "Perfect relief is not possible, except with time. You can not now realize that you will ever feel better. Is not this so? And yet it is a mistake. You are sure to be happy again. To know this, which is certainly true, will make you some less miserable now. I have had experience enough to know what I say; and you need only to believe it, to feel better at once."

Rarely does he allow himself one of Jefferson's outbursts against political treachery, but on August 23, 1864, he writes a note about the politically surging McClellan, who appears more likely to see victory as the Democrats' presidential candidate than he did on the battlefield. "This morning, as for some days past," Lincoln wrote, "it seems exceedingly probable that this Administration will not be re-elected. Then it will be my duty to so co-operate with the President elect, as to save the Union between the election and the inauguration; as he will have secured his election on such ground that he can not possibly save it afterwards." Lincoln asked members of his Cabinet to affix their names to the back of this paper without knowing what was on the front; only after defeating McClellan did he show them what they had signed. It was his ultimate economy of expression, a sort of magician's trick. He had gotten his men to produce a letter—which he hoped would coerce a victorious McClellan into working with the lame-duck administration—without their seeing, let alone writing, a word of it.

IN THE FIRST YEAR of the Civil War, after decades of trying to move the post farther and faster by steamship, rail and Pony Express, the U.S. government suspended mail delivery to the rebel states. On August 31, 1861, Lincoln's postmaster general, Montgomery Blair, directed that all Southern-bound mail henceforth be sent to the Dead Letter Office.

The missives of his sister, Mrs. Elizabeth Blair Lee, would have retained considerable liveliness even in that epistolary graveyard, but there was never much chance of their being shunted to such a destination. The war snapped Mrs. Lee's patriotism into a smart, four-year-long salute. This child of one border state (Kentucky) and resident of another (Maryland) knew many of the political and military principals on both sides of the conflict, but the Blairs and Gists (her mother's family) had been serving the Union since the Revolution, and Elizabeth was not going to break ranks now. Throughout the war she continued using her Washington home (today's Blair House) often enough to refer to Abraham Lincoln as "my opposite neighbor." Between Fort Sumter and Appomattox she sent her husband, the naval officer Samuel Phillips Lee (third cousin of the Confederate general), nearly a thousand letters, many in a light, satiric tone, nearly all of them distinguished by the author's sharp eye and shrewd good sense.

Elizabeth continues to see the rebels as her countrymen, with secession a sort of feverish disease that's got hold of them. Her compact account of how Jefferson Davis led his partisans out of the Senate on January 21, 1861, stands as one of the great descriptive passages in the war's literature:

> I never saw such an aroused audience when they left their places simultaneously—the Democratic side rose & surrounded them—But the Republicans ignored the whole scene & except 3 of them, all kept their seats & went on with business—looking stern & solemn—Mallory wept. [Clement] Clay shook all over—Yulee spoke as if choking with sorrow—Davis was firm & manly—but pale & evidently suffering—The ladies sat calmly—thro the whole—I wished in my heart for Old Hickory to arrest them all—it might save thousands of precious lives, so I thought & felt & so I did not weep tho' my head ached & so does my heart—

Six months later, at a dinner party given by her brother, she encounters William H. Russell, the same London *Times* journalist who had reported the Crimean horrors back in 1854, and she offers this "chuncky sample of John Bull" the sort of flinty resolve his dispatches had once roused in Florence Nightingale: "He remarked that the Southern women had more zeal than we Union women that they were making lint & bandages—& etc. I replied they were preparing to be whipped . . ."

Mrs. Lee resists the "dissipation" of novel reading for the writing of letter after letter. She compares running her household to a military campaign, a claim well supported by the plentiful news from her small home front: drought, smallpox and the sound of nearby drums can be found in a single letter composed on June 25, 1861. Elizabeth's most important company is her young son, Blair, a beautiful, good-natured child by his mother's reckoning, clearly a mama's boy by anxious circumstance. Elizabeth Lee is not a young bride: now in her mid-forties, she requires a pair of her husband's spectacles to read and write the letters moving between them. Age requires her to "matronize" the local single ladies at the opera, though her preference is for more serious pursuits, such as the Washington City Orphan Asylum, whose "directress" she becomes in 1862.

A reader is inclined to reach across battle lines—and the border of fiction—to regard her as an amalgam of Melanie and Scarlett, shouldering the former's sense of responsibility and unleashing, at least occasionally, the latter's sharp tongue. On a September day in 1863, with the rebels once again near the capital, she gives her husband a briskly sensible sign-off—"I have much to do—so good morning to you"—secure in their mutual devotion, more amused than irritated by some outsiders' assumptions about the marriage. When she overhears her niece doubting whether Samuel Lee has "ever made a pretty speech to me in my life," Elizabeth makes her presence known in order to "insist that you have said several very civil things to me in the course of the last 24 years."

The set of her jaw and the determination to keep her husband informed amid calamity also bring to mind the medieval Margaret Paston. Elizabeth reports her father's warning that "the long journey this letter has to take & the excitement of the times make caution essential." Francis Preston Blair, Sr., has been offering advice at the White House since Andrew Jackson's time, but Elizabeth doesn't depend on him for all the intelligence she passes on to Mr. Lee; she has her own direct observations to impart: "Mr. Seward dined here yesterday—& he mentioned that Every European Power had written to this Government letters of sympathy & *encouragement* England alone excepted." She tells her husband that people are "blue as indigo" over the loss of a Union ironclad; reports on the misbehavior of the Massachusetts Tenth as it passed through the area above Silver Spring; and expresses impatience with General Wool's handling of the New York draft riots. Still, thought of the continuing slaughters makes her "heart sick body sick," and her ability to feel sorrow over the rebels' suffering, too, only makes things worse. By the second year of the war "a *scare* is now [her] normal condition," and her thoughts run "turbid as the Mississippi water," the river up which her husband's outfit is fighting.

She keeps Lee apprised of all she's done to safeguard the Maryland house. The silverware and paintings have been packed up and "my own garden & Hen house will be my chief out door resorts—with Becky [a servant] & Blair trotting after me Father has followed the precaution you suggest for months past. He & our Coachman too *have* been armed—our horses are fast—& our neighbors reliable." When late in the war Jubal Early's Southern troops succeed in ransacking the place, she finds a note of apology left on the library mantel:

> A confederate officer, for himself & all his comrades, regrets exceedingly that damage & pilfering was committed in this house, before it was known that it was within our lines, or that private property was imperilled—Especially we regret that Ladies property has been disturbed, but restitution has been made, & punishment meted out as far as possible.

By this point she is stoical enough to admit that "if our own Army had swarmed over us & encamped there for two days—it would have been quite as bad for us."

More than the family's property, Elizabeth strives to protect and advance its reputation. She passes on to Samuel an encouraging rumor of opium use among the rival Frémonts and keeps him up to date about her efforts to secure him a better ship ("I will continue to jog"). She bitterly imparts news of David Porter's elevation to commodore and cries with disappointment when her husband fails to receive a promotion. (Lincoln appreciated the Blairs as a brave, if scrappy, clan, but the self-interested pitches of both Elizabeth and her father must have tried even the president's famous patience: "Father told me to night it was a matter he meant to talk over with the President—& to *follow up* until the end he most coveted was attained.")

The letters sent home by Samuel Phillips Lee become physical substitutes for his presence. Elizabeth lets young Blair interrupt his supper to hear them, sometimes "over & over." The boy will pat the pages "with his fat hand as he does living things he likes." His mother wishes she could "seal up some of [Blair's] merriment" in her replies; more realistically she hopes for strong winds behind the mail boat. Her plain, masculine penmanship, full of dashes instead of full stops when there's any punctuation at all, seems propelled by urgent gusts blowing from the left margin. Her brother-in-law pronounces her a better talker than a writer, a judgment she doesn't dispute. Indeed, some of what Elizabeth puts down on paper might have seemed more appealing if spoken, softened as it would have been by facial expression and gesture. One imagines the Lees playfully sparring when allowed the chance to be together. Since the war years offer few such face-to-face opportunities, they are lucky to have had important epistolary practice, twenty years before, while courting. Elizabeth's father hadn't wanted the match, and so Samuel Phillips Lee had sent letters to his future bride through an intermediary, using a made-up name: "Oh how often I have regretting [*sic*] sending them back to you," Elizabeth writes in 1863. "Stolen joys were very sweet—so I remember those letters with not half the repentance I ought—"

But different times call for different measures and manners. In 1864, Elizabeth reminds "Phil" that he once long ago asked her "never to read over what [she] had written," lest it lose its spontaneity. Now, she knows, he is "too overworked for such trespassing nonsense," and she will continue to make "all of my letters short and as plain as print."

After Phil's retirement, he and Elizabeth would have a quarter century for less urgent communication, as they lived together in Washington and Maryland until the death of Admiral Lee (he eventually got his promotion) in 1897. Elizabeth survived until 1906; thirty-six years after that, her grandsons discovered the letters in the hayloft at Silver Spring.

ON JANUARY 9, 1917, his first day ever in no-man's-land, Wilfred Owen received a letter from his mother. "It seems wrong," he replied, "that even your dear handwriting should come into such a Gehenna as this." If irony, as Paul Fussell demonstrates, was the chief mode of the very literary Great War, then the domestic communications sent by English mothers and sweethearts only added to it. Modern transport and the home front's proximity to the battlefield meant that letters often arrived inside a parcel with handkerchiefs that hadn't lost their crease and biscuits not yet gone stale. The psychic gulf between the two worlds would grow vast and bitter, as English soldiers gave up their limbs and sanity and lives just a boat-train's trip away from their own families. In his letters from France, Owen more than once reminds his mother that he is writing "while you are at Tea."

For all the speed and shortness of their journey, letters traveling back and forth across the Channel between 1914 and 1918 served all the ancient emotional functions of wartime correspondence. Owen's own dispatches alternate between grim frankness and filial reassurance, and on a couple of occasions he communicates his unit's position in a code arranged between him and his mother. Without the replies he receives from her, he declares, he should simply "give in." He cannot write her "without intensity" or without sometimes falling into a woozy biblical cadence, and on other occasions he dispatches blandishments that seem more a sweetheart's than a son's, dismissing all the competing charms that can be matched by the "little finger" of his "precious Mother." He knows they both "find letter writing a fitter mode of intimate communication than speaking," and he would like the pages he sends to substitute for something else as well: "because they are my only diary, I humbly desire you to keep these letters."

This gentle son of a Shrewsbury railroad superintendent—a boy drawn to botany, evangelical religion and, above all, Keats—was never a natural soldier. His 1915 enlistment in the Artists' Rifles was a "plunge," his first week of training marked by unexpected difficulties: "We had to practise Salutes (on Trees) this very morning. You would be surprised how long it takes to do the thing properly." His early wartime letters to Susan Owen, full of goodwilled self-mockery and jaunty exclamation points, chronicle a year of toughening that, he swears, has turned him into "a different being . . . from the lounger on divans, the reader of verse . . . the midday riser" that he used to be. But a touching haplessness remains evident to all latter-day readers, who must proceed through the correspondence with a terrible foreknowledge.

The poet's delicate nerves get scraped by a bullying sergeant major, "amusing enough in *Punch*, but not [when] viewed from the ranks." When he has to do a bit of officering himself, Owen feels distinctly uncomfortable: "I am 'commanding' numbers of wounded men, now restored," he writes from Milford Camp in Surrey on July 3, 1916: "It gives me a great deal of pain to speak severely to them, as now and again need is."

His first reports from the line show a mind and style suddenly stripped raw. The stark paragraphing of a letter written after a week spent holding a dugout near Beaumont Hamel already resembles those verses, shorn of Edwardian fat, now being produced by the war poets:

> I can see no excuse for deceiving you about these last four days.
> I have suffered seventh hell.
> I have not been at the front.
> I have been in front of it.

With its covering of snow, no-man's-land "is like the face of the moon chaotic, crater-ridden, uninhabitable, awful, the abode of madness." On January 19, 1917, Owen's company is "in a ruined village, all huddled together," his own mind wandering back home to Shrewsbury. Two weeks later, he reflects, with an amazement too exhausted to complete the sentence: "I used to consider Tankerville Street ugly, but now . . ."

In April, he will be harrowed by extended duty in the line at Savy Wood:

> For twelve days we lay in holes, where at any moment a shell might put us out. I think the worst incident was one wet night when we lay up against a railway embankment. A big shell lit on the top of the bank, just 2 yards from my head. Before I awoke, I was blown in the air right away from the bank! I passed most of the following days in a railway Cutting, in a hole just big enough to lie in, and covered with corrugated iron. My brother officer of B [Company], 2/Lt Gaukroger lay opposite in a similar hole. But he was covered with earth, and no relief will ever relieve him . . .

Even this has been sanitized for his mother. He admits to Susan Owen that a doctor is "nervous about my nerves," but asks that she "not for a moment suppose I have had a 'breakdown.'" Two days later, still at the Casualty Clearing Station, he concedes, as casually as he can manage: "*Some* of us have been sent down here as a little mad. Possibly I am among them."

He has, in fact, been shell-shocked, and only four days later, in a letter to his sister, does he reveal the grotesque full truth of what did him in: "You know it was not the Bosche that worked me up, nor the explosives, but it was living so long by poor old Cock Robin (as we used to call 2/Lt. Gaukroger), who lay not only near by, but in various places around and about, if you understand. I hope you don't!"

Suffering from nightmares, Owen is invalided to Craiglockhart War Hospital in Scotland, where—after mustering the courage to approach—he has his famous encounters with Siegfried Sassoon, the handsome huntsman-turned-poet, a half dozen years older and newly famous for his flamboyant protest against the war. "Shakespeare reads vapid" after the poems of Sassoon, Owen insists to his mother, pronouncing himself unworthy even "to light his pipe." The older poet offers some military-sounding literary advice: "the last thing he said was 'Sweat your guts out writing poetry!' 'Eh?' says I. 'Sweat your guts out, I say!' He also warned me against early publishing."

After two months of this mentoring, Sassoon leaves the hospital, prompting from Owen a sort of love letter, filled with hero worship but also self-protection: "Know that since mid-September, when you still regarded me as a tiresome little knocker on your door, I held you as Keats + Christ + Elijah + my Colonel + my father-confessor + Amenophis IV in profile . . . I love you, dispassionately, so much, so *very* much, dear Fellow, that the blasting little smile you wear on reading this can't hurt me in the least." Still, he urges Sassoon to confide this letter to the fire.

Two years earlier, when enlistment in the Artists' Rifles took him to London, Owen had excitedly noted how close he was to the informal headquarters of the new "Georgian poetry" movement.

"The Poetry Bookshop is about 7 mins. walk!" he told his mother. "There is a Reading this very night!" During his later convalescence, the connection to Sassoon and his own scattered publications expose him to some "first flickers of the limelight." He meets H. G. Wells and Arnold Bennett at the Reform Club and attends Robert Graves's wedding. His poems begin to move beyond the timid realm of discipleship and acquire a more authentic style. But if they become less self-consciously "Keatsian" (the early estimation of Poetry Bookshop owner Harold Monro), Owen himself remains a steadfast practitioner of the Romantic poet's advice for living.

He knows Keats's prescriptions from the earlier poet's letters, which he quotes and rereads and tries to keep on hand: "Please include in Parcel," he writes his father from one training camp, "Keats's *Letters.* (Vol. IV & V) (in Book*case*)." When Owen talks of how he turns into "whatever and whoever I see while going down to Edinburgh on the tram: greengrocer, policeman, shopping lady, errand boy, paper-boy, blind man, crippled Tommy, bank-clerk, carter, all of these in half an hour," a reader recognizes Keats's "Negative Capability," the chameleon-like empathy that led him into poetry. The Owen who declares excitement to be "always necessary to my happiness," and who announces "*I hate old age,*" realizes that there is "only one way to avoid" the latter—in some violent variant of Keats's early death.

"I go out of this year a Poet, my dear Mother," he writes on New Year's Eve 1917, after a year of transformation almost comparable to Keats's "living year" of 1819. Tennyson—whose music will remain detectable in even Owen's most unsparing war poems—now seems "a great child" to his twenty-four-year-old successor: "So should I have been," he declares, "but for Beaumont Hamel," a place he remembers as "cobbled with skulls." Graves counsels Owen to "outlive this war," because he's one of those who will "revolutionize English Poetry" once it's over. Owen can now even dare to see beyond Sassoon, whose poetry has lately "become a mere vehicle of propaganda."

For all his poignant careerism, Owen won't let himself overvalue publishing success, since his own subjects—the men fighting the war—regard print as "a dead letter." Their handwritten personal letters, which they compose all day and which Owen is called upon to censor by the hundred, are another matter. He sees the "hope of peace" expressed in each; the "'Daddys' . . . are specially touching, and the number of xxx to sisters and mothers weigh more in heaven than Victoria Crosses."

Owen's own letters show him becoming less evangelical and "more Christian," as he begins perceiving a pacifist light "which never will filter into the dogma of any national church." The nice young man grows less afraid of political blasphemy, too. While training in January 1916, long before arriving in France, he had reported home about one colonel's "brilliant lecture on the causes of the War." By June of the following year he lists his personal war aim as the "Extinction of Militarism *beginning* with Prussian"—and tells of observing a major refuse to get on a train with the explanation: "'I *eb*solutely decline, to travel in a coach where there are—haw—*Men*!" And by March 1918, with only months to live, Owen will characterize a boy who has just left school as "a creature of killable age."

He often imagines a life for himself after the war—as a flyer; or an antiques dealer; perhaps in the bungalow for which he draws up a design. But he resists exempting himself from the slaughter. At the Casualty Clearing Station in March 1917, shortly before being sent to Craiglockhart, he decides he would be "better able to do Service in a hospital than in the trenches. But I suppose we all think that." As 1917 ends, he knows he will have to go back to the front if he wants to describe the faces of the doomed, "more terrible than terror." He begins forcing himself to have the explicit battle nightmares from which he is supposed to be convalescing: "I do so because I have my duty to perform towards War."

The dates on the letters begin to click past in an awful countdown. A reader feels himself trying to thwart what's coming. Still in England in May of 1918, Owen glimpses a chance of staying there, as lecturer to a cadet battalion, thanks to a friend in the War Office; Sassoon even threatens to stab his protégé in the leg if he attempts returning to France. But as Owen writes his sister, in truthful self-ridicule: "I take myself solemnly now." By September he is back in the line, bearing a different sort of evangelical witness. Early in October he receives the Military Cross for action described in a citation: "On the Company Commander becoming a casualty, he assumed command and showed fine leadership and resisted a heavy counter-attack. He personally captured an enemy Machine Gun in an isolated position and took a number of prisoners." He tells his mother—everything reads like prefiguration now—that he "fought like an angel." His nerves, he further informs her, are this time "in perfect order." He tells the same to Sassoon but elaborates to his fellow soldier-poet on the reason for his calm: his senses have been "charred" into numbness. Dealing with the company's mail "I [now] don't take the cigarette out of my mouth when I write Deceased over their letters."

He composes his own last words home at six-fifteen p.m., October 31, 1918, preserving, with eerie immediacy, the conditions in which he writes them: "So thick is the smoke in this cellar that I can hardly see by a candle 12 ins. away, and so thick are the inmates that I can hardly write for pokes, nudges & jolts."

The Armistice was signed on November 11, the day Susan Owen received a telegram announcing that her son had been killed a week earlier. The power of his letters is such that one almost forgets it was their *enclosures*—the poems he sent with them—that made Wilfred Owen the Great War's one truly imperishable writer.

LATE IN THEIR long married life, Winston Churchill marveled to his wife, Clementine, about "all we have crashed through together." He could hardly overstate the matter: the Churchills' letters include public events from the *Titanic* to *Sputnik* as well as every phase of their own fifty-seven-year joint march from ardent youth to bemedaled decrepitude. "Je t'aime passionnément," writes Clemmie (who feels "less shy in French") in 1908; four decades and five hundred pages later in their collected correspondence, she'll be "so distressed about the truss" that's now a bother to Winston.

From the first, Winston Churchill understood that he could present himself to his wife without "the slightest disguise." His letters, however self-deprecating and full of affection, admit to a character "so devoured by egoism" that he "wd like to have another soul in another world & meet you in another setting, & pay you all the love & honour of the gt romances." But it was for this world that he was entirely made: "6 o'clock is a bad hour for me," he writes during one period of exile from the political center; "I feel the need of power as an outlet worst then." He falls behind in his letter writing only when too little, not too much, is going on around him.

For epistolary output and bumptious eloquence, his only American equivalent is Teddy Roosevelt, but Churchill's greatness as a letter writer is due in part to the kind of two-track character that made Pepys and Boswell his own nation's foremost diarists. Like them, he is wholly onto every appetite and piece of foolishness in his makeup but sometimes quite unable to squelch their appearance on paper. There is, for example, the trouble he has dislodging catchy tunes from his head. Several years after the Second World War, having been introduced to an applauding crowd in Morocco "to the strains of Lilli Marlene," he confesses to Clementine that he's "terrified of this getting into my mind again. I have several antidotes ready."

He emerges as the more likeable partner in the marriage. Clementine has high spirits, but no real silliness. She reassures her husband that the "tumultuous" life he gave her, all the "colour & jostle of the high-way," is a relief from the "straitened little by-path" she trod before meeting him, but it is her half-century-long lot to buck him up and rein him in—from extravagance (in rebuilding their country house, Chartwell), from too much closeness to questionable company (the newspaper baron, Lord Beaverbrook) and, especially, from hasty political choices. Oral spats are frequently patched up on paper, sometimes through the "house post," written communications from one room to another.

The couple fought fifteen election campaigns together, and Clementine's letters show her advice to be specific, shrewd and frequently indispensable. The more socially liberal of the two, she is

Winston's equal at sizing up his friends and foes: Lloyd George "is a barometer, but not a really useful one as he is always measuring his own temperature." During the early days of World War I, as First Lord of the Admiralty, Churchill takes the fall for the ill-starred Dardanelles campaign, descending to a level of political disgrace from which he might never have recovered without his wife's counsel. The letters they exchange after his decision to go as a soldier to the Western front are a blend of patriotism, ambition and mutual tenacity—really the heart of their long correspondence. In fact, it's these letters that mark Winston and Clementine as true heirs to the duke of Marlborough and Sarah, that eighteenth-century pair we now call "the first Churchills."

Sitting in the trenches, writing his letters "in a battered wicker chair within this shot-scarred dwelling by the glowing coals of a brazier in the light of an acetylene lamp," Churchill feels nothing like Owen's gathering horror. He pronounces the front a sort of personal therapy: "Amid these surroundings, aided by wet & cold, & every minor discomfort, I have found happiness & content such as I have not known for many months." A reader ends up believing him chiefly from Clementine's responses. She, too, contrasts politically poisonous Westminster with the supposed nobility of the battlefield, using the sort of hygienic terms favored by Rupert Brooke in his war sonnets: "The atmosphere here [in London] is wicked & stifling. Out where you are it is clean & clear."

And yet it is to politics that both she and Churchill know he must return. Winston urges her to "Keep in touch with the Government. Show complete confidence in our fortunes." While tending his fires on the home front, Clementine presses him to take command of a battalion instead of a brigade (it will look more modest) and, above all else, not to return too soon: "The present Government may not be strong enough to beat the Germans, but I think they are powerful enough to do you in, & I pray God you do not give the heartless brutes the chance . . . I could not bear you to lose your military halo." There is no surer sign of her love for Churchill's essential nature than the way this mother of three young children urges her husband to stay in the trenches. Her confidence "in your star" is so long-range that she implores him not to post the ill-considered letter he's written to the *Times*'s Lord Northcliffe: "If it goes it will form part of your biography in after times . . ."

During the next several decades, whether he's "in" or "out," Churchill's star remains the correspondence's chief theme and emotional focus. There is a great deal of domestic delight and discord—their son Randolph's impetuous electoral forays; their daughter Sarah's impetuous marriages—but nothing long distracts the letter writers from Churchill's own political life and its vast dramatis personae. In 1928, Churchill notes in the two-year-old Princess Elizabeth "an air of authority & reflectiveness astonishing in an infant"; he calls the Duchess of Windsor "Cutie." The Windsors' own correspondence—that sick-making pablum of baby talk and self-pity—could not provide more of a contrast to the Churchills'. Winston and Clementine may have their own pet names for each other—he's her "Pig" or "Pug," she's his "Cat"—but after a bit of epistolary cuddling it's always back to business.

Winston Churchill's manly, buoyant style is displayed to great effect in every decade. He moves easily between lofty parallelism ("How easy to evacuate. How hard to capture") and playful bombast: "I hope the Burgundy has reached you safely & that you are lapping it with judicious determination." Clementine, at her own most stylish moments, can bring Nancy Mitford to mind. Describing a fountain in the Italian Garden at Blenheim, the first Churchills' palace, she writes Winston: "The whole group now looks like a Pagan representation of the Assumption of the Virgin Mary attended by fallen members of the Salvation Army."

The early portions of the correspondence are the most orderly, sustained volleys of one letter replying to another. Later on, especially during the Second World War, dictation, haste and the need for secrecy take their toll. The two-way coded cable traffic between "Colonel and Mrs. Warden" is nothing like so absorbing as those exchanges from the Great War two decades earlier. "ALL WELL. HOPE YOU ARE NOT GETTING MUCH BOMBARDMENT," Churchill telegraphs from Naples in August 1944.

Mary Soames, the couple's youngest daughter and the editor of their letters, admits that during the later years "Winston himself could be maddening, and on occasions behaved like a spoilt child; but now there were times when Clementine harried him too much, and could be unreasonable and unkind." Still, the case for their uninterrupted devotion—through his second prime ministership, which took him past eighty, and through the pair's even later dramas of illness and enfeeblement—remains overwhelming. "Everyone has his day," Churchill told the House of Commons in 1952, "and some days last longer than others."

TO TURN ONE'S ATTENTION from Winston and Clementine's letters to the wartime correspondence of Mirren Barford and Jock Lewes is to move from a kind of practical royal marriage to a twentieth-century version of courtly love, in which neurosis mixes with ardor, and self-parody threatens to overrun self-sacrifice. Barford, a language student at Somerville College, Oxford, first encounters the twenty-six-year-old Lewes, a member of the British Council newly enlisted in the reserves, at a wedding in August 1939. After two meetings, they begin an exchange of letters that quickly takes on an intense, disorienting life of its own. At its plainest, their correspondence concerns Mirren's uncertainty about whether she should remain at university and Jock's eagerness to leave off training (with the Welsh Guards and then a commando unit) in order to see some action. But above these sublunary questions the two conduct a frantically Platonic romance, a substitute for the actual affair that circumstance and temperament won't permit them to have.

The Australian-raised Lewes is so handsome that when another male visits Mirren's room in Oxford, "he turns your photograph down because he says you look like Douglas Fairbanks, Jr." Making his own movie comparisons, the pure, dutiful Jock expresses a preference to be Ashley Wilkes instead of Rhett Butler with "his licentious ways." He lectures Mirren on the need to avoid "moral deterioration" and to persuade everyone "that we will and can fight not to the end but until we win." They must "cleave fast" to their "impractical ideals of understanding, generosity, beauty, love," the last of which can help to remake the world: "Whatever we touch will be hallowed for us and for those who see us."

It's not easy to imagine this paragon in the barracks, except perhaps in a bed short-sheeted by his fellow soldiers. Things would be better, he insists, if "half that mental energy and spiritual devotion . . . which we lavish on the pursuit of humour, comfort and convivial living" were put into training instead. Jock detaches himself from his comrades' "sordid" existence by reading the *Life of Johnson* and *Clarissa*, and he holds off reading Mirren's words until he can get a step or two away from the madding crowd: "I kept your letter till after dinner for I had seen the first sentence in the dim light of the hurricane lanterns and it was so like meeting you again in a dear dear garden at home that I almost recoiled from it there in that ribaldry."

Jock can write with such overelaborated lyricism that it's difficult to extract his meaning from the lofty tangle of clauses. Also prone to abstraction and treatise, he's liable to address his girl as if she were a foreign minister with whom he's conducting a bilateral negotiation: "I am here attempting to record in order that, quite apart from any intrinsic value in the record itself, we may be able to bring our minds to bear on the crux of the intricate and extremely important problems which now confront us both."

For her part, Mirren indulges in a few girlish outbursts, and she does remind Jock of her need for social activity and even the company of other young men. But mostly the poor thing struggles to stay on the path of purity. She can't pay attention to Michael de Chair, another suitor, when Jock is hovering like some gauzy "conscience" in a cartoon:

> between the two of you, somehow you make me feel like a very superior and refined prostitute. Mike gives me lovely presents because he adores to do it, yet, because you have rammed your nose in between Mike and me, the presents make me feel ashamed. I would rather be with you than with Mike, and those presents seem so like a less crude form of payment than bank notes. I try specially hard to be good with Mike; I make myself tolerate a

> rather sticky hand in the cinema. And why? Because Mike knows very well that he has slipped down a rung, but would rather have some signs of affection than the frigidity part of me wants to show him.

Mirren's effortful letters explore such matters as why intellectual work suits her better than the snares of art; Jock then critiques the letters as if they were term papers. She strains after sophistication and complexity, but her idea of honesty is very much a young person's: "You and I are so honest with each other, it becomes agony at times. But all the same, it leads to complete understanding which is a precious thing."

After a while the reader would like to go back in time, to some weekend when Jock has a pass, in order to get them drunk and book them a hotel room. But the results of such intervention would be uncertain, given Mirren's embarrassment about standing naked in front of Jock's photograph, and with Jock such a stickler for chastity that he wishes to proceed by "deliberate choice and not merely the dictation of desire." He defends to Mirren the ideal of male virginity, even though two women he consults don't think much of the concept, and despite what unfortunate imagery it leads him into: "I have not yet finished the forging of this ideal, though I have had it on the anvil often enough."

The Jock-Mirren letters are full of extended, tormented metaphors (Mirren's own virginity is a "Christmas stocking" not to be opened until the special day), as well as literary allusion. Jock will sign off as "Paris," and Mirren, depending on situation and mood, declares herself ready to be "Helen," "Penelope" or "Cassandra." Joy Street (the eventual title of their published correspondence) runs through a Bunyan-like terrain mapped out by the two of them; it's the cryptic capital of their emotional geography. By Jock's reckoning, the lovers' landscape also contains Casual Corner, Self Alley and Sentimental Gardens, not to mention a blue-leather corridor and some puzzling aquatic precincts. The correspondents' latter-day editor says he first guessed Joy Street to be "an allegorical representation of a specific place," before deciding "it described

Mirren and Jock's individual meetings." (The street's "beggar priest," he further concluded, is Lust.)

Those individual meetings are so few that the whole relationship becomes a sort of allegory, a massive psychological displacement in which the flesh is made word after word after word. Both lovers, to some extent, recognize this: Jock refers to a "grand game . . . playing the hide and seek of intention and expectation" from behind the "safety curtain of absence." All the sailors and soldiers and airmen, those former civilians that Mirren knew, seem to have "disappeared," their whereabouts just vaguely known, their persons "all so hopelessly unobtainable." She conducts her correspondence in a sort of fitful afterlife, and Jock himself comes to regard "a letter that arrives as something that has always existed, like a fossil that I come on in the desert, a message from another world."

Only the merest fragments of that other, real world—glimpses of Oxford, or of Mirren's alcoholic mother, or even just her own messy room—manage to penetrate the letters' separate realm. When Jock is sent with a commando unit to defend Tobruk in northern Africa, we do see him wearing khaki shorts and writing as he fights "a million flea bites"; but the military censors and his own taste for abstraction tend to dry up his chronicle. At the height of the Blitz, Mirren focuses for a moment on the real world's smashed houses and mad scramble for survival—the telephone "is always engaged because the family spends its time ringing up different members to make quite sure that no one is dead"—but she soon shifts attention to the infrastructure of her letter: "I'm sorry about those smudgy marks but I spent an anxious minute or so changing the ribbon."

By the middle of 1941, as Jock gets closer to the action—training parachutists for the desert winds by having them jump from the back of trucks—some of what he writes becomes more direct. There's even one astonishing eruption about "fucking" ("I wonder if we'd do it well; not at first I think"), and some decidedly more-ardent-than-usual endearments:

> To press you to me till I feel the very nipple of your breasts and the firmness of your thighs and sense the gracious gesture of their

> parting, to feel the agony of the longed for pain of passion, that nothing can satisfy but you. To lead you silently and through the dark to bed and there to enter, smooth and warm and thrilling until the madness of love's ecstasy engulfs us and sighing sleep into a world made whole.

One senses his new urgency in the frustration he expresses over the slow and erratic delivery of Mirren's letters: "when you think how you can change in a week . . ."

Mirren tries to speed up their exchange by exercising a kind of telepathy: "John, how could I reach your mind across these leagues of sea and desert? Somehow you've got to know, now, at once, how important it is that you should send a cable." The intensity of emotion seems to grow, and to the reader it begins at last to feel genuine. Mirren prepares herself for the worst ("If you die before we have had time to be together, at least I shall have the faith and love you have given me"), and Jock allows personal suffering to shatter his jutting, glass-jawed dutifulness:

> in the streets of Cairo the other night as I walked away from the film "Lady Hamilton" I cried in the dark; just for a moment tears and great baby sobs took hold of my throat and face and wrenched away my manhood. And when I had mastered them I went into a great shop and spent two lovely hours choosing two pieces of cloth for you. A flaming red velvet for Helen from America and an English silk and cotton print for Penelope.

The reader, knowing what's coming as surely as they do, finally gives himself over to these two young people trying so hard to act grown-up in the catastrophic place and time they've been assigned. Their needs and affinities and bravery become real only pages before the telegram arrives. Jock Lewes is killed on December 30, 1941, after his commando unit makes a raid that succeeds in destroying two German planes.

Little more than a month later, Mirren writes to his brother, David, a new doctor, telling him how Jock "seemed to charm all the shabbiness and mistrust" out of her. She reassures Dr. Lewes that she'll "have dozens of children and you can be godfather or whoosh out their adenoids for them—or do both. Take this letter for what it is worth and remember I was writing it"—at a quarter to two in the morning—"to me as well as to you."

Pain has awakened Mirren from her allegory; her writing seems suddenly straight ahead and clear-eyed, shocked into calmness and simplicity, like a person whose hair has gone white overnight. On March 4, 1943, she tells Jock's parents that she is ready to "live whole-heartedly again" now that she has subdued their son's memory and made it a "friend, philosopher, and guide." She announces plans to wed an American named Dick Wise and pledges "to call our first son Christopher John—do you like that?"

She kept her promise, and she kept the letters, in the back of a drawer. Michael T. Wise, the younger brother of Jock's namesake, published them three years after his mother Mirren's death in 1992.

"THE ECONOMIC SITUATION will hardly be improved by having a few million Poles for breakfast," writes a quietly disgusted Helmuth James von Moltke to his wife Freya on August 23, 1939. Having been drafted into the German Intelligence Service, this pious, aristocratic lawyer (only six years older than Jock Lewes) will just have to cope with it. "At bottom," he writes Freya seven months later, "my attitude to this war is that of an executor who is horrified to see heirs fighting over an inheritance that grows less and less because of the dispute."

Raised on a thousand-acre Silesian estate, this fastidious son of a Prussian count keeps himself as distant as possible from Nazi colleagues in the Abwehr. Moltke's collateral descent from Bismarck's most famous field marshal helps make possible his refusal to wear the military uniform that his colleagues favor. He tries to prevent violations of an international law that the regime employing him regards as a joke, and he attempts to arrange that those being subjugated by German conquest come under the control of the more civilized Wehrmacht instead of the SS.

By 1939, Moltke and Freya Deichmann, a banker's daughter, have been married for ten years. His letters home to her at Kreisau, the estate he's inherited, have a kind of bizarre double-agentry. The reader moves from the heading "Berlin, 25 August 1941" to a sentence noting how "Churchill has made a really great speech." The disjunction is reflected in Moltke himself and in the modern-day reader's constantly conflicted reaction to what he's reading: the letter writer seems both admirable and deluded, daring and craven, sometimes in the space of a paragraph. In July 1940, watching a "squabble of the various offices over the booty in the occupied territories," he can convince himself that he is "personally uninvolved in it" and thereby able to "enjoy . . . this clash of the vultures." Struggling, in the early days of the war, to limit pillage and deportation, he takes satisfaction in having "prevented so much evil and achieved so much good," knowing that to his superiors each of those words now means the opposite and that his success depends on no one's detecting what mercies he's been able to effect.

Constantly overrun by events, he continues at his post, stiff but moderately subversive, trying to convince himself that his conscience remains intact:

> This morning Schmitz and I fought hard in the Academy for German Law for the rights and status of the Poles in the area we occupy. Some really incredible theses were put forward, and Schmitz and I took turns responding. It was simply shocking. It's no use, unfortunately, but at least our honour was saved . . .

If this takes the idea of "working within the system" to a sleepwalking extreme, Moltke's occasional encounters with like-minded officials help to keep the bubble of denial from bursting within him. In August 1940, he finds himself in just-conquered Paris with General Alexander von Falkenhausen, the military commander for northern France and Belgium:

> He is an outstanding and courageous man and we talked mostly about the economic situation of Belgium, our spoliation of the

> country and its economic and political consequences. Finally he told me where he sees the limits of his collaboration and the point at which he will refuse to take any further part. From a human point of view it was all very encouraging . . .

Moltke himself decides not to shop in the occupied city.

By the following summer, the Final Solution begins to be discernible. "Again and again one hears reports that in transports of prisoners or Jews only 20% arrive." Moltke tells Freya that a whirlwind of "blood-guilt" is on its way to the German nation, but his moral response can only struggle to grow beyond the small, impotent gesture. On November 5, 1941, he takes a food parcel to "the last Jew I know" and declares that mankind's only chance lies in "maintaining the fundamental moral laws laid down in the 10 commandments." Still, the only specific prescription with which he can conclude this letter to Freya is that their sons begin saying grace at meals: "I think it would also improve table manners."

He expects the worst, for himself included. Noticing the deportation of ten thousand more Jews, he remarks that the "bearing of these people was good to see, and I can only hope that ours will be no worse when our turn comes." Yet he seems to stand still, like an animal caught in a blizzard. He fantasizes about a "secure peace" based on the rule of law, but must sometimes mock his own futile efforts during the catastrophe that is preceding it:

> Today I fought once more for the life of that officer, like a lion: the matter received the attention of Göring, Keitel, and probably the Führer; but at 1.15 it turned out that this officer does not exist, that we had all got excited about a hypothetical case. That was really funny and rather typical . . .

As the years pass, ever more horrifyingly, his bureaucratic detachment seems only to grow. He pays neurotic attention to the state of his desktop, passively fascinated by its orderly burden: "my production of paper in the last few weeks, since my return from Norway, has been gigantic. I wonder how it will all read in 10 years' time. Will I still like it?" Conceding his own rigidity, and the limits of his moral imagination, he suffers in Berlin from a terrible sort of claustrophobia, and yearns to be back at Kreisau with his family, "the apples & sheep . . . and the work in the fields."

Geographical displacement completes an unreality where he comes to "excel in the role of a spectator at my own funeral." Picking small battles—against the Nazification of a local kindergarten—he can fool himself about "astonishing progress" in his bigger, furtive ones on behalf of Jews and Russians. Still hanging on to his "honor," he seeks a reason or justification for everything, even his insomnia. Rationalization spins a dizzy sort of comfort: "that what I do is senseless does not stop my doing it, because I am much more firmly convinced than before that only what is done in the full recognition of the senselessness of all action makes any sense at all."

Moltke's letters to Freya carry a steady stream of cautionary advice—and warnings that things will soon be getting worse. Instructions about how to care for the lilacs and beehives at the family estate flesh out a more general request to "Stay with the work at Kreisau and look the other way." When a levy of "non-ferrous metals," a birthday tribute for the Führer, is about to be imposed, Moltke reminds Freya not to part with any relics of his ancestor, the field marshal.

The often robotic tone of these words from husband to wife reflects not only the author's natural formality but also an attempt to convey the illusion that they can both somehow bear what is clearly insupportable. The letters often sound like memoranda, or chapters of a philosophy paper, as Moltke works up new reasons to continue his course of conduct; to distinguish between personal survival and complicity; to ward off the feeling "that I have let myself be corrupted." What sounds like the worst sort of pomposity ("it gives me great satisfaction to think that many non-German women have your husband to thank for the continued existence of theirs") is more the desperate effort to give himself credit against an obligation that he knows—in his deeper, more honest being—can only be discharged by active resistance and, finally, his life.

Moltke acknowledges his tendency to write letters when he's

worn out. He recognizes the "schoolmasterish" quality of what he produces, as well as the one-track nature of his mind. The usual rhetorical compulsion to apologize for the inadequacy of one's letters seems, for once, right to the point here. Even so, some measure of intimacy weathers the storm of brutality and danger through which he must communicate. "My love, I'll stop," Moltke writes on May 26, 1940. "It is so nice to talk with you."

His secret talks with other often religious-minded dissenters—the "Kreisauers," as they would come to be known—are not the immediate cause of his arrest on January 19, 1944, but they will figure in his trial and execution. The group had concerned itself not with active resistance or plans for a coup but with its hopes for Germany's military defeat and subsequent inclusion in a united Europe. These abstract speculations manage to get Moltke killed, an irony that can't be lost on anyone who reads his tormented ruminations on the limits of active resistance. Only at his trial does Moltke seem to realize how, in a state so totalitarian as Nazi Germany, he has been guilty of resistance, however futile, all along:

> The beauty of the judgment on these lines is the following: It is established that we did not want to use any force; it is established that we did not take a single step towards organization, did not talk to a single man about the question whether he was willing to take over any post . . . We merely thought . . .

Some of his punctilio survives even in letters from prison—"My love, I really still owe you a report on the summer"—but there are signs, too, of a new, full-throated vitality, a vibrating doubleness that's more like the opposite of ambivalence: a simultaneous determination to resist and willingness to die.

Freya has always secreted Moltke's letters inside the well-maintained beehives at Kreisau. But her husband hopes that these last ones, recounting his show trial in January 1945, may gain the attention of the Reich's opponents and survivors. His final public letters are curiously more intimate—or at least naturally emotional—than many of the private, tortuously reasoned ones that preceded the author's arrest. Freed from the neurotic clutter that was for so long his mental hallmark, he writes of the trial with a straight-on narrative drive. The fearful, scrupulous official has achieved a sort of peaceful ecstasy: "I wonder if I am a bit high, for I can't deny that my mood is positively elated. I only beg the Lord in Heaven that he will keep me in it, for it is surely easier for the flesh to die like that. How merciful the Lord has been to me! . . . Your husband, your weak, cowardly, 'complicated,' very average husband, was allowed to experience all this."

Just before his execution on January 23, 1945, unshackled from secrecy and half measures, he writes from his most authentic self. "All the texts we love are in my heart and in your heart," he says in a final paragraph. The letters, taken out of the beehives after his captors themselves went to trial, remained Freya von Moltke's "greatest treasure" for the next six decades.

IN THE EARLY 1990S, like a long-dormant tubercular germ, war reactivated itself in the Balkans. In Sarajevo it broke out so suddenly that its Bosnian combatants found themselves lacking insignia, let alone armaments: "Men confront the [Serbian] nationalists' banners with anything—the Yugoslavian flag, photographs of Marshall Tito—they have been able to lay their hands on," wrote one student to her former professor. "Not out of nostalgia or any desire to return to the old ways but only because there are no new icons."

The besieged citizens of Sarajevo, who would capture the imagination of Westerners without measurably denting their indifference, never developed colors or a uniform. Their iconography, such as it became, was the debris of a dying city: broken glass, fallen wires, rats and bloodstains running on the sidewalk. A whole sophisticated population was shot and shelled into beggary, forced to chop up pianos for fuel. Dodging snipers and their own disbelief, lest that distract them from the business of survival, the city's letter writers succeeded in describing their charnel house with a nuance never caught on miles of outsiders' videotape, that flat news medium whose peculiar achievement can be to make everything feel like everything else.

Letters from Sarajevo was assembled by the Italian journalist Anna

Cataldi, who first served as a courier for some of the material she later anthologized. As she explained in 1993: "Cast like bread upon the waters, entrusted to anybody, even a complete stranger, who is able to leave the besieged city, stuffed into haversacks or into the pockets of chance travellers, and posted 'outside' to uncertain destinations (refugees' addresses tend to have only short-term validity), many letters are lost."

Writing to those who have fled across the Adriatic, Sarajevans will say that in return they would rather have a fax than a parcel, though a real letter, bearing scents and fingerprints, is even better: "I can't believe it, but your handwriting, your own beautiful handwriting, is here in my hands at this very moment! I have read your letter a thousand times at least. To touch something so fresh, smelling of the warm sea . . ." A group of mail-bearing Italian pacifists materialize more like angels than postmen: "When they started to produce letters from their rucksacks it never crossed my mind that there would be one for us too. We were so delighted, more than you can imagine. To us these pacifists seemed like supernatural beings that had descended from another planet to our incredibly gloomy, devastated city."

Circumstances impose a strange new set of epistolary conventions. One mother's jammed typewriter, like the young V. S. Naipaul's, will bat out only capital letters, which look more appropriate than accidental as they remain on the page: "THE SCHOOLS HERE ARE NOT GOING TO REOPEN SO I HOPE YOU WILL GO TO SCHOOL THERE AND THAT YOU WILL LEARN ITALIAN . . . I AM GOING TO FIND OUT ABOUT SENDING YOU TO AMERICA." Papa Zoran, Grandpa Nijaz, Mama Emira and brother Orhan all put their signatures to one letter, not just to add intimacy but also to let the girl who may or may not receive it "know beyond any doubt that we are all still alive." The old postcard envoi—"Wish you were here"—is now inverted: "I'm thinking about you, etc. etc. and I'm glad you're not here today. Because it would be daft to have a birthday party when the Chetniks [Serbian fighters] might start blazing away at any moment and wreck everything."

The siege also inverts people; one cannot predict who will or won't rise to each grisly occasion: "I have had good experiences too in this war. I have met some wonderful people and some have become personal friends. Some of my former friends I never want to see again." There are a thousand instant ways to be resourceful: "Asja and I very often see your husband. He's well, he's as handsome as ever, but feels lost without you. A few days ago he went to see Asja and said he couldn't remember your face. Asja reacted very swiftly and dug up one of your photos from somewhere and showed it to him."

In ordinary times, even a vivid personality may emerge only slowly from the letters it writes, not adding up to much until a reader nears the bottom of a thick, calm bundle. Sharpened by danger and privation, the Sarajevans make immediate, full-blown appearances in their outgoing mail. Lada, a teenager who complains that the lack of electricity is keeping her from the discos she used to frequent, survives on a rhetorical drumbeat of scatology and contempt. She's determined—in the almost comic translation of her bravado—to "bugger" and "stuff" all the "shit" she's being forced to live and see, including a CNN report about the city's starving zoo animals.

Pavle, a Bosnian fighter, sounds like Yeats's lofty, uncommitted Irish Airman ("I shoot at people I do not hate"), tying back his own long hair with one of his wife's ribbons and waiting for her letters. Writing to her is the central act of his day: "Yesterday I kept thinking that something was missing and couldn't imagine what it was until I remembered I hadn't written to you." He can be as gently fatalistic as Sullivan Ballou—"My darling, should they force me to my knees, should they prove themselves stronger than me, then know this, when I am no more, that I have loved you with a pure and honest love, an enormous love"—but more often an angry wildness animates him, a determination to survive and eventually forget. In the meantime, he does not spare her the details of all the blood and mud and shelling around him.

Cataldi's volume contains letters of despair and farewell and final communications that read like suicide notes, even though the victims were more nearly murdered. A father, one day before his death, writes his daughters: "Don't be angry with your papa because he has become so EMPTY. Completely EMPTY." A mother, her weight down to forty-eight kilograms [105 pounds], asks a son to forgive any "word or deed" of hers that ever hurt him. But even more remarkable are the letters displaying faith in the temporariness of all the carnage and want, letters that observe the birds "nesting in the holes made by the grenades!" Pavle, while mindful of the trees cut down from all the parks, sees how "weeds and shrubs are sprouting everywhere."

These private letters resonate with a power that the volume's "open" ones—to newspapers, to the president of the United States—failed to carry. For years, Sarajevo remained, in one recurring image, "the largest concentration camp in the world." The city's letters bear witness to the way, as Tatjana Sekulic told her old professor, the besiegers "lied to us, robbed us, destroyed our homes, forced us to die of starvation, refused to allow us to work, wounded and killed us, and all this to make us believe that we hate each other."

CHAPTER NINE *Prison*

. . . what else is there to do when you are alone for days in the dull monotony of a narrow jail cell than write long letters, think strange thoughts, and pray long prayers?

Martin Luther King, Jr.
"Letter from a Birmingham Jail" (1963)

POLITICAL OPTIMISTS assure us that the new communications technology is on its way to making the totalitarian state obsolete. Dictators won't be able to keep news from coming in or going out as they used to, not when a handful of keystrokes can start a digital prairie fire, and the chimes of incoming e-mail raise a louder, more energy-efficient, alarm than Paul Revere. But we are not there yet, and in many corners of the world the jailhouse letter and fearfully circulated petition remain the principal means of pushing against tyrannies still in place.

As the siege of Sarajevo began, Wei Jingsheng was entering his fourteenth year of imprisonment in China's gulag of "reform through labor" camps, the *laogai*. Like Lech Walesa an electrician by trade (the Beijing Zoo instead of a shipyard), Wei had been arrested in 1979 for his part in the poster-plastering Democracy Wall movement. Two years later, the prison authorities allowed him to write his first letter. They soon became a frequent addressee.

Wei approaches his jailers with a sly, Socratic logic: "I feel that even in prisons today, all actions should be explained. Saying there is 'no need to explain' to those who don't understand your reasons, and explaining things only to those who do, is a bit unreasonable in itself, wouldn't you say?" Self-mockery ("an ignorant young guy like myself") and gentle sarcasm are his preferred rhetorical modes, but in moments of more acute suffering he cannot stifle a cri de coeur: "I don't think it would be an exaggeration to say that you don't seem to care whether I live or die!" Still in his early thirties, he has loose teeth, heart disease, arthritis, periodontitis and a bad stomach. The authorities torture him with so many noises and interruptions that one of his letters to them takes ten days to write. "Why," he wonders, "can't I at least be treated like an ordinary political prisoner?" His bewilderment makes him ponder a mystery they are too dulled to see: "What hatred do these people feel toward me that makes them treat me so harshly? I am at an absolute loss to understand and don't know if even you know the reasons why or not."

He also writes to China's political leadership, delightedly pointing out how these naked emperors are following Goebbels and ignoring Marx. His best moments have him pretending to feel gratitude and humility:

> I was deeply moved to read in the paper how you've been having heart-to-heart discussions with young people, illustriously "showing concern for misled youths." It inspired me once again to take up "dissident political views" from yours, so please allow me to now take the liberty to express some of my dissatisfaction toward certain people and matters, in spite of my restricted vision and shallow understanding. I welcome your comments.

He congratulates General Secretary Hu Yaobang on a Twelfth Party Congress speech so "full of new ideas and very exciting . . . [that] it didn't put everyone to sleep despite its length." He closes as "Your most devoted hostile element," and probably even means it, since Hu was a relatively reform-minded chairman. (To the hardliner Jiang Zemin, Wei will sign off in his holy-fool mode: "So much for now! More next time.") When made to practice "self-criticism," he does so, wondering what better tactics he might have employed, when still free, against the people now demanding that he recant. "Our situations are very different," he tells Deng Xiaoping; "you are at the top of a billion people and I am at the very bottom—but life isn't easy for either of us. It's just that I am not the one making your life difficult, while you're the one making it hard for me." He doesn't fail to point out that Deng, who experienced his own suffering under Mao Zedong, ought to know better.

Not long before the June 1989 Beijing massacre, while students still fill Tiananmen Square, Wei addresses Prime Minister Li Peng on the subject of Tibet in the style of a backroom politician: "If you don't acknowledge people equally or don't even acknowledge their existence, then who the hell, may I ask, are you planning to negotiate with?" It is unlikely Wei knew very much of the students' momentary success, but one wonders if what did filter his way helped to raise the rare, and chilling, note he sounds at this point, one more appropriate to a man expecting power than still writhing beneath it: "I don't know what bastards gave Deng Xiaoping the lousy idea of postponing and thereby intensifying this urgent domestic problem that could basically have been solved quite easily, but they should be shot."

Year after year he writes to his sisters and brother, embarrassed by his dependence upon them for books and medicine as well as any information they have gleaned about his case. He cannot abide feeling useless nor understand why he's not permitted to work on the science projects he was planning while still at liberty. He does, after a transfer to an even harsher prison in the country's dry northwest, get the chance to raise rabbits, with whom he forms a "Get By Club": "the rabbits just get by; there's just enough coal to get by; and I just barely get by myself!" Imprisonment changes Wei's "old aversion for ball-point pens" into "a real love for them"; the ink cartridges in his Parker don't last long enough to write all the letters required to relieve his boredom, speak to his family and challenge the whims of his political masters.

His letters home may display some nostalgia for his childhood, but even these are tough-minded. He lectures one of his sisters, an aspiring painter, on what she must do to keep from being a second-rate artist in China's craven aesthetic climate and asks for no coddling in return. He urges his brother and sisters to invigorate him with their opposition: "If you have any disagreements or find fault with any of my views or arguments, then please write back and challenge me; there's no need to be polite . . . If you write back with a vigorous critique, it might help me break out of my apathetic mood." In fact, it is his lovingly quarrelsome family that he recommends to Deng Xiaoping as a political model for China: "Even I, being the great filial son that I am, have been known to talk back, and on occasion have even had to leave the family to cool off for a night or two . . . Can a family like this still unite to weather all manner of severe storms? The answer is: Absolutely yes."

For a brief period in 1993–1994, Wei Jingsheng was freed—perhaps as a sop to the International Olympic Committee, whom China was bidding to host the 2000 summer games. Before agreeing to his own parole, he demanded to see his prison file and found that it included any number of the letters that he had written and that the authorities had never posted. Those letters have now reached the West, and history, destinations Wei knew they were headed for all along, as he reminded his "old friend" Deng Xiaoping just after the Tiananmen Square massacre. What he had written several weeks before it would be his insurance policy with posterity; without such a letter of protest, "I would not only be unable to face the people who raised me and the teachers and parents who sustained me, but I could not face you who have bestowed so much honor upon me. I wouldn't be what I am today without you."

After Wei's re-arrest in 1994, his health worsened and he was forbidden to write even his family. A letter from the European Parliament awarding him the Sakharov Prize for Freedom of Thought was sent back, unopened, by his jailers. But when *The Courage to Stand Alone*, a collection of his letters, was published in May 1997, someone had the inspired idea to insert in each copy a postcard addressed to the White House that called for continued American pressure on the Chinese. The purchaser was invited to sign and mail it.

It can't have hurt: Wei Jingsheng was released from prison six months later and sent to the United States.

WHEN THE NEWLY FREED Wei held a press conference in New York, observers were struck by a certain merriment, even mischief—the same unlikely traits he had deployed in letters to his jailers. Putting this dissident into an American frame of reference made for some puzzlement, since the commanding demeanor of Martin Luther King remained the unerasable template for moral protest. And yet, if one returns to the long letter King wrote from the Birmingham city jail in April 1963—a document still much less well known than the speech he would give four months later—one finds him carrying out a sly, subversive strategy that had room for at least one bit of Wei's antic disposition.

King's words are addressed not to his jailers but to a group of eight clergymen whose published "Appeal for Law and Order and Common Sense" has just criticized the civil rights movement's illegal, if peaceful, provocations. As King rehearses historical precedent for his tactics and constructs an unhurried anatomy of just versus unjust laws, the stately pace of his letter rebuts the clergymen's call for patience—he's displaying it right now—more effectively than any particular point he makes about the movement's behavior toward the Birmingham city administration.

Begun in the margins of some newsprint and finished on stationery brought by his attorney, King's letter deploys its crucial word in the tenth paragraph. The word is "tension." It covers the creative sort that King has been putting into the streets and the stylistic kind he is now putting on paper. Tension is the medium in which he works. Outside jail, he stands "in the middle of two opposing forces in the Negro community"—middle-class complacency and the new Muslim militancy. He is similarly caught between "outright" white oppressors like Sheriff Bull Connor and the self-professed "white moderates," among whom his recipients no doubt count themselves. To King in his cell, they now appear as possibly a greater impediment than his fire-hosing foes; in fact, as the letter moves on, it becomes clear that King *is*, in the broad sense of things, writing to his jailers.

The letter's own rhetorical tension manifests itself as a series of one-two punches. Courtesy precedes attack; praise introduces complaint. King moves deliberately from the legalistic ("I am here because I have basic organizational ties here") to the transcendent: "Beyond this, I am in Birmingham because injustice is here." In the course of one sentence, he shifts from sounding like a social theorist to sounding like a prophet, exchanging jargon for poetry at the turn of a comma: "We are caught in an inescapable network of mutuality, tied in a single garment of destiny." In one more tense rhetorical pair, this time of poetic genres, King summarizes the transformation he seeks: the "pending national elegy" must become "a creative psalm of brotherhood."

The letter's essential warning—"Oppressed people cannot remain oppressed forever"—enacts itself in a drama of syntax, a single sentence hundreds of words long, a chain of semicoloned clauses, parallel instances of oppression that each begin with the word "when":

> . . . when you take a cross-country drive and find it necessary to sleep night after night in the uncomfortable corners of your automobile because no motel will accept you; when you are humiliated day in and day out by nagging signs reading "white" and "colored"; when your first name becomes "nigger" and your middle name becomes "boy" (however old you are) and your last name becomes "John," and when your wife and mother are never given the respected title "Mrs." . . .

All the "whens"—what grammar calls subordinate clauses—combine into one of King's marches, a swelling crowd of phrases determined to reach the predicate that will allow the sentence to breathe and be whole. After twenty-nine lines the grammar releases itself, by saying simply: "then you will understand why we find it difficult to wait."

And after more than fifteen pages, the letter, reaching its end, chooses not to explode but subside. It disarms itself—and its recipients—with quietness and a touch of self-mockery. "I must close now," King says, as if finishing up a casual note to his parents or a cousin, instead of concluding several thousand words that have just embodied his life's work. "Never before," he adds, "have I written a letter this long (or should I say a book?)" But even here, this teasing of himself only sets up some last purposeful taunting of his correspondents: "I'm afraid that [this letter] is much too long to take your precious time. I can assure you that it would have been much shorter if I had been writing from a comfortable desk . . ."

YEARS BEFORE THE TRIAL of Alger Hiss or the confirmation of Clarence Thomas turned Americans' ideological litmus paper one gaudy shade or the other, the case of Sacco and Vanzetti gave them a prolonged chance to put personal politics ahead of forensics. "In our side," wrote one of the immigrant defendants, "are the high-class professional[s] together with the labor unions, the humble, the Italians . . ." Across the divide, continued Bartolomeo Vanzetti, quoting the *New York World* in a letter to a supporter, "are business, money and power: business-men, small property owners, salesmen, butchers, bakers, storekeepers, the candle-stick makers, the members of the newest country club . . ."

Convicted of murdering the security guard and paymaster of a Massachusetts shoe factory, the fish peddler Vanzetti and his anarchist comrade Nicola Sacco spent seven years inside both prison and an emotional hurricane of protest, the movement that finally failed to halt their execution in the summer of 1927. Their "consciousness of guilt" (more likely, argues Richard Polenberg, about other radical activity than the murders) made up the soft legal center of an unconvincing case against them, but nothing—not the hundreds of thousands of dollars spent on their behalf, nor the later discovery of significant evidence that the murders may have been committed by a gang of career criminals—succeeded in getting them a new trial.

"That last moment belongs to us," Vanzetti told a newspaper reporter not long before his electrocution. "That agony is our triumph." It flung him into a long, haunting afterlife, plaguing his captors with doubt and his supporters with regret. Vanzetti's letters, along with a much smaller selection of Sacco's, were published fifteen months after the execution. They show the prison walls squeezing a crowd of personalities and voices, from the servile to the apocalyptic, out of the convict and onto the paper. "This enclosure affects my mind a great deal," he writes. "I feel dizzy and I am never in a good discreet mood to write." In the jumble of accumulating correspondence, a reader can witness all the different portions of Vanzetti's brain, as if it's already been sectioned by a coroner.

A week after his conviction, Vanzetti distinguishes between wanting "that the social wealth would belong to every umane [*sic*] creatures" and committing "robbery for a insurrection." His innocence, it should be noted, has been conceded even by some students of the case who conclude that Sacco was involved. Still, for all his professions of humility, Vanzetti admits to finding his righteousness "supremely sweet," and the letters occasionally burst open with messianic references to "two poor Christs" and his own "ascension to the Golgotha."

His correspondents are most often privileged women who have taken up his cause, and the underlying sexual tension—a sort of chained-up virility, the captured noble savage addressing his ladies bountiful—never leaves a reader's awareness for very long. Vanzetti explains, almost apologetically, that he cannot temper his radical views for Mrs. Hillsmith, lest he "repay your love, benefits, and sincerity with deceiveness and villancy"; and he cannot send Mrs. Blackwell the reminiscences of his mother that she's requested, not while "homicide impulses are hammering into my very heart and skull." The women send him fruit, books, flowers and Valentines, but nothing excites Vanzetti to gratitude like their color postcards, which he fixes to the walls of his cell: "Thank you for the picture of the road. I would walk it barefoot and light as a butterfly in spring days." When he sympathizes with Mrs. Evans's broken ankle or says he's glad to hear of another woman's salubrious surroundings, the effect will seem heroically kind—or Uriah Heepish—depending on what a reader believes about the author's innocence or guilt. "It was good of you to write me such a good and beautiful letter as yours of last," he replies to Mrs. Evans, "amid the troubles and botherings of a begining at a summer house."

Unable to share the false hopes of his supporters, he can't even hide expectations of doom from his mentor and inspiration, the socialist leader Eugene V. Debs: "I came near tearing the letter to pieces," he tells Alice Stone Blackwell, "when I thought of the sorrow that my words will cause to the Teacher's heart." But his letters have to rage and excoriate; they are the safety valve for Vanzetti's internal blast furnace, which always puts a formidable heat onto the page until it's time to sign off and "let go this raveing." From Judge Webster Thayer he expects nothing "other than some ten thousand volts divided in few times; some meters of cheap board and 4x7x8 feet hole in the ground"; and when he thinks of the axe with which he used to chop down trees, "a lust seizes [him] to get a mad delight and exaltation by using them on the necks and trunks of the men-eaters."

His reading includes Dante and Lincoln and Tagore ("Not a word in all these . . . beautiful poetries about social problems"), and he presents an unforgettable picture of himself with the two-volume *Rise of American Civilization* "at the light of one lamp, managing to avoid the window's bars shadows." With politics less analytic than lyrical ("my beautiful anarchy"), "bliss" remains a favorite word, and through much of his imprisonment, he's almost as likely to explode in praise of nature as in defiance of his tormentors.

For his loyal correspondents he fashions bits of black humor, as well as a gentler self-mockery about his difficulties with English, which still don't keep him from stretches of vivid, natural eloquence in these days when "life's oil is far from my lamp." Just as often, though, it's speechifying—the dull blade of any political movement—that enforces a phony rule over the page. During a transfer from Charlestown to Dedham for a court appearance, Vanzetti avidly looks out of the car, making at first a clear-eyed distinction between the employed and the out-of-work "by their way of walking"; but when it comes to a pair of young working-class women, perhaps sisters, he feels obliged to orate instead of depict: "Poor plebian girls, where are the roses of your springtime?" Similarly, he must "confess" to Mrs. Jack that he's given some of the surfeit of peaches she sent "to some unfortunate youths" in the prison.

As the half-dozen years of his confinement add up, Vanzetti's handwriting grows stiffer, less vital. But in the last six months of his life, while his and Sacco's convictions are reviewed and upheld, the letters come out of him at a frantic rate, sheet after sheet, as if they are all that can keep him alive. "Today I have written, written and written all the time," he informs Mary Donovan, a labor organizer on his Defense Committee. "Now it is late and I am tired. Yet I cannot help to write to you." Hours before his death, on August 22, 1927, he is still at it, composing a last apologia, knowing letter writing to be, in the absence of an ability to pray, the only meaningful activity left to him. Two years before, he had pronounced himself unable to see "how our stupid contingence shall inspire and fortify future revolutionists and prisoners." Now, in a last postscript, not so sure it must all be in vain, he asks the law professor H. W. L. Dana to help "in inserting our tragedy in the history under its real aspect and being."

A year later, when Sacco and Vanzetti were long dead, the letters took their impassioning place there. When one of the editors presented the published volume to the Massachusetts governor who had allowed the executions to proceed, the governor, upon realizing what he'd been handed, threw the book to the ground. Its falling pages contained Vanzetti's assertion to Mrs. Jessica Henderson that he "would not trust a feather of an anarchist sparrow to the *bon plesir*" of Governor Alvan T. Fuller.

THE EXECUTION-EVE LETTER is a genre unto itself: Dead Man Writing, to his loved ones or the world.

In 1603, James I put Sir Walter Raleigh in the Tower of London for plotting with the Spanish to pry James from his brand-new throne. In the letter that Raleigh is thought to have written his wife while waiting for his trial to begin, stoicism is nowhere to be found. "O intolerable infamy!" he cries, gnashing his teeth from paragraph to paragraph. "All my good turns forgotten, all my errors revived and expounded to all extremity of ill." Expecting the worst, he urges a posthumous practicality upon Besse, instructing her to forgive his enemies but only for the sake of their son's welfare. Any second marriage she makes should be "not to please sense, but to avoid poverty and to preserve thy child." She must regard a new spouse as only her "politic" husband; "let thy son be thy beloved, for he is part of me."

Once sentence has been passed, Raleigh writes again, "with the dying hand of sometimes thy Husband," calmly listing instructions on how he should be buried. Without actually retracting his advice about remarriage, he now proposes a less "politic" and more ethereal successor to himself: "Teach your son also to love and feare God whilst he is yet young, that the feare of God may grow with him, and then God will be a husband to you, and a father to him; a husband and a father which cannot be taken from you." He makes one request of his wife on his own behalf—that she attempt to retrieve letters he sent the Lords "wherein I sued for my life." He did so only for her sake, not his, and in language that now fills him with shame.

No such scruples seem to have troubled Sir Francis Bacon about the letter he wrote to James I from the Tower, some years later, after he'd been thrown in for an indefinite term on a bribery charge. We may associate Bacon with the rangy freedom of thought that led him to claim all knowledge for his province, but his epistolary plea is an oily masterpiece of servility and calculation. "Your Majesty's arm hath been over mine in council, when you presided at the table; so near I was: I have borne your Majesty's image in metal; much more in heart; I was never in nineteen years' service chidden by your Majesty . . . But why should I speak of these things which are now vanished? but only the better to express my downfall." And, of course, to spring his ruffled hide. "Help me (dear sovereign lord and master) and pity me so far, as . . . I that desire to live to study, may not study to live."

He certainly seems to have studied what works in this particular genre. Even those who express doubt about whether the king actually received this letter acknowledge that Bacon was out of the Tower—with another five years to live and study—within four days.

As it happens, Raleigh's head did not roll the morning after he wrote his wife. Lady Raleigh was instead brought to the Tower, where both husband and wife resided for a dozen years, until he was permitted to go looking for gold in the New World. When his mission to the Orinoco didn't succeed, he was again arrested and, finally, in 1618, beheaded. Two centuries later, Fyodor Dostoevsky's reprieve came in an even narrower nick of time. On December 22, 1849, upon the drill ground of the Peter and Paul Fortress, a death sentence, which would turn out to be false, was read to him and his radical compatriots. As he put it later that day in a letter to his brother: "we were told to kiss the Cross, our swords were broken over our heads, and our last toilet was made (white shirts). Then three were tied to the pillar for execution. I was the sixth. Three at a time were called out; consequently, I was in the second batch and no more than a minute was left me to live." During these supposed last moments, Dostoevsky was surprised to find his brother on his mind and to realize how much he loved him. Worried that Mikhail might think the sentence was carried out, Dostoevsky reassures him with this letter, whose writing he's been permitted instead of a visit.

Now preparing to serve four years in prison in lieu of his appointment on the scaffold, Dostoevsky is sick with scrofula and afraid he'll be forgotten by his brother's family. And yet, his letter to Mikhail is also giddy with a sense of resurrection: "I was today in the grip of death for three quarters of an hour; I have lived it through with that idea; I was at the last instant and now I live again!" Repenting the time he's wasted in the past, he determines to make the most of whatever chances lie ahead in exile and confinement. Like the imprisoned Raleigh, who found himself so agitated that his thoughts could not "dwell in one body" with his life, Dostoevsky understands that any hopes of surviving the time ahead depend upon the authorities' willingness to let him write. Otherwise the imaginings running riot inside him "will be extinguished in my brain or will be spilt as poison in my blood! Yes, if I am not allowed to write, I shall perish. Better fifteen years of prison with a pen in my hands!"

Four years and two months later, one week after completing his sentence of hard labor, he writes Mikhail a full, angry accounting of the filth, smells, vermin and brutality he's endured in Siberia. But his harshest words are reserved for his brother:

> I wrote you a letter through our official staff; you simply must have got it; I expected an answer from you, and received none. Were you then forbidden to write to me? But I know that letters are allowed, for every one of the political prisoners here gets several in the year. Even Dourov had some; and we often asked the officials how it stood about correspondence, and they declared that people had the right to send us letters. I think I have guessed the real reason for your silence. You were too lazy to go to the police-office, or if you did go once, you took the first "No" for an answer . . .

The anger and anxiety engendered by his brother's unwritten letters helped to fill *The House of the Dead*, begun in the prison hospital.

NEARLY ALL THE LETTERS in this last chapter have strong claims to be put in someplace earlier in the book. The conditions of prison intensify or invert the more ordinary human experiences of absence or love or complaint. Shame may do a fast alternation with religious ecstasy; the good-cop/bad-cop team that once secured the confession may now be an internal mechanism, something that seesaws between guilt and resentment on its own automatic switch.

In the early 1950s, Neal Cassady—that totem and prototype of the Beats—wrote manic letters that his biographer insists "astonished Kerouac and Ginsberg and convinced them that he was the one true writer among them." Cassady, however, was hoping the mails would bring more immediate satisfactions than long-range literary reputation: "His every letter to everybody during this period," writes the biographer, William Plummer, "included a request for grass: Did they have any? Would they send him some?" Arrested in 1958 for selling marijuana to some undercover policemen—or, more exactly, giving the officers three joints in return for a ride—Cassady wound up serving a two-year sentence, most of it in San Quentin, during which the letters he wrote to his wife, Carolyn, bounced as high and low and loud as a book-length Beat poem.

They're riddled with self-reproach; "a self pitious whale of a wail" is Cassady's own critique of one of them. Blaming his "shockingly selfish desire for marijuana's euphoria" for the slide that lost him his railroad-brakeman's job, landed him in prison and got his family thrown off the welfare rolls, he wonders: "Will I ever become a man?" Now past thirty, he determines to forsake the "sickniks" for whom he's been such a celebrated muse. He may protest the severity of his sentence by an alcohol-loving society that does not mind tormenting a poor pot smoker, but he'll retract even this complaint in a breast-beating postscript: "*last paragraph reveals resentment still to be overcome, am* sure *can do it in next 1/2 1000 days.*" The whole effect is jagged: at times his will seems truly broken, but he likes displaying its penitent pieces for the prison censor who'll see the letter before it leaves San Quentin.

The censor is again on Cassady's mind when he sends Carolyn an account of his erotic dreams: "suffice to say the last one ended, after much play, with us climaxing together as the book we were reading finished with the heavily printed words, ROAR, ROAR, ROAR: funny, what?" He worries that his wife's love is dwindling; pledges his fidelity; promises to make up for the past; gives her permission to divorce him; asks her not to visit; wonders if he still has a chance with her. His teasing attempts to lighten things up have a nervous undercurrent of hostility. When proposing a telepathic experiment that would have them attempt ten minutes of mental communication each day, Cassady instructs Carolyn to send him "a thought message" on the even-numbered days and on the odd-numbered ones to "blank [her] mind—blank*er* I mean, ha ha—to receive one from this devoted husband."

The live bomb of resentment, ticking between the lines of every letter, involves her refusal, after he'd been arrested, to bail him out by taking a second mortgage on their house in Los Gatos. When he instructs her on how to imagine his confinement, he sounds a bit like Dostoevsky writing Mikhail. There's an element of cruelty amid the cackling black humor:

> you might put car mattress in the bathtub, thereby making it soft, if not as long, at least much cleaner than my bug ridden bunk; bring Bim Eberline or, say, the even more negatively aggressive McGill woman [both were obese], then lock the door &, after first dragging 11 rowdy kids into our bedroom to parallel the 1,100 noisy ones housed in this particular cellblock. Of course you must remove the toilet seat, towel racks, cabinets; anything other than a small mirror & 4 ½' shelf—remaining almost motionless so as not to inadvertently irritate Armed Robber Bim, ponder past mistakes, present agonizing future defeats in the light of whatever insights your thus disturbed condition allows . . .

In the manner of most prisoners, he becomes inventively, obsessively chronological: "I've now circled the sun once from behind bars"; "With 1/2 a day less than 1/2 a year remaining, hence being almost down to Wino Time"; "exactly 1 1/4 million seconds to go." He types his letters standing up, letting the machine bounce on the springs of the cell's top bunk. His salutations give him the chance to entertain his small children ("Dearest Cherry cobbler Cathy, Jamhappy Jamie & Jellybean John") and to begin thanking Carolyn with the same sort of nutrient imagery used so long ago by the more reserved Wordsworths: "Dear Wife; Mucho Gratis for your Blessed Letter, it feed my heart's hunger beautifully well." He reminds her to rip off the San Quentin address before sharing a letter with the children, who have been told a different story of his whereabouts.

The letters dispatch news of Cassady's religious questing—his spontaneous invocations of Jesus, Mary Baker Eddy and Swedenborg, and somewhat more steady retreat toward the Catholicism in which he was raised. When Gavin Arthur (grandson of the 1880s president) fails to show up to conduct a comparative religion and philosophy class for the inmates, Cassady fills in and lectures to them on the psychic prophet Edgar Cayce. He embraces "perservering [*sic*] prayer" and even struggles to see the policeman who arrested him as an instrument of God's Will. But in his excited pilgrimage, he often seems more frightened than peaceful. He memorizes the names of all 262 popes, a desperate magical effort that continues far longer than the comfort he derives from news of John XXIII's Christmastime visit to an Italian jail.

Despite calling himself a "very very *Ex*-Beatster," Cassady can't stanch the alliterative flood of his own prose. One can almost picture Kerouac's famous roll of paper coursing through that typewriter on the top bunk. Carolyn is his "Dearest daft dove deliberately doubling deft devotion despite despair dripping dumbly down delicately dim decolletage . . ." His renunciations—of unprocreative sex, tobacco and pot—don't sound too convincing in a consonantal cascade: "that nicotine narcotic tobacco & that hardly more horrid Indian Hemp." The hipster and the paterfamilias, the man of the road and the struggling new square, have a comical clash on the page. The letters to his children can be gently, touchingly pedantic, full of vocabulary builders and math problems and explanations of the Four Freedoms; he goes so far as to emphasize good grammar and punctuation. But even in these prescriptive sentences, Daddy can't stop being Daddy-o.

His desire to go straight once he's released—so forced and so obviously doomed—makes him scorn the prospect of connecting with either old friends or new ones, as if each group is one more Lenten sacrifice he has to make. "I want to work myself to death, seriously, a kind of legitimate suicide; why? well, not being loving, cheerful, etc. & not being able to stand people or the world, about the only service left that I can perform is supporting you all . . ."

When he does get out, on Independence Day 1960, the old lures of North Beach and the new one of Ken Kesey are just outside the gates. He will be dead within eight years.

NORMAN MAILER'S CORRESPONDENCE with Jack Henry Abbott—a convict who spent twenty-five of his first thirty-seven years in prison—now stands as the novelist's own last hipsterish episode, a final existential burst before he settled into a paunchy gray eminence. Receiving Abbott's letters while writing *The Executioner's Song*, Mailer came to feel "all the awe one knows before a phenomenon."

In those letters, Abbott calls himself "state-raised," even though he acquired his considerable book-learning on his own: "nine-tenths of my vocabulary I have never *heard* spoken." His descriptions of life among a ferocious "new breed" of American convict can be quietly breathtaking. More literally so is his exposition of the technique one prisoner uses to stab another, as precise as Hemingway's account of hooking a trout:

> You are both alone in his cell. You've slipped out a knife (eight- to ten-inch blade, double-edged). You're holding it beside your leg so he can't see it. The enemy is smiling and chattering away about something. You see his eyes: green-blue, liquid. He thinks you're his fool; he trusts you. You see the spot. It's a target between the second and third button on his shirt. As you calmly talk and smile, you move your left foot to the side to step across his right-side body length. A light pivot toward him with your right shoulder and the world turns upside down; you have sunk the knife to its hilt into the middle of his chest.

Much of Abbott's rhetoric is defensively glazed with self-regard, but when he writes of the things he has lived and not about the politics he grabbed on to in desperation ("Communists *always* behave as anyone would expect real people in a real society to respond to one another"), he can seem dignified and commanding. Convict-versus-convict carnage seems more reasonable than mysterious after reading his book: "you are not killing in physical self-defense. You're killing someone in order to live respectably in prison. Moral self-defense."

He says that his letters to Mailer are the closest he's ever come to keeping a diary. When they were published in 1981, as *In the Belly of the Beast*, Mailer contributed a sincere but silly introduction on the subject of prisons: "Somewhere between the French Foreign Legion and some prodigious extension of Outward Bound may lie the answer, at least for all those juvenile delinquents who are drawn to crime as a positive experience." The novelist's faith helped win Abbott's conditional release from the Utah State Penitentiary a few weeks before the book's appearance, but a month later, Abbott was arrested for the murder of a young actor, Richard Adan. Mr. Adan had been skillfully stabbed in the chest.

DURING THE SAME ERA when Abbott's metamorphoses briefly intrigued the public, Jean Harris became even more famous for an even more improbable transformation.

For ten years after the headmistress of the Madeira School was sentenced to the Bedford Hills Correctional Facility for murdering her lover, the famous "diet doctor" Herman Tarnower, the letters she wrote to the journalist Shana Alexander functioned as Harris's "steam vent." *Marking Time*, a selection of them from 1989 to 1991, is not without Abbott's tendency toward apologia (Harris refers, for instance, to the "New York gulag"), but the collection is generally so much more measured and proceeds from an earlier lifetime so much more imaginable than Abbott's that it does manage to read like a collection of letters instead of documents.

Jean Harris's prison sufferings are undeniable: her depression; her fear of stroke; her failure to get one of the pardons handed out, year after year, at Christmastime. Her powers of evocation usually operate by inversion: the smaller the humiliation, the more finely observed and affecting her rendition will be. One day, for no reason, a favorite blouse is deemed an infraction of the rules: "suddenly its cowl neckline was called a turtleneck, and I couldn't see my visitor until I walked back up the hill to my cell to change it. I was too angry to sit and visit. For the first time in nine years I told them to send my visitor away." What she can never get used to is "being considered a liar and a cheat and being treated like one every day. A whole lifetime to the contrary is as nothing."

About prison's hierarchical chemistry, Abbott wrote: "Among themselves, the guards are human. Among themselves, the prisoners are human. Yet between these two the relationship is not human.

It is animal." If Bedford Hills is less brutal than the array of penitentiaries from which Abbott gained his experience, the general impossibility of relating to the guards still provides Jean Harris's letters with one of her major themes. The system runs on expensive, petty cruelties. Mulberries growing on the grounds of "this ridiculously overfenced pen" cannot be eaten because they are "supposed to go to waste." One guard, doing nothing to change Harris's opinion that the female officers are worse than the male, insists on calling her "Princess Di."

The "ladies" she refers to are her fellow inmates, with whom she has nothing and everything in common. The teaching she does—parenting classes—may be "a minor drop in the ocean," but a reader sees what was once a mere profession for Harris becoming something more like a true vocation. Thrown amidst sadder souls than she ever knew existed, she has enough respect for the ladies not to take them on their own terms: "How do you measure the emptiness of a life of, say, twenty-five or thirty years that has not somehow stumbled across the knowledge that birds build nests? Don't ask me who am I to look askance at another person's culture. Don't tell me a tree never grew in Brooklyn. Don't tell me they're street smart. Today I consider that an oxymoron. I've seen too many of the street smart, and heard them, too, to be moved by their much-touted smarts."

She learns humility during her dozen years at Bedford Hills, but one can't say she overdoes it or that the crisp contempt her old job sometimes required doesn't serve her even better in prison. If nothing else, it helps her make plain to Alexander a whole cellarful of unpleasant realities: "There's something about sharing a tub in an institution where herpes, gonorrhea, syphilis, and TB are on the rise and one in five test positive for the AIDS virus that quenches one's desire for a nice hot bath." A reader who appreciates her considerable wit can't help wondering what Harris, in her past life, might have said about her own crime, what bons mots she might have discharged, on better stationery, about the boarding-school head who iced her lover.

The new world she moves in is squalid and scary, but she does her best to be its Madame de Sévigné, evoking its elaborate customs and hidden structures. The longer letters become not manifestoes like Abbott's, but small essays. There's a mordant tour de force on the actual similarities of prisons and country clubs, and a primer of recidivism: "Prisons work the way companies do that build obsolescence into their products so you have to buy them again and again." She worries about the egocentrism of what she mails to Alexander—"what I care about, what I find interesting, what I just learned"—but the letters don't strike a third party that way, not when they contain the observations of someone with no choice in what she observes. They actually are a kind of grand, ongoing rise to the occasion.

It was a truly egocentric letter—a pained, frantic and pathetic one—that helped send Jean Harris to prison. At her trial in 1980–81, the district attorney attempted to establish deliberate intent in the murder of Herman Tarnower by introducing the "Scarsdale Letter," written to the doctor by Harris just before the shooting. It is a long cry against Tarnower's indifference; against the misbehavior of his new and, of course, younger mistress; and finally, against Harris's own neediness and vanished pride. She wrote to Tarnower for probably the same reason she shot him: relief.

"I am distraught as I write this—your phone call to tell me you preferred the company of a vicious, adulterous psychotic was topped by a call from the Dean of Students ten minutes later and has kept me awake for almost 36 hours. I had to expel four seniors just two months from graduation and suspend others. What I say will ramble but it will be the truth—and I have to do something besides shriek with pain." She lists Tarnower's "years of broken promises," involving everything from financial help with dentistry to the apartment in New York he never bought for the two of them. "It didn't matter all that much, really—all I ever asked for was to be with you—and when I left you to know when we would see each other again so there was something in life to look forward to. Now you are taking that away from me too and I am unable to cope."

Once displaced from his paltry attentions, she had to sustain their long-distance affair entirely at her own expense, financially and otherwise: "All our conversations are my nickels, not yours—and obviously rightly so because it is I, not you, who needs to hear your voice. I have indeed grown poor loving you, while a self-serving ignorant slut has grown very rich." The younger mistress's alleged harassments (cutting up Harris's clothes) and the older one's admitted retaliations ("I have, and most proudly so . . . ripped up or destroyed anything I saw that your slut had touched and written her cutesie name on") sound eerily like a preview of the pointless prison vendettas that lie ahead for Harris to witness.

Strung out on pills the doctor dispensed with his only evidence of liberality, Jean Harris began to feel desperate. "To be jeered at, and called 'old and pathetic' made me seriously consider borrowing $5,000 just before I left New York and telling a doctor to make me young again—to do anything but make me not feel like discarded trash—I lost my nerve because there was always the chance I'd end up uglier than before." Declarations like this one rendered her claim that she went to Tarnower's house to kill herself, not him—and that he died by accident in a struggle over the gun—almost plausible.

After her conviction, Jean Harris would use the prison mails to provide herself with another, less explosive, release ("I write because there's no one to talk with, except you, my friend") and also to do a bit of good from where she was. Her new return address commanded attention when seen by recipients like Barbara Bush, her fellow Smith alumna, to whom Harris wrote about childcare legislation in May of 1990. In her 1981 book about the shooting and trial, Diana Trilling argued that prison might afford Jean Harris an opportunity to be "splendid" than she had never had before. At moments in *Marking Time* she comes close.

THE BLOATED, graying debtor who died in the Hôtel d'Alsace with a few friends and some champagne (a pleasure he referred to by its slang name "Boy") had for the previous quarter century dispatched letters with as much deliberateness as he had squandered life. We shall never know how many of Oscar Wilde's letters were destroyed in 1895 during fits of puritanical rage and fear by their once-delighted recipients, but when Sir Rupert Hart-Davis's collection of the surviving correspondence appeared in the early 1960s, W. H. Auden—who believed such publications were generally an invasion of privacy and who a decade later would ask that his own letters be destroyed by all who had them—pronounced Wilde's letters an exception: "From the beginning [he] performed his life and continued to do so even after fate had taken the plot out of his hands. Drama is essentially revelation; on the stage no secrets are kept. I feel therefore, that there is nothing Wilde would desire more than that we should know everything about him."

Wilde's early letters from Oxford roll along on the gentle sort of humor he would later banish to make room for wit. To his mother and his friends Reginald Harding and William Ward, he writes mostly of college routine, vacation travels, and a flirtation with Roman Catholicism: "I now breakfast with Father Parkinson, go to St Aloysius, talk sentimental religion to Dunlop and altogether am caught in the fowler's snare, in the wiles of the Scarlet Woman—I may go over in the vac." He didn't. At the end of his life he would still be a self-aware sucker for ceremony and costume. From Rome, in April 1900, to Robbie Ross:

> Yesterday a painful thing happened. You know the terrible, the awe-inspiring effect that Royalty has on me: well, I was outside the Caffè Nazionale taking iced coffee with *gelato*—a most delightful drink—when the King drove past. I at once stood up, and made him a low bow, with hat doffed—to the admiration of some Italian officers at the next table. It was only when the King had passed that I remembered I was *Papista* and *Nerissimo*! I was greatly upset: however I hope the Vatican won't hear about it.

In the Oxford letters, Wilde hasn't yet learned to throw away a line or resist explaining his own jokes, and the bombast still hasn't gone successfully over the top. What survives from his first brief London period (1879–1881) is still more ambitious than outrageous. (In between responding to and issuing invitations, he sends his verses to Arnold, Browning—and Gladstone.) It's only during his 1882 trip to America that Wilde discovers his true ability to perform, both on the platform and in the mails. The buoyant poseur and paradox-maker is now up and running. "They were dreadfully disappointed at Cincinnati at my not wearing knee-breeches," he informs his lecture agent, and his confidence only grows as he moves further west. In San Francisco, where four thousand people meet him at the depot, he is "really appreciated—by the cultured classes." By the time he is back in Boston, after famously charming the Colorado silver miners, his name is six feet high on the placards, "printed it is true in those primary colours against which I pass my life protesting, but still it is fame, and anything is better than virtuous obscurity." The same bons mots, self-plagiarized, begin showing up in several letters all at once.

Returning to London, he declares that "society must be amazed," but for a time, though he's rising at a fast, steep grade now, he does what is expected of him, editing *Woman's World* and marrying Constance. (The only surviving letter of any length to her is a pleasant, entirely conventional, love note.) He so delights in his children that he urges Norman Forbes-Robertson to "get married *at once!*" But the paradoxes at the heart of his wit begin emptying themselves toward perfection. As he writes Arthur Conan Doyle, "I throw probability out of the window for the sake of a phrase, and the chance of an epigram makes me desert truth."

The letters from 1890 often argue the moral case for *Dorian Gray*, and in a running battle with the *St. James's Gazette*, Wilde defends his novel in a way that previews his response to the marquess of Queensberry's eventual provocation: "To say that such a book as mine should be 'chucked into the fire' is silly. That is what one does with newspapers." The next few years give Wilde his successful comedies, his money and fame, and the spoiled-brat love of his life, Lord Alfred Douglas, first mentioned as being "quite like a Narcissus—so white and gold . . . he lies like a hyacinth on the sofa, and I worship him." By 1893, Wilde is tossing off homosexual slang ("Who on earth *is* the editor? He must be rented") and writing

Bosie the purple letter that will be used against him during the Queensberry trial: "it is a marvel that those red rose-leaf lips of yours should have been made no less for music of song than for madness of kisses. Your slim gilt soul walks between passion and poetry."

The rush to disaster has its giddy charm. Wilde vacations at Babbacombe Cliff in February 1893 with his sons, Bosie, and Bosie's tutor, Campbell Dodgson, reveling in this all-male world of boys and children. He fantasizes about the "Babbacombe School"—he is the headmaster, and this is the evening schedule:

> 5. Tea for headmaster and second master, brandy and soda (not to exceed seven) for boys.
> 6–7. Work.
> 7.30. Dinner, with compulsory champagne.
> 8.30–12. Écarté, limited to five-guinea points.
> 12–1.30. Compulsory reading in bed. Any boy found disobeying this rule will be immediately woken up.

Bosie, however, must be asked not to "make scenes . . . They kill me, they wreck the loveliness of life."

By 1894, Wilde understands that in his own novel, "Basil Hallward is what I think I am: Lord Henry what the world thinks me: Dorian what I would like to be—in other ages, perhaps." Just a year later, Queensberry will be throwing down his misspelled but quite unlibelous card ("To Oscar Wilde posing as a somdomite"), and its recipient will be going off "to fight with panthers." Only a few emergency telegrams and notes will remain to be written before it's time for the letters dispatched from Her Majesty's prisons. "With what a crash this fell!"

The prison commissioners had decreed in 1887 that the "permission to write and receive Letters is given to Prisoners for the purpose of enabling them to keep up a connection with their respectable friends and not that they may be kept informed of public events." But Wilde pronounces the letters from his friend Robbie Ross "messengers between me and that beautiful unreal world of

Art where once I was King," and in one of his reformist communications to the *Daily Chronicle* in 1898, he decries the "habit of mutilating and expurgating" prisoners' mail. Wilde's own prison letters chiefly concern the debilitating effects of confinement, relations with Bosie, his fears (entirely wrong) about his place in history, and preparations for his release—a trauma complicated by what he considered the legal and financial ineptitude of friends. He picks oakum, suffers from an abscess of the ear, and is harrowed by the everything-in-its-place regulations of cell-keeping: "Dear Robbie, I could not collect my thoughts yesterday, as I did not expect you till today. When you are good enough to come and see me will you always fix the day? Anything sudden upsets me."

Publication of his letters by the venal, limelight-loving Bosie is a new worry, since "[t]he gibbet on which I swing in history now is high enough." He resents his ex-lover's new status as the "Infant Samuel" and imagines the Queensberry family looking "on the whole thing merely as a subject for sentiment or reminiscence over the walnuts and the wine." At first, trying to stay alive emotionally, he clings to his love for Bosie, but as time goes on and the latter never visits or writes, Wilde concentrates on Douglas's treachery. Invective begins to serve him better than expressions of longing, though the high spirits he fakes for his more loyal correspondents make for the most touching letters he writes.

Self-awareness comes and goes. He is frightened, repentant, vindictive, practical, mystical. Nature "will hang the night with stars so that I may walk abroad in the darkness without stumbling, and send the wind over my footprints so that none may track me to my hurt: she will cleanse me in great waters, and with bitter herbs make me whole." *De Profundis* spends much time lamenting past glories and shoring up the author's cultural status, but this long letter is at its best when attacking Bosie, the nominal recipient, and when Wilde is mixing compliments to others into the pity for himself:

> When I was brought down from my prison to the Court of Bankruptcy between two policemen, Robbie waited in the long dreary corridor, that before the whole crowd, whom an action so sweet

> and simple hushed into silence, he might gravely raise his hat to me, as handcuffed and with bowed head I passed him by. Men have gone to heaven for smaller things than that.

Wilde's letters from Berneval on the French Channel coast, written just after his release with much false optimism and a horror of recidivism, are the hardest for a reader to bear. The ex-convict expects the good air, wholesome food and the practice of little personal economies to save him from repeating his "days of gilded infamy." But even though he will manage to compose "The Ballad of Reading Gaol," within a year he will have to admit: "I don't think I shall ever really write again. Something is killed in me. I feel no desire to write. I am unconscious of power. Of course my first year in prison destroyed me body and soul. It could not have been otherwise." In one of his feminine, submissive letters to Frank Harris, he admits that he has "lost the mainspring of life and art, *la joie de vivre.*"

If this realization was his first real achievement, understanding Bosie came next. The attacks on him in *De Profundis* could not preclude Wilde's "psychologically inevitable" return to him in Naples in 1897. At first he would claim it was for inspiration, but the truth comes in an explanation to Robbie Ross: "Of course I shall often be unhappy, but still I love him: the mere fact that he wrecked my life makes me love him." One feels that Wilde has finally found a paradox instead of forced one. As predicted, Bosie remains spiteful and profligate as always ("He apparently goes to the races every day . . . he has a faculty of spotting the loser, which, considering that he knows nothing at all about horses, is perfectly astonishing") and for much of the time Wilde is alone.

In his last years, he comes to more realistic conclusions about his sexual nature. Shortly after his release, he is "thankful and happy to be able to say" that he has no attraction to a twenty-nine-year-old ex-Reading convict who comes to spend a week with him; the following year he's back to defending homosexual love to Ross as "more noble than other forms"; and soon after that he simply decides to get what pleasure he can from it. Playing with one of

Charles Reade's titles, he writes: "How evil it is to buy Love, and how evil to sell it! And yet what purple hours one can snatch from that grey slowly-moving thing we call Time! My mouth is twisted with kissing, and I feed on fevers. The Cloister or the Café—there is my future. I tried the Hearth, but it was a failure." He settles on the café. "I know that there is no such thing as changing one's life," he declares toward the end; "one merely wanders round and round within the circle of one's own personality." But the reader of his letters gets steadily closer to the center, to what the newspapers, determined to deprive him of even the simple honorific "Mister," called "the man Wilde."

In the struggle for money, he sells options on the same play to several buyers and turns out some of his most charming prose ever in the form of notes to his shrunken but most essential public—the friends he asks for money. Begging letters become his chief means of expression: "I am going to write a Political Economy in my heavier moments. The first law I lay down is 'Wherever there exists a demand, there is *no* supply.'" He reports having made a "pilgrimage" to the chapel of Notre Dame de Liesse—fifty yards from his hotel—and talks of the boy guide Robbie has left him with: "Omero is his name, and I am showing him Rome." He thanks Reginald Turner for the gift of a clock (part of the optimistic apparatus of Berneval) in sentences as delightful as any in his fairy tales: "It is most sweet of you to give it to me, and you will be pleased, and perhaps astonished, to hear that it is quite beautiful, and has a lovely face and wonderful slim restless hands, yet it is strangely punctual in all its habits, business-like in its methods, of ceaseless industry, and knows all that the sun is doing." Three days later: "The clock *still goes;* and is quite astounding in its beauty and industry. It even works at night, when no one is watching it."

On February 1, 1899, Wilde wrote Leonard Smithers, his last publisher, that he was autographing copies of *The Importance of Being Earnest* in the hope of making a little money: "One . . . has a smudge of ink on it, but as I have initialled the smudge, which I made myself, it must count as a *remarque.* You might ask one and sixpence extra for that copy." On February 6, 1981, both the smudged copy and the letter were sold at Christie's in New York. Price: $8,500.

THE STIFFEST UPPER LIP is required to quote, with any real belief, Lovelace's famous assertion that stone walls do not a prison make. The ordinary mortal is more likely to reverse the proposition and declare that a prison hardly requires walls of stone. The plasterboard of little offices and unhappy homes will do just as well. Charles Lamb, whose "Distant Correspondents" got this book going, marched between two confinements nearly every day for thirty-three years. In the mornings he set off for his clerkly job keeping track of vessels sent forth by the East India Company. He earned what it took to support himself and the sister he came home to—the occasionally mad Mary, who had slain their mother in a fit. Lamb could dispatch his own fanciful ships, gay little skiffs that didn't betray their turbulent origins, only at night. Some of the essays we best remember, "A Dissertation on Roast Pig" and even "Distant Correspondents," got started as private communications to friends like Coleridge.

We love Lamb for his constant susceptibility, the excitement of his feelings by food ("how beautiful and strong those buttered onions come to my nose!"), tobacco, and certainly drink. But the gusto never proceeds from anything like ease. Unworthiness prompts his sympathies for the wretched ("I killed a rat the other day by punching him to pieces, and feel a weight of blood upon me to this hour"), and melancholy often keeps him from being genial company. The food he loves is usually better eaten alone, and this bachelor so known for his love of teeming London—who writes Wordsworth that man was lucky to have sinned his way out of the too-green Garden of Eden—takes many of his urban delights from a solitary remove: "The wonder of these sights impells me into night-walks about [London's] crowded streets, and I often shed tears in the motley Strand from fulness of joy at so much Life."

His devotion to those who are out of their minds is a kind of propitiation against the threat madness presents to his own shaky nature. With his friend Thomas Manning about to go preach the gospel in China, Lamb resorts to telltale black humor—"perhaps, you'll get murder'd, and we shall die in our beds with a fair literary reputation"—knowing that the possibilities of sudden violence are probably greater right in Inner Temple Lane. Once Manning has become a distant correspondent halfway 'round the world, Lamb cries wolf to lure him home. Some of the false alarms are broad enough ("St. Paul's Church is a heap of ruins"), but others are sufficiently pointed to unsettle even a man doing the Lord's work: "Scarce here and there one will be able to make out your face; all your opinions will be out of date, your jokes obsolete, your puns rejected with fastidiousness as wit of the last age." The urgency beneath the comedy comes from Lamb's desire for Manning's "steadiness and quiet, which used to infuse something like itself into our nervous minds. Mary called you our ventilator."

Mary's mental episodes, "twelve or thirteen weeks every year or two," take "a tedious cut out of a life." Lamb hopes for the best and blames himself for anything else. On one occasion he declines an invitation from Coleridge—hardly a rock himself—by explaining that the poet has "a power of exciting interest, of leading all hearts captive, too forcible to admit of Mary's being with you." And yet he credits his childhood friend with developing everything worthwhile in his own character.

When the essayist and poet George Dyer experiences a fit of insanity in 1801, it is Lamb who takes him in: "He came thro' a violent rain with no neckcloth on, and a *beard* that made him a spectacle to men and angels, and tap'd at the door," Lamb tells his friend John Rickman. "I shall not be sorry when he takes his nipt carcase out of my bed . . . but I will endeavour to bring him in future into a method of dining at least once a day." When Lamb finds himself living alone, it is usually madness and death that have created the situation. On May 12, 1800, he writes Coleridge:

> Hetty [a servant] died on Friday night, about eleven o'clock, after eight days' illness; Mary, in consequence of fatigue and anxiety, is fallen ill again, and I was obliged to remove her yesterday. I am

> left alone in a house with nothing but Hetty's dead body to keep me company. To-morrow I bury her, and then I shall be quite alone, with nothing but a cat to remind me that the house has been full of living beings like myself. My heart is quite sunk, and I don't know where to look for relief.

A sheet of stationery would often suggest itself. On it, the cheer he prepared for others could also be sent to himself. Lamb is letter writing's great whistler in the dark, his productions a singing kettle put on for both writer and recipient. We grab for their gossip; their overstuffed descriptions ("each individual flake presents a pleasing resistance to the opposed tooth"); their harmless japes, in which a man so hemmed in by circumstance can tinker with reality. In April 1829, he complains to Henry Crabb Robinson: "I have these three days been laid up with strong rheumatic pains, in loins, back, shoulders. I shriek sometimes from the violence of them. I get scarce any sleep." In his next letter, he admits that this was all just one-upmanship to irritate the genuinely rheumatic Robinson: "I have no more rheumatism than that poker . . . The report of thy torments was blown circuitously here from Bury. I could not resist the jeer." Nor, one suspects, the chance to provide himself with relief, if only from an affliction he must imagine in order to banish.

Lamb deprecates his letters for a tedium they never have ("dull up to the dulness of a Dutch commentator on Shakespeare") and more honestly apologizes for the scarcity of time he has to write them. Innumerable distractions keep him from "epistolary purposes"; chief among them is his job, which he curses to Wordsworth in 1822:

> Thirty years have I served the Philistines, and my neck is not subdued to the yoke. You don't know how wearisome it is to breathe the air of four pent walls without relief day after day, all the golden hours of the day between 10 and 4 without ease or interposition . . . these pestilential clerk faces always in one's dish.

He wishes "for a few years between the grave and the desk," but when they finally arrive, he makes a difficult adjustment. He now writes letters to pass the time he never had: "I pity you for over-work," he writes Bernard Barton in 1829, "but I assure you no-work is worse. The mind preys on itself, the most unwholesome food . . . I have killed an hour or two in this poor scrawl."

But Lamb had always hated getting to the end of a letter. "Things come crowding in to say, and no room for 'em," he'd written Manning decades earlier before returning to the difficult life beyond the margins of his stationery. If the letters of Keats, his younger contemporary, are prescriptions for living, tickets into the world, Lamb's mood-driven miniatures are respites *from* it, little globes unto themselves, complete and welcoming and, for all that, still hard to bear:

> The rooms where I was born, the furniture which has been before my eyes all my life, a book case which has followed me about (like a faithful dog, only exceeding him in knowledge) wherever I have moved—old chairs, old tables, streets, squares, where I have sunned myself, my old school,—these are my mistresses.

Even now, he is the distant correspondent from whom we would most like to hear.

Selected Bibliography

Abbott, Jack Henry. *In the Belly of the Beast: Letters from Prison.* Introduction by Norman Mailer. New York: Random House, 1981.

Agee, James. *Letters of James Agee to Father Flye.* New York: George Braziller, 1962.

Appignanesi, Lisa, and John Forrester. *Freud's Women.* New York: Basic Books, 1993.

Baker, Ray Stannard. *Woodrow Wilson: Life and Letters. Youth Vol. 1: 1856–1890.* Garden City, N.Y.: Doubleday, 1927.

Barford, Mirren, and Jock Lewes. *Joy Street: A Wartime Romance in Letters, 1940–1942.* Edited by Michael T. Wise. Foreword and commentary by Alan Hoe. Boston: Little, Brown, 1995.

Basler, Roy P., ed. *Abraham Lincoln: His Speeches and Writings.* Preface by Carl Sandburg. Cleveland and New York: World Publishing Co., 1946.

Black, Jeremy. *The English Press in the Eighteenth Century.* Philadelphia: University of Pennsylvania Press, 1987.

Bloch, Michael, ed. *Wallis and Edward: Letters, 1931–1937: The Intimate Correspondence of the Duke and Duchess of Windsor.* New York: Summit, 1986.

Block, Zachary. "An Evangelista for Our Times," *Brown Alumni Magazine,* May/June 2004, p. 75.

Bokenkotter, Thomas. *A Concise History of the Catholic Church.* Revised and expanded edition. New York: Doubleday, 2004.

Boyd, Brian. *Vladimir Nabokov: The American Years.* Princeton: Princeton University Press, 1991.

Burlingame, Michael. "The Trouble with the Bixby Letter," *American Heritage,* July/August 1999, pp. 64–67.

Burroughs, William S. *The Letters of William S. Burroughs: 1945–1959.* Edited and with an introduction by Oliver Harris. New York: Viking, 1993.

Byron, George Gordon. *The Selected Letters of Lord Byron.* Edited with an introduction by Jacques Barzun. New York: Grosset & Dunlap, 1953.

Carroll, Andrew, ed. *Letters of a Nation: A Collection of Extraordinary American Letters.* New York: Broadway Books, 1997.

Carroll, Donald, ed. *Dear Sir, Drop Dead!: Hate Mail Through the Ages.* New York: Barnes & Noble, 1993.

Cassady, Neal. *Grace Beats Karma: Letters from Prison 1958–60.* Foreword and notes by Carolyn Cassady. New York: Blast Books, 1993.

Cataldi, Anna, ed. *Letters from Sarajevo: Voices of a Besieged City.* Translated by Avril Bardoni. Rockport, Mass.: Element, 1994.

Chekhov, Anton, and Olga Knipper. *Dear Writer, Dear Actress: The Love Letters of Anton Chekhov and Olga Knipper.* Edited and translated by Jean Benedetti. New York: Ecco, 1997.

Chesterfield, Philip Dormer Stanhope, Earl of. *Letters to His Son.* New York: Dingwall-Rock, 1925.

Churchill, Winston, and Clementine Churchill. *Winston and Clementine: The Personal Letters of the Churchills.* Edited by Mary Soames. Boston: Houghton Mifflin, 1999.

Clemens, Samuel L. *The Selected Letters of Mark Twain.* Edited with an introduction and commentary by Charles Neider. New York: Cooper Square Press, 1999.

Colette, Sidonie Gabrielle. *Letters from Colette.* Selected and translated by Robert Phelps. New York: Farrar, Straus and Giroux, 1980.

Congdon, Kirby. *Crank Letters.* New York: The Smith, 1986.

Coward, Noël. *The Letters of Noël Coward.* Edited and with commentary by Barry Day. New York: Knopf, 2007.

Cumming, John, ed. *Letters from Saints to Sinners.* New York: Crossroad, 1996.

Cyr, Miriam. *Letters of a Portuguese Nun: Uncovering the Mystery Behind a Seventeenth-Century Forbidden Love.* New York: Miramax, 2006.

Daum, Meghan. "Virtual Love," *The New Yorker,* August 25 & September 1, 1997, pp. 80–89.

Davis, Lennard J., ed. *Shall I Say a Kiss? The Courtship Letters of a Deaf Couple, 1936–1938.* Washington, D.C.: Gallaudet University Press, 1999.

De Toledano, Ralph, ed. *Notes from the Underground: The Whittaker Chambers–Ralph de Toledano Correspondence, 1949–1960.* Washington, D.C.: Regnery, 1997.

Dickens, Charles. *Charles Dickens' Uncollected Writings from* Household Words, *1850–1859.* Edited with an introduction and notes by Harry Stone. Bloomington: Indiana University Press, 1968.

———. *The Dent Uniform Edition of Dickens' Journalism,* Vol. 2. Edited by Michael Slater. Columbus: Ohio State University Press, 1996.

Dostoevsky, Fyodor. *Letters of Fyodor Michailovitch Dostoevsky to His Family and Friends.* Translated by Ethel Colburn Mayne. Introduction by Avrahm Yarmolinsky. New York: Horizon Press, 1961.

Emerson, Ralph Waldo. *The Selected Letters of Ralph Waldo Emerson.* Edited by Joel Myerson. New York: Columbia University Press, 1997.

Emery, Jane. *Rose Macaulay: A Writer's Life.* London: John Murray, 1991.

Etkind, Marc. . . . *Or Not to Be: A Collection of Suicide Notes.* New York: Riverhead Books, 1997.

Faulkner, William. *Thinking of Home: William Faulkner's Letters to His Mother and Father, 1918–1925.* Edited by James G. Watson. New York: Norton, 1992.

Fénelon, François de Salignac de la Mothe. *Letters of Love and Counsel.* Selected and translated by John McEwen. New York: Harcourt, Brace & World (A Helen and Kurt Wolff Book), 1964.

Fitzgerald, F. Scott. *Letters to His Daughter.* Edited by Andrew Turnbull. Introduction by Frances Fitzgerald Lanahan. New York: Scribner's, 1965.

Flaubert, Gustave, and George Sand. *Flaubert-Sand: The Correspondence.* Translated by Francis Steegmuller and Barbara Bray, with a foreword by Francis Steegmuller. Based on the edition by Alphonse Jacobs with additional notes by Francis Steegmuller. New York: Knopf, 1993.

Forster, E. M. *Selected Letters of E. M. Forster. Vol. 1, 1879–1920.* Edited by Mary Lago and P. N. Furbank. Cambridge, Mass.: Belknap Press of Harvard University Press, 1983.

———. *Selected Letters of E. M. Forster. Vol. 2, 1921–1970.* Edited by Mary Lago and P. N. Furbank. Cambridge, Mass.: Belknap Press of Harvard University Press, 1985.

Fox, Margalit. "Helene Hanff, Wry Epistler of '84 Charing,' Dies at 80," *The New York Times,* April 11, 1997, p. B12.

Gelernter, David. *Drawing Life: Surviving the Unabomber.* New York: The Free Press, 1997.

Grant, Michael. *Saint Peter.* New York: Scribner, 1995.

Greene, Graham. *Yours Etc.: Letters to the Press.* Selected and introduced by Christopher Hawtree. London: Penguin, 1991.

Griffin, Farah Jasmine. *Beloved Sisters and Loving Friends: Letters from Rebecca Primus of Royal Oak, Maryland, and Addie Brown of Hartford, Connecticut, 1854–1868.* New York: Knopf, 1999.

Grimes, William. "'Dear Abby' Doesn't Live Here Anymore," *The New York Times,* March 30, 1997, Styles section, pp. 27, 30.

Hamilton, Ian. *Keepers of the Flame: Literary Estates and the Rise of Biography from Shakespeare to Plath.* Boston: Faber and Faber, 1994.

Hanff, Helene. *84, Charing Cross Road.* New York: Grossman (Viking), 1975.

Harlow, Alvin F. *Old Post Bags: The Story of the Sending of a Letter in Ancient and Modern Times.* New York and London: Appleton, 1928.

Harris, Jean. *Marking Time: Letters from Jean Harris to Shana Alexander.* New York: Macmillan, 1991.

Hearn, Lafcadio. *The Japanese Letters of Lafcadio Hearn.* Edited by Elizabeth Bisland. Boston and New York: Houghton Mifflin Company. The Riverside Press, Cambridge, 1910.

Hopkins, Gerard Manley. *The Letters of Gerard Manley Hopkins to Robert Bridges.* Edited by Claude Colleer Abbott. London: Oxford, 1935.

Hyde, Louis, ed. *Rat & the Devil: Journal Letters of F. O. Matthiessen and Russell Cheney.* Hamden, Conn.: Archon Books, 1978.

Ibn Abbad of Ronda. *Letters on the Sufi Path.* Translation and introduction by John Renard. New York: Paulist Press, 1986.

Jameson, Storm, ed. *London Calling.* New York and London: Harper & Bros., 1942.

Jefferson, Thomas. *The Family Letters of Thomas Jefferson.* Edited by Edwin Morris Betts and James Adam Bear, Jr. Charlottesville: University of Virginia Press, 1986.

———. *Writings.* Edited by Merrill D. Peterson. New York: Library of America, 1984.

Karlinsky, Simon, ed. *The Nabokov-Wilson Letters: Correspondence Between Vladimir Nabokov and Edmund Wilson, 1940–1971.* New York: Harper & Row, 1979.

Kasson, John F. *Rudeness and Civility: Manners in Nineteenth-Century Urban America.* New York: Hill and Wang, 1990.

Keats, John. *Complete Poems and Selected Letters.* Edited by Clarence DeWitt Thorpe. New York: The Odyssey Press, 1935.

Kenyon, Olga, ed. *800 Years of Women's Letters.* Foreword by P. D. James. New York: Penguin Books, 1994.

Kermode, Frank, and Anita Kermode. *The Oxford Book of Letters.* Oxford and New York: Oxford University Press, 1995.

Lamb, Charles. *The Portable Charles Lamb: Letters and Essays.* Edited and with an introduction by John Mason Brown. New York: Viking, 1949. Reprinted 1965.

———. *Selected Letters of Charles Lamb.* Edited by G. T. Clapton. New York: George H. Doran Co., 1924.

Landers, Ann. *Ann Landers Says: Truth Is Stranger.* Englewood Cliffs, N.J.: Prentice-Hall, 1968.

Larkin, Philip. *Selected Letters of Philip Larkin, 1940–1985.* Edited by Anthony Thwaite. London: Faber and Faber, 1992.

Lee, Elizabeth Blair. *Wartime Washington: The Civil War Letters of Elizabeth Blair Lee.* Edited by Virginia Jeans Laas. Foreword by Dudley T. Cornish. Urbana and Chicago: University of Illinois Press, 1991.

The Letters of Abelard and Heloise. Translated with an introduction by Betty Radice. London: Penguin Books, 1974.

Lewis, C. S. *Letters to an American Lady.* Edited by Clyde S. Kilby. Grand Rapids, Mich.: William B. Eerdmans Publishing Co., 1967.

Lincoln, Abraham. *Selected Speeches and Writings.* New York: Library of America, 1992.

Lovric, Michelle. *Love Letters: An Anthology of Passion.* New York: Shooting Star Press, 1994.

Macaulay, Rose. *Letters to a Friend, 1950–1952.* Edited by Constance Babington-Smith. New York: Atheneum, 1962.

McCarthy, Mary, and Hannah Arendt. *Between Friends: The Correspondence of Hannah Arendt and Mary McCarthy, 1949–1975.* Edited and with an introduction by Carol Brightman. New York: Harcourt, 1995.

McEwan, Ian. *Atonement.* New York: Doubleday (Nan A. Talese), 2002.

McGuire, William, ed. *The Freud/Jung Letters: The Correspondence Between Sigmund Freud and C. G. Jung.* Translated by Ralph Manheim and R. F. C. Hull. Abridged by Alan McGlashan. Princeton, N.J.: Princeton University Press, 1994.

Mallon, Thomas. *A Book of One's Own: People and Their Diaries.* New York: Ticknor & Fields, 1984.

———. "Read a Book and Write a Letter," *The New York Times Book Review,* October 12, 1986, pp. 1, 24–25.

Marx, Groucho. *The Groucho Letters: Letters from and to Groucho Marx.* New York: Simon & Schuster, 1967.

Mencken, H. L. *The New Mencken Letters.* Edited by Carl Bode. New York: Dial Press, 1977.

Merton, Thomas, and Czeslaw Milosz. *Striving Towards Being: The Letters of Thomas Merton and Czeslaw Milosz.* Edited by Robert Faggen. New York: Farrar, Straus and Giroux, 1997.

Miller, Henry, and James Laughlin. *Selected Letters.* Edited by George Wickes. New York: Norton, 1996.

Milton, John. *The Familiar Letters of John Milton.* Edited by Donald Lemen Clark. Translated by David Masson. *The Works of John Milton,* Vol. XII. New York: Columbia University Press, 1936.

Mitford, Jessica. *Decca: The Letters of Jessica Mitford.* Edited by Peter Y. Sussman. New York: Knopf, 2006.

Mitford, Nancy. *Love from Nancy: The Letters of Nancy Mitford.* Edited by Charlotte Mosley. Boston and New York: Houghton Mifflin, 1993.

Morris, Edmund. "This Living Hand," *The New Yorker,* January 16, 1995, pp. 66–69.

Nabokov, Vladimir. *Vladimir Nabokov: Selected Letters, 1940–1977.* Edited by Dmitri Nabokov and Matthew J. Bruccoli. New York: Harcourt Brace, 1989.

Naipaul, V. S. *Between Father and Son: Family Letters.* Edited by Gillon Aitken. New York: Knopf, 2000.

Newkirk, Pamela. *A Love No Less: More Than Two Centuries of African American Love Letters.* New York: Doubleday, 2003.

Nightingale, Florence. *Ever Yours, Florence Nightingale.* Edited by Martha Vicinus and Bea Nergaard. Cambridge, Mass.: Harvard University Press, 1990.

Norton, Rictor, ed. *My Dear Boy: Gay Love Letters Through the Centuries.* San Francisco: Leyland Publications, 1998.

O'Conner, Patricia T., and Stewart Kellerman. "Virtual: Welcome to the E-mail Combat Zone," *The New York Times Magazine,* August 11, 2002, p. 22.

O'Connor, Flannery. *The Habit of Being*. Selected and edited by Sally Fitzgerald. New York: Farrar, Straus and Giroux, 1979.

Oudes, Bruce, ed. *From: The President: Richard Nixon's Secret Files*. New York: Harper & Row, 1988.

Owen, Wilfred. *Selected Letters*. Edited by John Bell. Oxford and New York: Oxford University Press, 1985.

Perelman, S. J. *Don't Tread on Me: The Selected Letters of S. J. Perelman*. Edited by Prudence Crowther. New York: Viking, 1987.

Perkins, Maxwell E. *Editor to Author: The Letters of Maxwell E. Perkins*. Selected and edited, with commentary and an introduction by John Hall Wheelock, and a new introduction by Marcia Davenport. New York: Scribner, 1979.

Phillips, Charles, and Alan Axelrod. *My Brother's Face: Portraits of the Civil War in Photographs, Diaries, and Letters*. Foreword by Brian C. Pohanka. San Francisco: Chronicle Books, 1993.

Plummer, William. *The Holy Goof: A Biography of Neal Cassady*. Englewood Cliffs, N.J.: Prentice-Hall, 1981.

Pool, Daniel. *Dickens' Fur Coat and Charlotte's Unanswered Letters: The Rows and Romances of England's Great Victorian Novelists*. New York: HarperCollins, 1997.

———. *What Jane Austen Ate and Charles Dickens Knew: From Fox-Hunting to Whist—The Facts of Daily Life in Nineteenth-Century England*. New York: Simon & Schuster, 1993.

Proust, Marcel. *Selected Letters, Vol. 2, 1904–1909*. Edited by Philip Kolb, translated with an introduction by Terence Kilmartin. New York: Oxford University Press, 1989.

Rand, Ayn. *Letters of Ayn Rand*. Edited by Michael S. Berliner. Introduction by Leonard Peikoff. New York: Dutton, 1995.

"Red Letter Day," *People*, August 27, 2001, p. 98.

Rilke, Rainer Maria. *Letters to a Young Poet*. Translated by M. D. Herter Norton. New York: Norton, 1993. Originally published 1934.

Robson, John M. "Marriage or Celibacy?: A Victorian Dilemma," in *Papers for the Millions: The New Journalism in Britain, 1850s to 1914*. Edited by Joel H. Wiener. New York and Westport, Conn.: Greenwood Press, 1988.

Roosevelt, Franklin D. *F.D.R.: His Personal Letters, 1928–1945*. 2 vols. Edited by Elliott Roosevelt, assisted by Joseph P. Lash. Foreword by Eleanor Roosevelt. New York: Duell, Sloan and Pearce, 1950.

Roosevelt, Theodore. *A Bully Father: Theodore Roosevelt's Letters to His Children*. With a biographical essay and notes by Joan Paterson Kerr. Foreword by David McCullough. New York: Random House, 1995.

Rosa, Paul. *Idiot Letters: One Man's Relentless Assault on Corporate America*. New York: Doubleday (A Main Street Book), 1995.

Rose, Phyllis. *The Year of Reading Proust: A Memoir in Real Time.* New York: Scribner, 1997.

Ross, Harold. *Letters from the Editor: The New Yorker's Harold Ross.* Edited by Thomas Kunkel. New York: The Modern Library, 2000.

Sacco, Nicola, and Bartolomeo Vanzetti. *The Letters of Sacco and Vanzetti.* Edited by Marion Denman Frankfurter and Gardner Jackson. With an introduction by Richard Polenberg. New York: Penguin, 1997. Originally published 1928.

Sackville-West, Vita. *The Letters of Vita Sackville-West to Virginia Woolf.* Edited by Louise DeSalvo and Mitchell A. Leaska. New York: Morrow, 1985.

Sangharakshita. *Through Buddhist Eyes: Travel Letters.* Birmingham, Eng.: Windhorse Publications, 2000.

Schulz, Bruno. *Letters and Drawings of Bruno Schulz.* Edited by Jerzy Ficowski. New York: Harper & Row, 1988.

Schuster, M. Lincoln, ed. *A Treasury of the World's Great Letters.* New York: Simon & Schuster, 1940.

Sévigné, Madame de (Marie de Rabutin Chantal). *Selected Letters.* Translated and with an introduction by Leonard Tancock. London: Penguin, 1982.

Shaw, Bernard, and Mrs. Patrick Campbell. *Bernard Shaw and Mrs. Patrick Campbell: Their Correspondence.* Edited by Alan Dent. New York: Knopf, 1952.

Shipley, David, and Will Schwalbe. *Send: The Essential Guide to Email for Office and Home.* New York: Knopf, 2007.

Singer, Godfrey Frank. *The Epistolary Novel: Its Origin, Development, Decline, and Residuary Influence.* New York: Russell & Russell, 1963. Originally published 1933.

Smith, Dinitia. "Dear Web Pal: These Letters Must End," *The New York Times,* January 6, 2001, p. B19.

Smith, Ira R. T., with Joe Alex Morris. *"Dear Mr. President . . .": The Story of Fifty Years in the White House Mail Room.* New York: Julian Messner, Inc., 1949.

Stewart, Elinore Pruitt. *Letters of a Woman Homesteader.* Foreword by Gretel Ehrlich. Illustrations by N. C. Wyeth. Boston: Houghton Mifflin, 1988. Originally published 1914.

Super, R. H. *Trollope in the Post Office.* Ann Arbor: University of Michigan Press, 1981.

Tapert, Annette. *The Brothers' War: Civil War Letters to Their Loved Ones from the Blue and Gray.* New York: Times Books, 1988.

Thornton, Tamara Plakins. *Handwriting in America: A Cultural History.* New Haven and London: Yale University Press, 1996.

Trilling, Diana. *Mrs. Harris.* New York: Harcourt Brace Jovanovich, 1981.

Vermorel, Fred, and Judy Vermorel. *Starlust: The Secret Life of Fans.* London: W. H. Allen, 1985.

Virgoe, Roger. *Private Life in the Fifteenth Century: Illustrated Letters of the Paston Family.* New York: Weidenfeld & Nicolson, 1989.

Von Moltke, Helmuth James. *Letters to Freya, 1939–1945.* Edited and translated from the German by Beate Ruhm von Oppen. New York: Vintage, 1995.

Wade, James, and Stuart Wade. *Drop Us a Line . . . Sucker! The Prank Letters of James and Stuart Wade.* New York: Carroll & Graf, 1995.

Wei Jingsheng. *The Courage to Stand Alone: Letters from Prison and Other Writings.* New York: Viking, 1997.

Welty, Eudora. "Why I Live at the P.O.," *The Collected Stories of Eudora Welty.* New York: Harcourt, 1980, pp. 46–56.

West, Nathanael. *Miss Lonelyhearts.* New York: New Classics, 1933.

Wilde, Oscar. *The Letters of Oscar Wilde.* Edited by Rupert Hart-Davis. London, 1962.

———. *More Letters of Oscar Wilde.* Edited by Rupert Hart-Davis. New York: Vanguard, 1985.

Williams, Tennessee. *Five O'Clock Angel: Letters of Tennessee Williams to Maria St. Just, 1948–1982.* With commentary by Maria St. Just. Preface by Elia Kazan. New York: Knopf, 1990.

Wilson, Edith Bolling. *My Memoir.* New York and Indianapolis: Bobbs-Merrill, 1939.

Wilson, Edmund. *Letters on Literature and Politics, 1912–1972.* Selected and edited by Elena Wilson. Introduction by Daniel Aaron. Foreword by Leon Edel. New York: Farrar, Straus and Giroux, 1977.

Wilson, Woodrow, and Edith Bolling Galt Wilson. *A President in Love: The Courtship Letters of Woodrow Wilson and Edith Bolling Galt.* Edited by Edwin Tribble. Boston: Houghton Mifflin, 1981.

Woollcott, Alexander. *The Letters of Alexander Woollcott.* Edited by Beatrice Kaufman and Joseph Hennessey. New York: Viking, 1944.

Wordsworth, William, and Mary Wordsworth. *The Love Letters of William and Mary Wordsworth.* Edited by Beth Darlington. London: Chatto & Windus, 1982.

Wright, Frank Lloyd. *Letters to Apprentices.* Selected and with commentary by Bruce Brooks Pfeiffer. Fresno: The Press at California State University, 1982.

Zane, J. Peder. "A Rivalry in Rabble-Rousing as Letter Writers Keep Count," *The New York Times,* June 19, 1995, p. D5.

Zinsser, William. *Extraordinary Lives: The Art and Craft of American Biography.* New York: American Heritage, 1986.

Index

Permissions Acknowledgments

Grateful acknowledgment is made to the following for permission to reprint previously published material:

Alfred A. Knopf: Excerpts from *Between Father and Son: Family Letters* by V. S. Naipaul, edited by Gillon Aitken, copyright © 1999 by V. S. Naipaul; excerpts from *Letters to Freya, 1939-1945* by Helmuth James Von Moltke, translated by Beate Ruhm von Oppen, translation copyright © 1990 by Alfred A. Knopf, a division of Random House, Inc. Reprinted by permission of Alfred A. Knopf, a division of Random House, Inc.

Columbia University Press: Excerpts from *The Selected Letters of Ralph Waldo Emerson*, edited by Joel Myerson (New York: Columbia University Press, 1997). Reprinted by permission of Columbia University Press.

Farrar, Straus and Giroux, LLC and Harold Matson Co., Inc.: Excerpts from *The Habit of Being: Letters of Flannery O'Connor*, edited by Sally Fitzgerald, copyright © 1979 by Regina Cline O'Connor. Reprinted by permission of Farrar, Straus and Giroux, LLC and Harold Matson Co., Inc. on behalf of the Mary Flannery O'Connor Charitable Trust.

Farrar, Straus and Giroux, LLC: Excerpts from *Striving Towards Being* by Thomas Merton and Czeslaw Milosz, edited by Robert Faggen. Letters copyright © 1997 by The Merton Legacy Trust. Letters by Milosz copyright © 1997 by Czeslaw Milosz. Reprinted by permission of Farrar, Straus and Giroux, LLC.

Gallaudet University Press and Lennard Davis: Excerpts from *Shall I Say a Kiss?: The Courtship Letters of a Deaf Couple, 1936-1938*, edited by Lennard J. Davis, copyright © 1999 by Lennard Davis (Washington, DC: Gallaudet University Press, 1999). Reprinted by permission of Gallaudet University Press and Lennard Davis.

Houghton Mifflin Harcourt Publishing Company: Excerpts from *A President in Love: The Courtship Letters of Woodrow Wilson and Edith Bolling Galt*, edited by Edwin Tribble, copyright © 1981 by Edwin Tribble. All rights reserved. Reprinted by permission of Houghton Mifflin Harcourt Publishing Company.

Richard Hyde: Excerpts from *Rat & the Devil: Journal Letters of F. O. Matthiessen and Russell Cheney*, edited by Louis Hyde (Hamden, CT: Archon Books, 1978). Reprinted by permission of Richard Hyde.

Little, Brown & Company: Excerpts from *Joy Street* by Michael Wise, copyright © 1995 by Michael T. Wise. Reprinted by permission of Little, Brown & Company.

Oxford University Press: Excerpts from *Selected Letters* by Wilfred Owen, edited by John Bell (New York: Oxford University Press, 1985). Reprinted by permission of Oxford University Press.

Penguin Books Ltd.: Excerpts from *Selected Letters* by Madame de Sévigné, translated with an introduction by Leonard Tancock, copyright © 1982 by Leonard Tancock (Penguin Classics, 1982). Reprinted by permission of Penguin Books Ltd.

Princeton University Press: Excerpts from *The Freud/Jung Letters: Correspondence Between Sigmund Freud and C.G. Jung*, edited by William McGuire, translated by Ralph Manheim and R.F.C. Hull. Reprinted by permission of Princeton University Press.

Scribner and Harold Ober Associates Inc.: Excerpts from *F. Scott Fitzgerald: Letters to His Daughter*, edited by Andrew Turnbull, copyright © 1963, 1965 by Frances Scott Fitzgerald Lanahan. Copyrights renewed 1991 by Eleanor Lanahan, Matthew J. Bruccoli, Samuel J. Lanahan, Joanne J. Turnbull, Joanne T. Turnbull, and Frances L. Turnbull. Copyright © 1993 by Eleanor Lanahan, S. J. Lanahan, and Cecilia Ross. Reprinted by permission of Scribner, a division of Simon & Schuster, Inc. and Harold Ober Associates Inc.

Viking Penguin: Excerpts from *The Courage to Stand Alone* by Wei Jingsheng, translated by Kristina M. Torgeson, copyright © 1997 by Wei Jingsheng. Reprinted by permission of Viking Penguin, a division of Penguin Group (USA) Inc.

The Wylie Agency LLC: Excerpts from *Letters of James Agee to Father Flye* by James Agee, copyright © 1962 by The James Agee Trust (New York: George Braziller, 1962). Reprinted by permission of The Wylie Agency LLC.

ABOUT THE AUTHOR

Thomas Mallon is the author of seven novels, including *Fellow Travelers, Bandbox, Henry and Clara* and *Dewey Defeats Truman.* Among his nonfiction books are studies of diaries (*A Book of One's Own*), plagiarism (*Stolen Words*) and the Kennedy assassination (*Mrs. Paine's Garage*). A frequent contributor to *The New Yorker, The Atlantic Monthly* and other publications, he lives in Washington, D.C.

A NOTE ON THE TYPE

This book was set in Janson, a typeface long thought to have been made by the Dutchman Anton Janson, who was a practicing typefounder in Leipzig during the years 1668–1687. However, it has been conclusively demonstrated that these types are actually the work of Nicholas Kis (1650–1702), a Hungarian, who most probably learned his trade from the master Dutch typefounder Dirk Voskens. The type is an excellent example of the influential and sturdy Dutch types that prevailed in England up to the time William Caslon (1692–1766) developed his own incomparable designs from them.

Composed by Creative Graphics
Allentown, Pennsylvania

Printed and bound by RR Donnelley
Harrisonburg, Virginia

Designed by M. Kristen Bearse